中国侨联文化交流部指导

北美枫香书局

# 100年北美华人移民史

张 西 主编

中国华侨出版社
·北京·

## 图书在版编目（CIP）数据

100年北美华人移民史/张西主编. —北京：中国华侨出版社，2023.5

书名原文：100 YEARS OF CHINESE IMMIGRATION IN THE UNITED STATES AND CANADA

ISBN 978-7-5113-8924-4

Ⅰ.①1… Ⅱ.①张… Ⅲ.①华人—移民—历史—北美洲 Ⅳ.①D771.038

中国版本图书馆CIP数据核字（2022）第213987号

著作权合同登记号 图字：01-2022-6104号

## 100年北美华人移民史

主　　编：张　西
责任编辑：高文喆　桑梦娟
经　　销：新华书店
开　　本：787毫米×1092毫米　1/16开　印张：27.25　字数：295千字
印　　刷：北京鑫益晖印刷有限公司
版　　次：2023年5月第1版
印　　次：2023年5月第1次印刷
书　　号：ISBN 978-7-5113-8924-4
定　　价：150.00元

中国华侨出版社　北京市朝阳区西坝河东里77号楼底商5号　邮编：100028
发行部：（010）64443051　传　真：（010）64439708
网　址：www.oveaschin.com　E-mail：oveaschin@sina.com

如发现印装质量问题，影响阅读，请与印刷厂联系调换。

# 序言

　　1785年，3名中国海员乘坐美国商船"帕拉斯号"从广州抵达美国东海岸巴尔的摩，成为最早抵达美国的华人。自此，北美地区就有了华人的印记。从19世纪中叶的淘金热潮，到修建太平洋铁路；从美国加利福尼亚州的种植园，到加拿大维多利亚港；从险山深壑中的日夜劳作，到反法西斯战场上的英勇作战……华人在北美地区留下了坚实的历史足迹，做出了卓越的历史贡献。

　　然而，彼时的华人却不断遭受歧视与压迫。频发的暴力排华事件、大规模排华运动、长达半个多世纪的全国性《排华法案》……北美华人在异国他乡饱受屈辱。但他们没有向命运低头，凭借着坚韧不拔之精神冲决命运之桎梏，用血与泪书写了一部可歌可泣又气贯长虹的奋斗史诗。如今，这段历史虽被诸多学者研究，却鲜为公众熟知。

　　为了让更多人尤其是华裔新生代了解这段历史，北美枫香文化中心做了一件非常有意义的事，他们策划并实施了《100年北美华人移民史》手绘本项目，希望通过华裔青少年视角解读和呈现北美华人的百年移民历程。

　　项目发起人旅美剧作家、导演张西女士在撰写绘本故事时翻阅了大量史料，并求教于数位华人历史学者，以期更好地还原华人先辈的历史印记。这位在美国华裔社会颇具影响力的女性学者，怀着赤子之心，沿着北美华人的足迹，把百年前华人先辈的历史印迹串联成一段段耐人寻味的故事。这些故事无不折射出中华儿女勤劳勇敢、热爱和平、不屈不挠、自强不息的高尚品格。

　　该项目一经启动便吸引了众多华裔青少年参加。70名6～16岁有绘画基础的华裔青少年，历时一年，用画笔再现了华人在北美地区淘金、修铁路、遭遇排华、卷入南北战争以及"一战"和"二战"的艰辛历程，更记录了

100 Years of Chinese Immigration in the United States and Canada

1785—1947年华人对北美地区的建设和发展做出的巨大贡献。

华裔青少年用画笔与百年前的华人先辈展开了一场超越时空的对话。孩子们读懂了先辈为北美地区的建设发展乃至世界和平所贡献的聪明才智，倾注的辛勤汗水，付出的巨大牺牲。透过一幅幅生动的画作，我们不仅能看到华裔青少年卓越的绘画天赋，触摸到他们纯真的美丽心灵，更能感受到他们对先辈的真挚情感。透过一幅幅饱含真情、有些还略显稚嫩的画作，我们能看到孩子们对华人移民北美历史和文化的探究、理解，以及对未来的笃定。感谢张西女士、北美枫香文化中心以及参与绘本项目的华裔青少年为生动再现北美华人百年移民史所做的努力。

今天，我们庆幸生活在伟大的新时代，中国人受奴役受屈辱的日子已经一去不复返了。我们始终珍爱和平，维护和平，追求国家统一和民族复兴。抚今追昔，令人感慨万千。时代的沧桑巨变证明，唯有一个强大的中国，才是海外侨胞力量的来源和坚强的后盾。未来，中国前进的脚步不会停歇，开放的大门会越开越大。对海外侨胞而言，无论海角天涯，强大的中国永远伴你远行。

希望该绘本能激励更多人以史为鉴，砥砺前行；鼓舞更多人尤其是海外华裔新生代走近他们的父辈祖辈，深入探寻先辈进取、勤劳、开放、包容、奉献的历史，更好地了解先辈为当地经济社会发展所做出的贡献，成为华侨华人故事的讲述者和传播者，推动中外文化交流，讲好中国故事，传播好中国声音，推动中外民心相通和中外文明交融，为推动构建人类命运共同体贡献侨界力量！

中国侨联副主席

程学源

2023年1月12日

# 前言

# 《100年北美华人移民史》手绘本

　　这是北美枫香文化中心在新冠肺炎疫情暴发期间研发的一个服务于青少年的公益项目。70名6～16岁、有绘画基础的华裔画童，历时1年，绘画了290幅关于美国、加拿大、墨西哥华人的百年移民故事，并最终由北美枫香书局出版。

　　这是以锲而不舍的网上搜集资料碎片的方法，沿着北美华人的足迹线，把1785年到1947年这160多年的历史印迹串起来，撰写的一本手绘本读物。它的特点是故事性强，画面生动，青少年容易理解。它不是通常意义上的学术研究论著，请勿高估它的科学性和严谨性，也不要低估它的常识性和普及传播功用。虽然，能搜索到的历史人物和照片有的并不清晰，但它是北美华人百年移民史，也是北美移民历史！不能跳过或忽略。

　　本书中，我通常以一个人名或事件为线索和切入点，反复查阅资料后再还原和拼凑历史真相，在这个过程中，我曾数次咨询请教"美华史记"创始人之一黄倩、纽约历史学者郭代伟、《黑色道钉》纪录片导演周敏、自由摄影人李炬、《还原美国华人历史》作者原文彬、亚利桑那华人口述历史学者张肇鸿，以及从已过世的加华移民史学者黎全恩教授的文章里也获得启发，他们均对我完成该手绘本有过帮助，特此致谢。

　　感谢年轻的绘画指导老师陈泓颖，她研究生毕业来到枫香实习，就赶上这个项目，正好施展了她那不凡的才华；也要感谢加拿大绘画指导老师宿裴致，

I

她带领阳光画苑学员，为整个项目贡献了最优秀的画作；更要感谢波士顿剑桥中文学校和新泽西家长俱乐部，均承担了部分绘画任务；最后感谢画童们的家长，帮忙承担了图片说明的英文翻译，没有他们的热情帮助，手绘本不可能顺利出炉。

感恩我和画童们都没有虚度疫情期间的日子。这是一个没有先例的、在摸索中完成的文化工程，虽然为此耗去整整一年时间，也未寻求一分钱赞助，但在这个项目里枫香和画童们都得到了不同程度的成长。

大部分画童天赋异禀，在专业老师的指导下，均能根据历史老照片进行二度创作，该项目还意外地挖掘出部分画童使用电脑软件绘画的天赋。

希望手绘本能让更多海外华人以史为鉴，找到自己在当下的定位而少困扰；希望更多的华裔后代从中找到自信和从容。我会老去，画童们也会老去，可我们图文并茂的艺术再现画面，将永远都在这里！

北美枫香文化中心将分年度、分批次培训青少年们看图说话的技能。疫情过后，由画童们组成的"华裔移民史青少年讲师团"，将在北美各地进行巡回讲演和画展，浅显易懂地传播这群先驱们对北美社会的贡献，他们应该被记住！

因为很多历史照片来源于网络，查不到版权出处，如果哪段文字或图片的使用引起版权质疑，请联系我们，我们会真诚妥善地解决。邮箱：namccct@gmail.com。

张　西<br>
2022年2月28日<br>
于美国康州

# 目  录
# Contents

## 第一部分　移民篇
## Part One　Immigration

**第一章**　最早到达北美的华人　/ 3
Chapter 1　The First Chinese Arriving in North America

**第二章**　北美淘金华人　/ 15
Chapter 2　Chinese for Gold Rush in North America

**第三章**　北美早期唐人街　/ 25
Chapter 3　Early-stage Chinatowns in North America

## 第二部分　华工篇
## Part Two　Chinese Workers

**第四章**　太平洋铁路构想　/ 37
Chapter 4　Concept of the Pacific Railroad

**第五章**　华人来美修铁路缘由　/ 55
Chapter 5　Reasons for Chinese to Come to America to Build Railways

**第六章**　华工劳作　/ 67
Chapter 6　Chinese Laborers at Work

**第七章**　华工生活　/ 111
Chapter 7　Life of Chinese Workers

**第八章**　排华浪潮　/ 123
Chapter 8　The Chinese Exclusion Tide

**第九章**　华工去向　/ 143
Chapter 9　The Next Direction of Chinese Workers

i

## 第三部分　战争篇
## Part Three　The Wars

**第十章**　美国南北战争中的华人 / 167
Chapter 10　Chinese in the American Civil War

**第十一章**　美墨边境战中的华人 / 185
Chapter 11　Chinese in the Mexican-American War

**第十二章**　"一战"中的美国华人 / 189
Chapter 12　American Chinese in World War Ⅰ

**第十三章**　"一战"中的加拿大华人 / 195
Chapter 13　Canadian Chinese in World War Ⅰ

**第十四章**　欧洲战场 / 201
Chapter 14　European Battlefield

**第十五章**　亚洲战场 / 233
Chapter 15　Asian Battlefield

**第十六章**　华裔飞虎队 / 261
Chapter 16　Chinese Flying Tigers

**第十七章**　华裔女军人 / 301
Chapter 17　Chinese Female Soldiers

**第十八章**　家族参战 / 323
Chapter 18　Families in the War

**第十九章**　加华军人 / 345
Chapter 19　Canadian Chinese Soldiers

## 第四部分　融入篇
## Part Four　Integration

**第二十章**　美加百年杰出华人 / 367
Chapter 20　Centurial Outstanding Chinese in the United States and Canada

**第二十一章**　华人之友 / 413
Chapter 21　Chinese Friends

**附　录** / 427
Appendix

# 第一部分　移民篇

# PART ONE
# IMMIGRATION

# 第一章 最早到达北美的华人

## Chapter 1　The First Chinese Arriving in North America

◎《旧中国贸易》 张云想 画
*Old China Trade* by Yunxiang Zhang

第一部分　移民篇
Part One　Immigration

**旧中国贸易**

商船带去了水獭皮、酒、松脂和夏威夷木材，又从中国带回茶叶、瓷器和丝绸。那时的欧洲，能使用中国瓷杯品中国茶，是贵族的象征。这段"旧中国贸易"持续了半个多世纪，直到1840年鸦片战争爆发。

**Old China Trade**

Merchant ships took otter skins, wine turpentine, and Hawaiian wood with them, and brought back tea, china, and silk from China. In Europe at that time, it was a symbol of nobility to be able to use Chinese porcelain cups to taste Chinese tea. This "old China trade" lasted for more than half a century until the outbreak of the Opium War in 1840.

100年北美华人移民史

100 Years of Chinese Immigration in the United States and Canada

◎《最早抵美的三名华人》　　　　　　　　　　　　　　张云想　画
　　The First Three Chinese People to Arrive in the United States　　by Yunxiang Zhang

## 最早抵美的三名华人

"中国皇后号"商船停靠广州期间，大胆的爱尔兰冒险家约翰·奥多奈尔和他的商船"帕拉斯号"（Pallas，也译为"智慧女神号"）正好也在广州。船主常年穿梭于印度和中国，他通过"中国皇后号"船长得知了美国的商机，便火速在广州购买了大批中国货，又招募了三名广东台山船员，与另外的印度和东南亚的船员们一起为"帕拉斯号"服务。1785年1月，"帕拉斯号"从广州离港启航驶往美国，这是第一艘从广州始发的直航美国的商船。该商船于1785年8月9日驶入马里兰巴尔的摩港。然而发了大财的船长，决定不再继续到中国做生意。他没有

# 第一部分 移民篇
Part One  Immigration

支付船员们回国的路费，致使他们流落在巴尔的摩街头。一名叫霍林斯沃斯（Levi Hollingsworth）的商人伸出援手，把他们带到费城，向当时的最高立法机构——大陆会议提出申请资助水手们。据史料记载，三名中国水手留在了东岸，成为首批在美国定居的华人。

**The First Three Chinese People to Arrive in the United States**

During the "Queen of China" docking in Guangzhou, a daring Irish adventurer named John O'Donnell and his merchant ship "Pallas", translated as "Goddess of Wisdom" as well, also happened to be in Guangzhou. The ship owner travels between India and China all year round. He learned about the business opportunities in the United States through the captain of the Queen, so he quickly bought a large number of Chinese goods in Guangzhou and recruited three crew members from Taishan, Guangdong, along with other Indian and Southeast Asian crew members to serve the "Pallas". In January 1785, the "Pallas" set sail from Guangzhou for the United States, which was the first merchant ship to sail directly to the United States from Guangzhou. The merchant ship entered Baltimore, Maryland, on August 9, 1785. However, the captain, who had made a fortune, decided not to continue doing business in China. He even didn't pay the crew to back home, making them to live on the streets of Baltimore. A businessman named Levi Hollingsworth reached out, took them to Philadelphia and submitted an application to the top legislature at the time, the Continental Congress, to fund the sailors. According to historical records, three sailors stayed on the east coast, becoming the first Chinese to settle in the United States.

◎《"中国皇后号"商船》　　　　　　　　　　　　　　　　　　　　杜馨予　画
　"China's Queen" Merchant Ship　　　　　　　　　　　　　　　　by Claire Du

## "中国皇后号"商船

据余颖娉的《早期飘洋过海踏入美国的华人》文章记载，1784年2月22日，美国的"中国皇后号"三桅杆帆商船，从纽约启程，经过半年航程，于当年8月28日抵达中国广州，从此揭开了中美直接贸易的序幕。

## China's "Queen" Merchant Ship

According to the article *Early Chinese Who Crossed the Ocean and Entered the United States* written by Yingping Yu, the American three-masted merchant ship "Queen of China" set out from New York on February 22, 1784, and arrived in Guangzhou, China on August 28, 1784 after a half year voyage. From then on, direct trade between China and the United States began.

第一部分　移民篇
Part One　Immigration

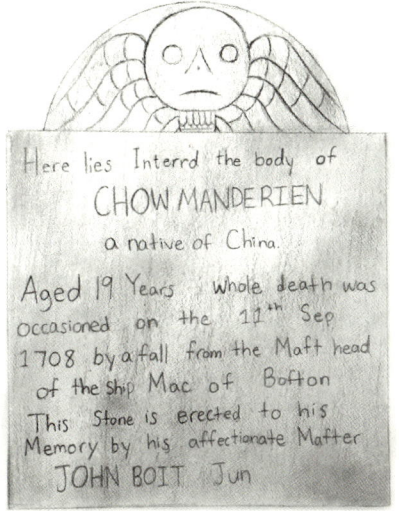

◉《波士顿公园里的华人少年墓地》
Chinese Juvenile Cemetery in Boston Park

姚嘉璐　画
by Jessica Yao

## 波士顿公园里的华人少年墓地

1798[①]年9月，一位叫Chow Zhou的19岁中国少年水手，从波士顿港口商船"麦克号"的桅杆上坠落致死，船主把他安葬在波士顿公园内的中央埋葬地。

船主名字是约翰·小博伊特，出生于波士顿。他的父亲来自英格兰，是早期的航海家，曾探险发现了位于今天华盛顿州的哥伦比亚河，并与合伙人从哥伦比亚河捕河狸卖往中国，同时购买茶叶与丝绸运到美国。他在1794—1796年间环游世界，是"旧中国贸易"的先行者。

## Chinese Young Adult's Cemetery in Boston Park

In September 1798, a 19-year-old Chinese sailor named Chow Zhou fell from the mast of the Mike's ship in Boston Harbor and then died. The ship's owner buried him at the central burial grounds in Boston Park.

The ferry owner was John Boit Jr. He was born in Boston, and his father was an early sailor from England. John's father explored the Columbia River in Washington State. In the Columbia River, he and his partner caught beavers and sold them together to China, while importing tea and silk to the United States. He traveled around the world between 1794 and 1796 and is the forerunner of "the Old China Trade".

---

[①]　画中应为1798年。

◉《最早抵美的华人女子梅阿芳》　　　　　　　　　　宋波菲　画
*A Fang Mei, the First Chinese Woman to Arrive in the United States*　　by Sophia Song

第一部分 移民篇
Part One  Immigration

**最早抵美的华人女子梅阿芳**

1834 年，一名叫梅阿芳的小脚女子被"华盛顿号"商人卡恩兄弟带到美国，她是记录在案的第一个踏入美国的华人女子。卡恩兄弟将年仅 16 岁的梅阿芳包装成一位清朝公主——皇帝的女儿，在城里的商业地段公园广场 8 号 (Park Place 8) 装饰了一间中国风格的沙龙，让梅阿芳在里面接待体面的绅士和淑女。沙龙门票为 25 美分。完全迥异的外貌与生活习惯吸引着西方人的猎奇心。卡恩兄弟的做法在当时曾受到媒体抨击，认为将人与商品一起展出很不人道。史料记载，梅阿芳在翻译陪同下，曾前往费城、华盛顿，还被美国总统安德鲁·杰克逊会见过，后定居波士顿。

**A Fang Mei, the First Chinese Woman to Arrive in the United States**

In 1834, a small-footed woman named A fang Mei (A fong Moy) was brought to the United States by Brother Kahn, a merchant of the ship "Washington". She was the first Chinese woman on record to arrive in the United States. The Kahn brothers decorated a salon in Chinese style at Park Place 8, a commercial area of the city, and presented this 16-year-old Afang Mei as a Qing Dynasty princess, the emperor's daughter, to entertain decent gentlemen and ladies. Salon ticket was 25 cents. The completely different appearance and living habits attracted the curiosity of Westerners. But the media at the time criticized the Kahn brothers was saying it was inhumane to display people alongside merchandise. According to historical records, Afang Mei, accompanied by a translator, went to Philadelphia and Washington, was met by US President Andrew Jackson, and then settled in Boston.

◉ 《最早的华人茶商》  姚嘉璐 画
   The Earliest Chinese Tea Merchants  by Jessica Yao

## 第一部分　移民篇
Part One　Immigration

### 最早的华人茶商

1850年，中国的道光皇帝驾崩，咸丰皇帝登基。而在美国，华人茶商亚寿已经当上两家茶叶店的老板——一家在纽约州的奥尔巴尼市，另一家在波士顿市中心。1851年，亚寿参加了在伦敦水晶宫举办的伦敦工业博览会，并担当中国展台的翻译。从英国博览会回来后，1853年，亚寿与德裔美国女子路易莎在南波士顿的圣马修教堂结婚，此前他受洗成为基督徒。美国各大媒体都刊登了这条爆炸性新闻。

1860年，亚寿成为首位加入美国籍的华人，并成为首位以中国名字出现的美国选民。1878年5月，与亚寿生活25年、共同养育了一双儿女的妻子去世。同年9月，亚寿告别波士顿，返回故乡广东。

图为亚寿在纽约奥尔巴尼市和波士顿茶叶店的广告。

### The Earliest Chinese Tea Merchants

In 1850, Emperor Daoguang of China died and Emperor Xianfeng ascended the throne. While in the United States, Yashou became the owner of two tea shops. One was in Albany, New York; the other was in downtown Boston. In 1851, Yashou participated in the London Industrial Fair held at the Crystal Palace in London and acted as a translator for the Chinese booth. After returning from the British Exposition, Yashou married a German-American woman called Louisa at St. Matthew's Church in South Boston in 1853, after he was baptized as a Christian. Major American media have published this breaking news.

In 1860, Yashou was the first Chinese to become an American citizen. He also became the first American voter appearing with a Chinese name. In May 1878, his wife, who lived with Yashou for 25 years and raised a pair of children with him, died. In September of the same year, Yashou bid farewell to Boston and returned to his hometown in Guangdong.

The picture shows the advertisements of Yashou in Albany, New York, and Boston tea shops.

（译文 / 姚嘉璐　责编 / 贾晋平）

◎《最早的华人雕像广告》　　　　　　　　　姚嘉璐　画
　 The Earliest Advertisement for Chinese Statues　　by Jessica Yao

## 最早的华人雕像广告

19 世纪 40 年代，波士顿瑞鼎茶叶店老板为了吸引顾客，同时强调自己的茶叶产地正宗，特意在店门口放了一座半个真人大小的中国人雕像。那时波士顿的人口不足 14 万人。

## The Earliest Chinese Statues as Advertisement

In the 1840s, in order to attract customers and emphasizing his authentic tea origin, an owner of the Boston Ruiding Tea Shop purposefully placed an authentic, half-life Chinese statue in front of the store. At that time, Boston's population was no more than 140,000 in total.

（译文 / 姚嘉璐　责编 / 贾晋平）

# 第二章　北美淘金华人

## Chapter 2　Chinese for Gold Rush in North America

◉《首批华人群体抵达加州》　　　　　　　　　　　　　　　　程子宁　画
First Batch of Chinese Arrive in California　　　　　　　　　by Zining Cheng

## 首批华人群体抵达加州

1785年，三名华人船员落地马里兰州后，陆续有个别华人被美国商船带到美国。加州发现金矿的消息传出后，1848—1852年，由于两广地区长达十余年的太平天国运动、广东四邑地区遭遇大旱、水灾和饥荒，为了谋生，2.5万名华人分批次抵达加州金山。

## First Batch of Chinese Arriving in California

In 1785, after three Chinese sailors landed in Maryland, some Chinese were brought to the United States by American merchant ships. After the news of the discovery of gold mines in California, between 1848 and 1852, due to the Taiping Rebellion that lasted for more than ten years in Guangdong and Guangxi, and the severe drought, flood and famine in Siyi area, in order to make a living, 25,000 Chinese arrived in Jinshan, California in batches.

第一部分　移民篇
Part One　Immigration

◉ 《内华达山脉发现金子》　　　　　　　　　　　程子宁　画
　　*Gold found in Sierra Nevada*　　　　　　　　　by Zining Cheng

## 内华达山脉发现金子

　　1846 年，美国与墨西哥爆发战争，1948 年，战争结束。美国获得加州、内华达、犹他、科罗拉多、亚利桑那、新墨西哥和怀俄明部分地区，一跃成为跨大西洋和太平洋的大国。同年，一位叫詹姆斯·威尔逊·马歇尔的人，在内华达山脉的一个锯木场发现了黄金。

## Gold found in Sierra Nevada

　　War broke out between the United States and Mexico in 1846 and ended in 1948. The United States won areas such as California, Nevada, Utah, Colorado, Arizona, New Mexico and parts of Wyoming, and became a transatlantic and Pacific power. The same year, a man named James Wilson Marshall discovered gold at a sawmill in the Sierra Nevada.

◎《加州淘金潮》　　　　　　　　　　　　　　　　　　　　毛笛　画
　*California Gold Rush*　　　　　　　　　　　　　　　　　by Di Mao

### 加州淘金潮

　　加州发现金子的消息迅速传遍全世界。1848—1849年，短短两年时间，加州移民的数量从400人激增到9万人。19世纪60年代中期，大约30万人从世界各地涌入加州，史称"淘金潮"。

### California Gold Rush

News of the discovery of gold in California quickly spread around the world. From 1848 to 1849, in just two years, the number of immigrants in California surged from 400 to 90,000. In the mid-1860s, about 300,000 people poured into California from all over the world, known as the "Gold Rush" in history.

第一部分　移民篇
Part One　Immigration

◎《淘金华人陈明》　　　　　　　　　　　　　　邓依然　画
　Chinese Gold Rusher Chen Ming　　　　　　　by Melissa Deng

**淘金华人陈明**

　　1847年，首位中国广东人陈明来到加州淘金。最初，在亚美利加河河床上可以轻易找到沙金，于是陈明很快就发了大财。随后，陈明给同村老乡捎去口信，去加州能发财的消息很快在当地各个宗族间传播，淘金热使无数人变卖了田地、耕牛以换取前往美国的船票。没钱的则会和中间人签下契约劳工，抵美后打工还钱。

**Chinese Gold Rusher Chen Ming**

　　In 1847, the first Chinese Cantonese, Chen Ming, came to California to pan for gold. Initially, alluvial gold was easily found on the bed of the American River. Chen Ming quickly made a fortune. Later, Chen Ming sent a message to his fellow villagers in his hometown. The news that he had make a fortune in California quickly spread among the local clans. Countless people sold their fields and cattle in exchange for ferry tickets to the United States. Those who had no money signed an indentured labor contract with middlemen. They would work after arriving in the United States to pay back the money.

● 《华人不能购买采矿权》　　　　　　　　　　　　　钟骐励　画
　Chinese Cannot Buy Mining Rights　　　　　　　　by Qili Zhong

## 华人不能购买采矿权

　　淘金过程中，华人遭到美国白人的诸多歧视，每当华人发现高产量的金沙河段时，就被白人赶出产金地带，只能开采已经淘过两三次的废旧坑穴。因为根据加州矿区规定，华人不能购买采矿权。

　　据记载，1848—1849年，淘金华人仅775名，人均月收入150美元左右。华人们发现，这份苦力活的收入远高于在国内务农。攒下钱后，他们又通过中间人将其他同族接到加州，并为新来的同胞提供翻译和简陋住房。

　　于是，随着抵美华人越来越多，华人会馆应运而生，并逐渐形成后来的六大会馆。这些会馆极具地域性，如中山人的阳和总会馆、客家人的宁阳总会馆等。

　　据资料显示，1857年1月至1858年6月，共有35条船从香港驶向旧金山。其中，成人男子9907人，成年女子699人，男童11人。

第一部分　移民篇
Part One　Immigration

**Chinese Cannot Buy Mining Rights**

During the gold panning process, the Chinese were discriminated against by the white Americans. Whenever the Chinese discovered the high-yielding golden sands, they were driven out of the gold-producing areas by the whites, and they could only mine the abandoned pits that had been panned two or three times. Because according to California mining regulations, the Chinese cannot buy mining rights.

According to records, from 1848 to 1849, there were only 775 gold rush Chinese, with a per capita monthly payment of about 150 US dollars. The Chinese found that the income of this coolie was much higher than that of farming in the country. So, they quickly formed a group and established the Association of Hometowns. After saving the money, they brought other kin to California through middlemen, and provided translators and poor housing for the newcomers.

So more and more Chinese arrived in the United States, Chinese guild halls came into being and gradually formed the later six assembly halls. These guild halls were regionally-based, such as the Yanghe General Hall of the Zhongshan people and the Ningyang General Hall of the Hakka people.

According to data, from January 1857 to June 1858, a total of 35 ships sailed from Hong Kong to San Francisco, including 9,907 adult men, 699 adult women, and 11 boys.

◉《香港港口》　　　　　　　　　　　　　　　　　　陈乃仪　画
Hong Kong Port　　　　　　　　　　　　　　　　　　by Nia Chen

**加拿大发现金矿**

　　1858 年，加拿大卑诗省（即不列颠哥伦比亚省）的菲莎河以及新西敏市发现金矿后，加拿大掀起淘金热。美国金山的华人，还有广东台山开平等地的华人，纷纷涌来，成为第一批华人掘金队伍。到 1860 年，卑诗省的华人已达 4000 人。

　　1862 年，第二次淘金热兴起，第二批华人又涌入，直到 1870 年退潮时。淘金华人在获得执照后，他们简陋的小木屋和帐篷到处林立。

　　据考古学者称，加拿大淘金热时，约 2000 名华人涌向温哥华北面的巴克维尔镇，占当地人口的一半。

**Gold Found in Canada**

In 1858, after the discovery of gold mines in the Fraser River in British Columbia and New Westminster, Canada set off a gold rush. The Chinese in Jinshan, the United States, and the Chinese in Kaiping, Taishan, Guangdong and other places, flocked to become the first group of Chinese gold-digging teams. By 1860, the Chinese in British Columbia, Canada had reached 4,000.

第一部分 移民篇
Part One  Immigration

◎《淘金华人的木屋》
*Chinese Gold Rusher's Hut*

赵汉黎 画
by Hailey Zhao

When the second gold rush started in 1862, the second group of Chinese came again until 1870, when the tide fell. After the license was granted to the Chinese gold rusher, humble log cabins and tents popped up everywhere.

According to archaeologists, during the Canadian Gold Rush, about 2,000 Chinese, nearly half the local population, flocked to the town of Barkerville, north of Vancouver.

（译文/毛笛 责编/黄丽芳）

# 第三章　北美早期唐人街

## Chapter 3　Early-stage Chinatowns in North America

# 100年北美华人移民史
100 Years of Chinese Immigration in the United States and Canada

◉ 《旧金山唐人街》　　　　　　　　　　　　　马倩芸　画
　　*San Francisco Chinatown*　　　　　　　　　by Annissa Ma

第一部分　移民篇
Part One   Immigration

### 旧金山唐人街

1848年，首批华人抵达加州淘金后，为了连接华人与美国社会，华人们自然而然地以金山的都板街（Grant Avenue）为中心，建起了全美历史最悠久的唐人街（Chinatown, San Francisco）。

图为1866年的旧金山唐人街。

### San Francisco Chinatown

Chinatown in 1848, after the first group of Chinese arrived in California to rush for gold, in order to meet the need for connecting the Chinese and the American society, the Chinese people spontaneously built up the oldest Chinatown in Grant Avenue, Duban Street, San Francisco as the center.

The picture shows Chinatown in 1866, San Francisco.

◉《华人单身社区》　　　　　　　　　　　　　喻玲珑　画
　*Chinese Singles Community*　　　　　　　　by Annie Yu

## 华人单身社区

　　1882年，因为《排华法案》的限制，为了养家糊口，旧金山唐人街的华人们有家不敢回，担心回去就无法再回来打工赚钱养家。因此，第二次世界大战前的唐人街中男性居多。

## Chinese Singles Community

　　In 1882, because of the restrictions of the "Chinese Exclusion Act", to work for the families, the Chinese people in San Francisco's Chinatown chose not to go back to their homes, for fear that they would not be able to return to work to earn money to support their families. As a result, there were more men than women in Chinatowns before World War II.

第一部分　移民篇
Part One　Immigration

◉《唐人街杂货店》　　　　　　　　　　　　　　　　　　马倩芸　画
　*Grocery Store in San Francisco Chinatown*　　　　　　by Annissa Ma

## 唐人街杂货店

　　早在1807年，广东商人就把丝绸、陶瓷、海味、烟草等产品带到美国通过杂货铺售卖。1846年，旧金山市政府正式成立时，华人已在旧金山繁衍生息，杂货店和中餐馆成为唐人街必不可少的场所。

## Grocery Store in San Francisco Chinatown

　　As early as 1807, Cantonese merchants brought silk, ceramics, seafood, tobacco and other products to the United States for sale through grocery stores. In 1846, when the city government of San Francisco was formally established, the Chinese had already prospered in San Francisco, and grocery stores and Chinese restaurants had become important places for people.

◎《加拿大早期唐人街》　　　　　　　　　　　　　马倩芸　画
　*Canada's First Chinatown*　　　　　　　　　　by Annissa Ma

## 加拿大早期唐人街

1842 年后,一批广东台山人从香港进入加拿大。

1858 年,卑诗省的菲莎河谷发现金子,吸引了许多旧金山淘金华工和广东台山人来此。于是,加拿大最早的唐人街就在卑诗省维多利亚市建立。

## Canada's First Chinatown

After 1842, people from Guangdong and Hongkong immigrated to Canada.

In 1858 British Columbia, there was a rumor said that there was gold found in the Fraser Valley, many Chinese immigrants rushed to Canada to find gold. Canada's earliest China Town was found in British Columbia.

第一部分 移民篇
Part One　Immigration

◉《波士顿唐人街》　　　　　　　　　　　　　　　　　宋毕昕　画
　　Boston Chinatown　　　　　　　　　　　　　　　　by Anthony Song

## 波士顿唐人街

1870 年，华工大批涌入马萨诸塞州。为了取代罢工的工人，75 名 20 岁左右的中国人被马萨诸塞州的北亚当斯的一家制鞋场雇佣。他们暂住在平安巷，渐渐便形成波士顿唐人街。

这个区域占地五亩，有三条主街，近百家店铺，近一半人口为亚裔。

## Boston Chinatown

In 1870, Chinese laborers poured into Massachusetts in large numbers. 75 Chinese, who were in their 20s, were hired by a shoe factory in North Adams, Massachusetts to replace the striking workers. These people settled in Ping on Alley, which gradually became Boston's Chinatown. This area covers an area of five acres, with three main streets, nearly 100 shops, and nearly half of the population is Asian.

100 Years of Chinese Immigration in the United States and Canada

◉《纽约唐人街》　　　　　　　　　　　　　　　　马倩芸　画
　*New York Chinatown*　　　　　　　　　　　　　by Annissa Ma

第一部分　移民篇
Part One　Immigration

**纽约唐人街**

据记载，1858年，一名叫阿肯（Ah Ken）的广东商人是首位抵达纽约的华人。据说他在柏路开了一间香烟店，在纽约街头贩售三毛钱一根的香烟，提供点烟纸和油灯给顾客使用。后来他又在勿街经营一间旅馆，租赁房间给初到此地的华人，这里渐渐形成唐人街。1870年时，纽约唐人街只有200名华人。

排华时期，2000余名美国西海岸的华人迁移到东岸打工，到1882年，已有7000余名华人生活在唐人街区域的披露街、勿街和宰也街。

图为1909年的纽约唐人街区域的Doyers街。

**New York Chinatown**

According to records, in 1858, a Cantonese businessman named Ah Ken was the first Chinese to arrive in New York. It is said that he opened a cigarette shop in Park Road, selling a thirty-cent cigarette on the streets of New York, providing cigarette lighters and oil lamps for customers to use. Later, he ran a hotel in Mott Street and rented rooms for the Chinese who came here for the first time. The place gradually formed a Chinatown. In 1870, there were only 200 Chinese in New York's Chinatown.

During the era of Chinese exclusion, more than 2,000 Chinese from the west coast of the United States migrated to the east coast to work. By 1882, more than 7,000 Chinese lived in the disclosure Street, Mott Street and Zai Ye Street in the Chinatown area.

The picture shows New York Chinatown in 1909, Doyers street.

# 100年北美华人移民史
100 Years of Chinese Immigration in the United States and Canada

◉《圣何塞唐人街》
*San Jose Chinatown*

张云想　画
by Yunxiang Zhang

## 圣何塞唐人街

1866年，华人在加州圣何塞市建唐人街。1870年发生大火，唐人街被烧毁。之后，新迁来的500名华人，再建唐人街。

1887年，华人移民多达1400人。然而，《排华法案》颁布后，唐人街因被定为"公害"而被人纵火烧毁。之后，华人再建唐人街。

图为加州圣何塞南端，那里曾是华工的聚集地，而今成为圣克鲁斯主街。

## San Jose Chinatown

In 1866, the Chinese built Chinatown in San Jose, California. In 1870, a fire broke out and Chinatown burned down. After that, the new-arrivals of 500 Chinese rebuilt the Chinatown.

In 1887, as many as 1,400 Chinese immigrated. However, after the enactment of the *Chinese Exclusion Act*, Chinatown was set on fire because it was designated a "public nuisance". After that, the Chinese built Chinatown again.

The picture shows the southern end of San Jose, California, which used to be a gathering place for Chinese workers and is now the main street of Santa Cruz.

（译文/毛笛　责编/黄丽芳）

# 第二部分　华工篇

# PART TWO
# CHINESE WORKERS

# 第四章　太平洋铁路构想

Chapter 4　Concept of the Pacific Railroad

◉《东岸到西岸需要半年时间》  赵君艺 画
Six Months from East to West   by Victoria Zhao

## 第二部分　华工篇
## Part Two　Chinese Workers

**东岸到西岸需要半年时间**

19世纪30年代，从美国东岸到西岸需要花费半年的时间。

美国南北向交通一直比较发达，然而东西向的交通一直困扰美国人。那时的美国，从纽约坐马车穿越内华达山脉到旧金山需要3～6个月；从纽约坐船绕过南美的合恩角再到旧金山需要半年；从纽约乘船经巴拿马丛林到旧金山需6～9个月。

**Six Months from East to West**

In the 1830s, it took about half a year from the east coast to the west coast.

North-south traffic in the United States had been relatively developed, but the east-west traffic had always troubled Americans. The trip from one coast to another was very long and hard. At that time, in the United States, it took 3—6 months to travel from New York to San Francisco by horse-drawn carriage. It took half a year to travel from New York to San Francisco via Cape Horn in South America by boat. It took 6—9 months from New York to San Francisco through the Panama jungle by boat.

◎《阿萨·惠特尼》  陈子鉴 画
　　Asa Whitney  by Kent Chen

## 第二部分　华工篇
## Part Two　Chinese Workers

### 阿萨·惠特尼

阿萨·惠特尼（Asa Whitney）首次发文主张修建一条从密歇根湖到俄勒冈州的跨大陆铁路。并于1847年向美国国会提交了提案。

出生于美国康涅狄格州的干货商人阿萨·惠特尼于1843年乘坐一艘狭窄的帆船，花了153天到达广东。缓慢的旅程让他痛苦不堪，他想到，如果能从纽约修一条铁路直达旧金山，再从那里坐船直达中国，岂不有利于东西方贸易往来？

1844年在回美国的途中，他草拟了修建美国东西两岸铁路的议案。

1845年，惠特尼率领8名队员调查了设想的铁路路线沿线。为了寻求企业家和政治家的支援，他分发地图和小册子，向联邦议会陈述了大陆横贯铁路的建设计划。但是，当时美国爆发了南北战争，计划没能实现。

### Asa Whitney

Asa Whitney published a paper advocating the construction of a transcontinental railroad from Lake Michigan to Oregon. He submitted a proposal to the US Congress in 1847.

In the year 1843, Asa Whitney, a dry goods merchant from Connecticut, USA, sailed on a narrow sailboat to China. His journey to China took 153 days, and his final destination was Guangdong. The slow journey made him miserable. He began to consider: Wouldn't it be good if a railroad could be built from New York to San Francisco? It would be helpful if there be a direct ship to China? These thoughts was the beginnings of his plan.

On his way back to the United States in 1844, he drafted a proposal for the building of the East-West Railway.

In 1845, Whitney led a team of eight person to in vestigate the land, where he had wanted the railroad to be built on. In order to seek the support from entrepreneurs and politicians, he distributed some maps and pamphlets, and presented the plans for the Transcontinental Railroad to the Federal Parliament. However, when the Civil War broke out in the United States, the plans were forced to pause.

◉ 《唐纳大队》　　　　　　　　　　　　　　　　　　　毛笛　画
*The Donner Party*　　　　　　　　　　　　　　　　　　by Di Mao

第二部分　华工篇
Part Two　Chinese Workers

## 唐纳大队

19 世纪 40 年代，前往西部的移民者倍增。1846 年春，乔治·唐纳、雅各·唐纳以及詹姆斯·瑞德三大家族以及来自田纳西的莫菲家族、德国移民柯赛堡家族等共 87 人，组成一个西进大队，从美国伊利诺伊州的春田市出发，计划用半年时间移民到加州。他们需要走完 3000 千米，在大雪封山前翻越内华达山。但一场提早到来的风雪将这几个家族困在海拔 2000 米的地方，接近半数成员冻死或饿死，部分生存者靠食人存活。第二年救援队找到他们时，只剩 48 人到达加州。后来他们称这个不知名的雪山为唐纳山峰。20 年后，就是这个峰顶，埋葬了许多铁路华工。

## The Donner Party

In the 1840s, immigration to the West doubled. In the spring of 1846, a total of 87 people, including the people of George Downer, Jacob Downer and James Reid families, the Murphy family from Tennessee, and the German immigrant Kosseberg family, formed a westward team to immigrate from Springfield City, Illinois to California in half a year. In order to do this, they needed to cover 3,000 kilometers, and should cross the Sierra Nevada before the snow capped the mountains. However, an early snowstorm trapped the families at an altitude of 2,000 meters. Nearly half of the members died of freezing or starvation, and some people survived by eating human. The following year, when rescue teams found them, only 48 arrived in California. Later they called this unnamed snow-capped mountain Donner Peak. Twenty years later, it was at this peak that many Chinese railway workers were buried.

◉《铁路之父》　　　　　　　　　　　　　　　　　　祝云姝　画
*Father of the Transcontinental Railroad*　　　　　　　by Maggie Zhu

第二部分　华工篇
Part Two　Chinese Workers

**铁路之父**

西奥多·朱达 1826 年生于康涅狄格州的布里奇波特，是一名牧师的儿子。在他 12 岁时，父亲过世。他的一个哥哥去西岸淘金，另一位哥哥参军。他 13 岁时，以全校第一名的成绩毕业于伦斯勒理工学院，这是世界上第一家私人建立的工程学院。

20 岁时，他就名扬天下，因为他参与了多条铁路线、桥梁和运河的建设。比如特洛伊和斯克内克塔迪铁路以及被称为现代工程奇迹的尼亚加拉峡谷等。

1854 年，他遇见一位在美墨战争中当过上校的商人。为了方便从内华达山脉把银矿运出来，这个商人建议朱达修一条从加州首府萨克拉门托到福尔松的"托溪谷"铁路。

**Father of the Transcontinental Railroad**

Theodore Judah was born in Bridgeport, Connecticut, in the year 1826. He was the son of a priest.

When he was just 12 years old, his father died. One of his older brothers went to the West Bank to pan for gold, the other brother joined the army. At the age of 13, Judah graduated from Rensselaer Polytechnic Institute, the first engineering school established by private in the world.

At the age of 20, he became famous for his involvement in the construction of several railway lines, bridges and canals, such as the Troy and Schenectady Railroad and the Niagara Gorge, which were known as modern engineering marvels.

In 1854, he met a businessman who had been a colonel in the Mexican-American War. He suggested that Juda build the "Tor Creek" railway from Sacramento, California, to Folsom, so that the transportation of silver mines from the Sierra Nevada would be more convenient.

◉ 《铁路测绘》 张馨雅　画
　　The Genius Engineer by Xinya Zhang

**铁路测绘**

　　修建托溪谷铁路的过程中,朱达萌生了要修一条横贯东西大陆的 4000 千米长的铁路计划。当他四处宣讲这个计划时,他被人们称为"疯子朱达"。

　　1856 年,他在华盛顿参加了联邦议会的大厅活动,书写建议书,发给阁僚和议员等有影响力的人们。

　　1859 年 9 月,在旧金山召开了第一次太平洋铁路会议,朱达被选为特使。12 月他回到华盛顿,在凯皮特尔·希尔大厦的一角设立了办公室。他代表太平洋铁路会议与詹姆斯·布坎南总统会面,并在联邦议会上发言。

　　1860 年,朱达回到加利福尼亚,调查了通过铁路越过内华达山脉的路径。然而在他再次返回东岸的路途中,他得了黄热病,37 岁病逝于纽约。

第二部分　华工篇
Part Two　Chinese Workers

**The Genius Engineer**

During the construction of the "Tor Creek" Valley Railway, Judah came up with a plan to build a 4,000-kilometer railway across the East and West continents. He was called "Mad Judah", because he kept running around telling everyone his plans.

In 1856 he went to Washington and participated in the halls of the Federal Assembly, where he wrote proposals and sent them to influential people such as cabinet ministers and congressmen.

In the September of 1859, the first Pacific Railroad Conference was held in San Francisco, Judah was selected as the deputy. He returned to Washington in December and set up an office in a corner of the Capitol Hill Building, where he met with President James Buchanan on behalf of the Pacific Railroad Conference and addressed the Federal Assembly.

In 1860, Judah returned to California to research a path by rail across the Sierra Nevada. However, on his way back to the East Coast, he caught yellow fever and died in New York at the age of 37.

100 Years of Chinese Immigration in the United States and Canada

◎《林肯与〈太平洋铁路法案〉》　　　　　　　　　　　　　　　贾佳茵　画
　 *Lincoln and the Pacific Railroad Act*　　　　　　　　　　　　by Kaela Jia

第二部分　华工篇
Part Two　Chinese Workers

**林肯与《太平洋铁路法案》**

1859 年，总统候选人林肯在爱荷华州演讲时遇到铁路工程师格伦维尔·道奇（Grenville M. Dodge），并向他求证："横贯大陆的铁路应该从哪里开始它的起点？"

南北战争期间，时任美国总统林肯想把西部的矿产物资以及兵源投入东部战场。1862 年，美国国会出台了《太平洋铁路法案》。

**Lincoln and the Pacific Railroad Act**

In 1859, presidential candidate Lincoln, while speaking in Iowa, met railroad engineer Grenville M. Dodge. He asked him, "Where should the transcontinental railroad begin?"

During the Civil War, Lincoln, then president of the United States, wanted to send the minerals and soldiers from the west to the eastern battlefield. In 1862, Congress passed the *Pacific Railroad Act*.

◉《中央太平洋铁路公司董事》 吴雨芮 画
*Chairperson and Shareholders of Central Pacific Railroad Company* by Sherry Wu

第二部分　华工篇
Part Two　Chinese Workers

**中央太平洋铁路公司董事**

1863年，时任加州州长利兰·斯坦福（Leland Stanford）及夫人珍妮创办了中央太平洋铁路公司，另有三位股东和一名工程师加盟。他们是亨廷顿、霍普金斯、克洛克和35岁的总工程师朱达。

1863年1月8日，连接美国东西的横贯大陆铁路正式动工兴建。

**Chairperson and Shareholders of Central Pacific Railroad Company**

In 1863, the Governor of California, Leland Stanford and his wife Jenny Stanford founded the Central Pacific Company. Three other shareholders and an engineer joined. They were Huntington, Hopkins, Kroc and 35-year-old chief engineer Judah.

On January 8, 1863, the first Pacific Railroad in the history of the United States was officially constructed.

◉《铁路承建商》　　　　　　　　　　　　　　　　　　　　　高晨曦　画
　*Transcontinental Railroad Participating Companies*　　　　　by Chenxi Gao

## 铁路承建商

　　横贯东西大陆的 4000 千米长的铁路主要由三家公司承包修建：

　　1. 最西端从萨克拉门托到旧金山奥克兰的路段 200 千米，由西太平洋铁路公司承担。

　　2. 联合太平洋公司从爱荷华州与内布拉斯加相交界的奥马哈开始，向西修筑铁路。该公司是美国政府直接扶持的半国有企业。所雇佣的劳工，大部分为逃饥荒而来美国的爱尔兰移民。

3. 中央太平洋公司从加州的萨克拉门托开始，往东修铁路。当时预计双方汇合的时间是14年后，地点是太浩湖附近，也就是加州和内华达州的交界处。虽然中央太平洋公司只修600多千米铁路，而联合太平洋公司修了2000多千米。但前者比后者的难度高了很多。从萨克拉门托到太浩湖，要经过内华达雪山（Sierra Nevada），内华达雪山不仅长年积雪还遍布悬崖峭壁。而后者的区域，一半以上是平原，剩下一半在落基山里，但也有足够多的山谷和隘口可以利用，施工难度要小得多。

**Transcontinental Railroad Participating Companies**

The 4,000-kilometer railway across the east and west continents was mainly contracted by three companies:

1. The westernmost 200-kilometer section from Sacramento to San Francisco and Oakland was undertaken by the Western Pacific Railroad Company.

2. Union Pacific Company began building railroads westward from Omaha, where Iowa and Nebraska meet. The company was a semi-state-owned enterprise directly supported by the US government. Most of the workers employed were Irish immigrants who came to the United States to escape famine.

3. The Central Pacific Company built a railway from Sacramento, California to the east. At that time, it was expected that the two companies would meet in 14 years, near Lake Tahoe, which is the junction of California and Nevada. The Central Pacific only built more than 600 kilometers of railway, while Union Pacific built more than 2,000 kilometers. However, the tosk of former was much more difficult than the latter. From Sacramento to Lake Tahoe, you have to pass through the Sierra Nevada, which is not only covered with snow all year round but also covered with cliffs. For Union Pocific, more than half of the area are plains, and the remaining half are in the Rocky Mountains, where there are enough valleys and passages can be used. The construction was much less difficult.

（译文/潘洁祾 责编/陈虹）

# 第五章 华人来美修铁路缘由

## Chapter 5　Reasons for Chinese to Come to America to Build Railways

● 《白人劳工短缺》　　　　　　　　　　　陈睿斌　画
White Labor Shortage　　　　　　　　　　by Ruibin Chen

## 白人劳工短缺

中央太平洋铁路公司的进程并不顺利。

从西往东，耗用两年时间，只挺进43英里，到达纽卡斯尔（New Castle）时，工程便停滞了。因为前方进入了内华达山脉地质最坚硬、地矿最复杂的布鲁默高地，所以白人劳工们纷纷离开，转向赚钱更容易的农场、矿山。工地上只剩下不到300个工人，还常常罢工抗议。为此，中央太平洋铁路公司决定扩招5000名铁路劳工，但广告贴出后，只有几百名白人劳工来应聘，白人劳工严重短缺！

第二部分　华工篇
Part Two　Chinese Workers

**White Labor Shortage**

The process for the Central Pacific Railroad was not smooth.

From west to east, it took two years to advance merely 43 miles before it reached New Castle. When it did, the construction came to a standstill. As the front entered the Bloomer Heights, the hardest and most complex geological place in the Sierra Nevada, the white laborers left one after another, leaving for farms and mines where it was easier to make money. Less than 300 workers remained on the site, and they often went on strike in protest. Due to this issue, the Central Pacific Railroad Company decided to recruit 5,000 railway workers, but after the advertisement was posted, only a few hundred white workers applied for the job, and there was a serious shortage of white workers!

◉《雇用华工争议》　　　　　　　　　　　　　　　　　祝云姝　画
　*Disputes Over Hiring Chinese Workers*　　　　　　　　by Maggie Zhu

**雇用华工争议**

　　中央太平洋铁路公司负责实际建造铁路以及人力资源管理的股东查尔斯·克罗克（Charles Crocker）与淘金华工有过接触，他看中华工的勤劳朴实。1865年2月，他建议雇用华工，但与公司总裁斯坦福以及施工监督斯托尔布瑞吉在试用华工问题上发生争执。斯坦福认为太平洋铁路是美国历史上最伟大的工程，怎能让血统低贱的种族插手！何况身强力壮的白人都干不了，这些面黄肌瘦、留辫子的中国人，能干什么！克罗克反驳说："难道你们不知道吗，这些中国人在数千年之前，就修建过世界上最伟大的人造工程——长城，还有什么是建不成的？"最后斯坦福同意，先雇少量的华人来试试。

第二部分　华工篇
Part Two　Chinese Workers

**Disputes Over Hiring Chinese Workers**

　　Charles Crocker, the shareholder of the Central Pacific Railroad, who was in charge of the actual construction of the railway and the management of human resources, had worked with the gold mining Chinese workers. He saw the industriousness and simplicity of the Chinese workers. In February 1865, he suggested that they should hire Chinese laborers, but the company president Stanford and the construction supervisor Stolbridge had a dispute over the trial employment of Chinese workers. Stanford believed that the Pacific Railroad had been the greatest project in American history, there should be no way a low-blood race intervene. What's more, since even the strongest white men couldn't do the job, it was impossible that a group of Chinese men, with yellow faces, thin muscles and braid, to accomplish it. Crocker retorted, "Don't you know that these Chinese people built the greatest man-made project in the world, the Great Wall? Since they had built the Great Wall, thousands of years ago. What else can't they build? " He reasoned, "We can try some Chinese."

# 100 Years of Chinese Immigration in the United States and Canada

◎《劈开布鲁默高地》 张馨雅 画
*Split the Bloomer Heights* by Xinya Zhang

第二部分 华工篇
Part Two  Chinese Workers

**劈开布鲁默高地**

1863年1月8日，连接美国东西部的横贯大陆铁路正式动工兴建。第一批50名试用华工陆续到达铁路工地。

华工不计较比白人劳工低5美元，二话不说，就在工地搭起帐篷，第二天就开始用简单的铲子、镐和黑火药干活。他们炸开坚硬的石头与粘质的土块，硬生生从山中间劈出一条路——深63英尺，底部宽达12英尺，长800英尺。仅用七个月，他们就开凿了从Dutch Flat到Donner Lake之间的收费马车车道，打通了中央太平洋铁路的物流通道，攻克了中央太平洋铁路上第一个难关工程，创造了"世界第八大奇迹"——布鲁默堑。

**Split the Bloomer Heights**

50 trial Chinese workers as the first group arrived at the railway construction site one after another. On January 8, 1863, a construction of the transcontinental railroad connecting the east and west of the United states began.

The Chinese laborers didn't mind being paid $5 less than white labor set up tents at the construction site without any hesitation, and the next day they started working with simple shovels, picks and dynamite. They blasted the hard stones and sticky soil block, then cut a path through the middle of the mountain, which was 63 feet deep, 12 feet wide at the bottom, and 800 feet long. In only seven months, they dug the toll carriage lane from Dutch Flat to Donner Lake, opened up the logistics channel of the Central Pacific Railway, overcame the first difficult project on the Central Pacific Railway, and completed "The Eighth Wonder of the World" —Bloomers Cut.

◎《送别》 陈乃仪 画
Farewell by Nia Chen

## 送别

中央太平洋铁路公司意识到,他们需要成千上万的华工。不久,铁路工地需要招募5000个华工的广告迅速贴满了旧金山的大街小巷。但却只招到3000名华工,人数远远不够。于是,中央太平洋铁路公司决定到广东征召2000名华工。并以每月26～31美元的月薪吸引了大批台山、开平、新会青壮年前来应征。

当时的中国正值清末,战乱不断,地震、洪水、饥荒,民不聊生,每个成人平均月收入一块银圆。为了生存,青壮年们从香港乘船,踏上背井离乡之途。

许多人不知道,这一挥手就是永别。

第二部分　华工篇
Part Two　Chinese Workers

**Farewell**

The Central Pacific Railroad realized they could have thousands of Chinese laborers to work for them, as they worked so hard and did things much faster than other laborers. Before long, advertisements that 5,000 Chinese laborers should be recruited at the railway site filled the streets of San Francisco. However, only 3,000 Chinese workers were recruited. The numbers were far from enough. Then the Central Pacific Railroad Company decided to recruit 2,000 Chinese workers in Guangdong. With a monthly salary of $26—$31 a month offered, it attracted a large number of young adults in Taishan, Kaiping and Xinhui.

In China, at the end of the Qing Dynasty, continuous wars, earthquakes, floods and famines kept attacking the people. The average monthly income of adult was one silver dollar each. In order to survive, young and middle-aged people took boats from Hong Kong and embarked on a journey to the foreign lands.

Many people didn't know that this trip was to say goodbye to their hometowns, and that it was the last time they would see their loved ones.

◉《万余华工应征来美》 祝云姝 画
*Million Chinese Recruited to be Railroad Worker* by Maggie Zhu

## 万余华工应征来美

1865年夏，首批2000名特招的华工到达美国旧金山，招聘公司预支了一笔路费，如果是乘蒸汽船来的，一张船票是40美元；如果是乘帆船来的则是25～35美元。这批华工大都是从广州市以南的珠江口离开家乡的。这笔钱需要以每月5%的利息分期从月薪中扣除。

香港到旧金山的海上航行一般需要35～40天，许多中国人一上岸就遭到攻击或抢劫。

1865—1869年，1.2万～1.4万名华工抵美。他们绝大多数来自广东台山、开平、新会等。1866年铁路工地的华人超过1万人，而白人劳工不足2000人。

# 第二部分　华工篇
## Part Two　Chinese Workers

**Million Chinese Recruited to be Railroad Worker**

To the company's delight, more than 10,000 Chinese workers applied to come to the United States and work.

In the summer of 1865, the first group of 2,000 specially recruited Chinese workers arrived in San Francisco. The job agencies had already paid the travel fee in advance. If they came by steamboat, a ticket was $40; if they came by sailboat, it was $25-$35. Most of the Chinese workers left their hometowns from the Pearl River estuary, south of Guangzhou. The travel fee needed to be deducted from the salary in installments of 5% per month.

The sea voyage from Hong Kong to San Francisco usually took 35-40 days, and many Chinese were attacked or looted as soon as they got ashore.

From 1865 to 1869, about 12,000 to 14,000 Chinese laborers arrived in the United States. Most of them were from Taishan, Kaiping and Xinhui, Guangdong Province. In 1866, there were more than 10,000 Chinese working on the railway construction site. The American laborers were less than 2,000.

（译文 / 潘洁棱　责编 / 陈虹）

# 第六章　华工劳作

## Chapter 6　Chinese Laborers at Work

◉《艰难工程》　　　　　　　　　　　　　　　　　　　　　　宋毕昕　画
　The Tough Project　　　　　　　　　　　　　　　　　　　by Anthony Song

**艰难工程**

　　1862 年美国总统林肯批准通过了《太平洋铁路法案》，该法案规定由联合太平洋铁路公司和中央太平洋铁路公司共同承建横贯大陆的太平洋铁路，美国国会决定以发行国债的方式筹集修路资金，并获准发行面值 100 美元的股票，数量多达 100 万张。

　　参与修建太平洋铁路的公司从政府那里获得的土地，比整个得克萨斯州的面积还要大。所以两家铁路公司都想加快建设速度以获得更多的利益。

　　太平洋铁路西线在加州部分总长约 130 英里，虽然仅占总里程的五分之一，但这里有崇山峻岭，而且终年飘雪，是最难修的一段。

第二部分 华工篇
Part Two  Chinese Workers

**The Tough Project**

In 1862, US President Lincoln signed *the Pacific Railroad Act* and made it a law. It authorized the Union Pacific and Central Pacific Railroad Company to build the Transcontinental Pacific Railroad jointly. The Congress decided to raise funds to finance the project by issuing government bonds. They also authorized the federal government to issue the stocks with a face value of $100, the amount of which reached up to one million.

The companies in charge of building the Pacific Railroad acquired land from the government, with a total area larger than the whole state of Texas. This motivated the two companies to speed up construction so that they could gain more profits.

The total length of the west line of the Pacific Railroad in California was 130 miles. Even though it only accounts for one-fifth of the total length of the railroad, this part of the line was the most difficult to build because there were lofty mountains and high ranges, covered with snow all year long.

◉《马车拉土》　　　　　　　　　　　　　　　　　　　　　　周子婷　画
　　*Pulling Soil with Horse-Drawn Carts*　　　　　　　　　　　　　by Helen Zhou

## 马车拉土

　　由于当时的蒸汽机火车马力不够大，连5度的坡也爬不上，所以沿线遇到山就要挖洞，见到坡就要开沟，而华工用最简陋的马车拉土的方式开始修建铁路。

## Pulling Soil with Horse-Drawn Carts

　　The power of the steaming train was so low at that time that it couldn't even climb up a road with five degrees of slope. Therefore, wherever there was a mountain or slope, Chinese workers needed to dig tunnels or ditches. Even so, Chinese workers started building the railroad using the simplest tools such as horse wagons to transport rocks and earth.

第二部分　华工篇
Part Two　Chinese Workers

◉《西部路段的主要劳工》　　　　　　　　　　　　　　　　肖禹睿　画
　*Main Laborers in the Western Section*　　　　　　　　　　by James Xiao

## 西部路段的主要劳工

从 1865 年到 1869 年的四年间，有 1.2 万 ~ 1.4 万名华工参加筑路工程，占铁路工人总数的 90%。

## Main Laborers in the Western Section

From 1865 to 1869, generally 12,000 to 14,000 Chinese workers toiled for the railroad construction, accounting for 90% of the total workers.

◉《修建 50 座桥梁》　　　　　　　　　　　　　　　　　　　祝云姝　画
　*Construction of 50 Bridges*　　　　　　　　　　　　　　　　by Maggie Zhu

**修建 50 座桥梁**

　　从西部往东修建的路段是最艰难的工程，铁路向东要穿越海拔 2100 米的内华达山脉，而最初的 40 英里都必须在崇山峻岭中穿行，需要建设 50 座桥梁和 10 条隧道。

**Construction of 50 Bridges**

　　The most challenging part of the project was the line from the west to the east, where the railroad went through the Sierra Nevada Mountains, which were 2,100 meters above sea level. The first forty miles of the line had to be built through the mountain ranges, involving the construction of fifty bridges and ten tunnels.

第二部分 华工篇
Part Two　Chinese Workers

◉《在悬崖峭壁施工》　　　　　　　　　　　　　贾佳茵　画
　　*Construction on the Cliffs*　　　　　　　　　　　by Kaela Jia

**在悬崖峭壁施工**

　　合恩角犹如一堵花岗岩石墙。它的下部是垂直光滑、深达 1000 英尺（合 304.8 米）的悬崖峭壁。

**Construction on the Cliffs**

　　Cape Horn is like a giant granite wall. The lower part is a steep and slippery cliff with a depth of a thousand feet (304.8 meters).

100 Years of Chinese Immigration in the United States and Canada

◎《锤子和钢钎》
*Hammer and Steel Drill*

宋毕昕　画
by Anthony Song

### 锤子和钢钎

　　华工腰系绳索，身悬半空，用锤子和钢钎先凿出一条险峻的小道，然后再费劲地逐步向里扩展，开凿出一条能够行驶车辆的通道。

### Hammer and Steel Drill

　　Chinese workers tied a rope around their waists and hung in the air, using hammers and steel chisels to carve out small roads in the mountains. Then they slowly expanded the roads to allow for the passing of wagons.

第二部分　华工篇
Part Two　Chinese Workers

◎《作业流程》　　　　　　　　　　　　　　张天阳　画
　 *Workflow*　　　　　　　　　　　　　　 by Andrew Zhang

**作业流程**

　　图为华工在峭壁上凿出隧道的作业流程。

**Workflow**

　　This image shows the workflow of Chinese workers when digging tunnels on the cliff.

75

◉《跌下山崖》　　　　　　　　　　　　　　　胡锦海　画
　　Fall off a Cliff　　　　　　　　　　　　　　by Elmer Hu

## 跌下山崖

　　在悬崖峭壁作业的华工，一旦系着他们的绳索被磨断或被炸断，他们就有跌下山崖的危险。这导致铁路劳工成为那个年代风险最高的职业。如果不是为了养家糊口，谁愿意用生命换这份工钱？

## Fall off a Cliff

　　Chinese workers who worked on the cliff always bore the risk of falling off the cliff if the rope around their waist was worn off or broken due to an explosion. This made railroad workers the most hazardous occupation then. If not for making ends meet for their families, who would like to risk their lives working on this job?

第二部分　华工篇
Part Two　Chinese Workers

◉《遭遇 44 次暴风雪也不停工》　　　　　　　　　　　毛笛　画
*Working in 44 Blizzards*　　　　　　　　　　　　　　by Di Mao

**遭遇 44 次暴风雪也不停工**

　　1866 年的冬天暴风雪多达 44 次，来自广东的华工几乎没见过雪。但工地并没有因为暴雪而停工。每个白人工头管理二三十个华工，每天分三班轮流上工；白人劳工每天工作 8 小时，分两班轮流上工。

**Working in 44 Blizzards**

　　The harsh winter of 1866 brought 44 blizzards, which shocked the Cantonese workers, who had rarely seen snow before. However, the construction was not halted because of this. Every white worker was assigned to charge twenty to thirty Chinese workers, divided into three shifts each day, whereas white workers worked eight hours per day with two shifts.

77

◉《雪崩埋没了很多华工》  韩赫颐 画
*Chinese Workers Buried by the Avalanche*  by Helen Han

**雪崩埋没了很多华工**

　　1867年寒冬，雪崩埋没了一间华工营地，里面有18名工人。50名工人挖了近12个小时，才救出其中15名工人。还有一次，20名华工在雪崩中丧生，当春天发现尸体的时候，他们的手中还紧紧握着铲子和镐。

**Chinese Workers Buried by the Avalanche**

　　During the brutal winter of 1867, an avalanche buried a camp accommodating 18 Chinese workers. Fifty workers spent 12 hours and saved 15 workers. In another incidence, twenty Chinese workers lost their lives in an avalanche. When their bodies were found in spring next year, some hands were still holding shovels and spades.

第二部分 华工篇
Part Two  Chinese Workers

◉《铺设 60 千米冰雪道》
Sixty-kilometer Ice Trail

王彦博　画
by Yanbo Wang

### 铺设 60 千米冰雪道

　　1867 年冬天，美国气温下降到零下 23℃，工程运输因气候陷入停顿，美国工程师们也束手无策。但聪明的华工竟然铺了一条 60 千米长的冰雪道，他们利用光滑的路面拖运物资，这样，不仅没有中断运输，反而加快了工程进度。

### Sixty-kilometer Ice Trail

　　In the winter of 1867, the temperature dropped to negative 23°C, halting all transportation for the project. When the American engineers felt helpless to cope with this challenge, the brilliant Chinese workers managed to build a sixty-kilometer-long ice trail to tow the supplies, which greatly facilitated the progress of the whole project.

◎《修建防雪棚》
*Build A Snow Shelter*

宋毕昕 画
by Anthony Song

**修建防雪棚**

为了避免雪崩，华工在开隧道时，利用农耕经验和技术，设计和修建了高大的防雪工棚，这相当于给路基铁轨做一个罩子将其保护起来。

**Build A Snow Shelter**

In order to mitigate the impact of the avalanche, Chinese workers used their experiences and skills in farming to design and build giant anti-snow work tents. These tents covered up the railway and its foundation and protected them well.

第二部分　华工篇
Part Two　Chinese Workers

◎《木质防雪墙》
*Wooden Snowproof Wall*

宋毕昕　画
by Anthony Song

## 木质防雪墙

　　华工沿着铁路在容易发生雪崩的地方搭建起 60 千米的木质防雪墙，保障了工程的顺利进行。

## Wooden Snowproof Wall

　　Chinese workers constructed wooden anti-snow walls for sixty kilometers along the railroad, where avalanches often occurred.

81

◉ 《爆破台》  王其顼 画
Fort Point Cut  by Alice Wang

## 爆破台

开山挖沟就要爆破，而所有牵扯爆破的危险工作主要由华工来做，这个爆破台下埋着众多华工的辛酸经历。

## Fort Point Cut

Digging a tunnel through a mountain required an explosive. Chinese workers did all the risky work related to explosive danger. The miserable experiences of many Chinese workers were buried underneath the explosion sites.

第二部分　华工篇
Part Two　Chinese Workers

◎《危险的烈性炸药》　　　　　　　　　　　　　　毛笛　画
　*Dangerous High Explosives*　　　　　　　　　　by Di Mao

## 危险的烈性炸药

　　由于传统的黑火药在坚硬的岩土中效果不佳，为了赶工程进度，1867年2月，中央太平洋铁路公司请来英国人詹姆斯·豪顿（James Howden），让其在6号隧道工程施工现场试制作硝酸甘油。

　　图为试用烈性炸药的危险场景。

## Dangerous High Explosives

The traditional black powder didn't work well on hard granite. Not to delay the construction progress, the Central Pacific Railroad Company asked James Howden to make and test out nitroglycerin on the site of Tunnel 6 in the February of 1867.

This image shows the scary scene when examing explosives.

◉ 《爆炸事故频发》　　　　　　　　　　　　　　　　胡锦海　画
　 *Frequent Explosions*　　　　　　　　　　　　　　　by Elmer Hu

**爆炸事故频发**

　　1846年，诺贝尔发明硝酸甘油炸药。由于它的危险性，加州政府禁运硝酸甘油。但是1866年4月，在中央太平洋铁路工地，却要求华工冒险试用硝酸甘油，这导致爆炸事故频发。

**Frequent Explosions**

　　Nobel invented nitroglycerin as an explosive in 1864. Due to its danger, California government prohibited transporting nitroglycerin. However, on the Central Pacific Railroad construction site, Chinese workers were required to use the nitroglycerin, which led to frequent explosive accidents.

第二部分　华工篇
Part Two　Chinese Workers

◉《生命代价》　　　　　　　　　　　　　　　　　　　　贾佳茵　画
　Life Lost　　　　　　　　　　　　　　　　　　　　　　by Kaela Jia

## 生命代价
　　随着烈性炸药的使用，工程进度是加快了，但是许多华工却因此受伤甚至丧命。

## Life Lost
　　With the usage of powerful explosives, the construction progress had been accelerated. However, many Chinese workers got injured or even died from them.

◉《挖出一个竖井》　　　　　　　　　　　　　　　　　　　张馨雅　画
　*Dig a Shaft*　　　　　　　　　　　　　　　　　　　　by Xinya Zhang

## 挖出一个竖井

　　1866 年 11 月底，尽管积雪深近 50 英尺，但沿线隧道工程依旧全部铺开。

　　为了加快建设速度，华工决定从隧道两头同时掘进，先挖出一个竖井，底端与隧道地面平行，再往两边作业展开。光是挖那口竖井，就用去了 85 天。再加上山上全是坚硬的花岗岩。最初的阶段，华工每天只能推进一英尺。

## Dig a Shaft

At the end of November of 1866, the project of digging tunnels was carried out without any delay, although the snow accumulated up to fifty feet.

To accelerate the construction, Chinese workers decided to dig from two sides of the tunnel simultaneously. They dug down a well from the top at first until the bottom of the well was aligned with the expected tunnel floor. Then, they dug from the bottom of the well towards two sides to build a tunnel. It took 85 days, just to dig the well. The mountain was made up of granite rocks. At the beginning, Chinese workers could complete up to a foot every day.

第二部分 华工篇
Part Two  Chinese Workers

◎《打通第一个隧道》　　　　　　　　　　　陈子鉴　画
　 The First Chiseled Tunnel　　　　　　　　　by Kent Chen

**打通第一个隧道**

　　华工被分成了3组，每组三四十人。他们24小时不停地轮流换班，13个月后终于打通了隧道。

**The First Chiseled Tunnel**

　　Chinese workers were divided into three groups, each of which comprised thirty to forty people. These three groups of workers shifted to work for 24 hours. After 13 months, the tunnel was finally completed.

◎《送水工人》
*A Water Delivery Worker*

韩赫颐　画
by Helen Han

## 送水工人

8号隧道是另一个使用硝酸甘油爆破的隧道。图为一名华工为在隧道内昼夜轮流值班工作的华工送水。

不像其他族裔劳工爱喝生水，因为华工每天煮热水泡茶喝，所以较少得疟疾。

## A Water Delivery Worker

Tunnel 8 is another tunnel dug with nitroglycerin as the explosive. This image shows a Chinese worker carrying drinking water to those who worked on shifts continuously.

Unlike the workers from other racial groups, who liked drinking faucet water, Chinese workers brewed and drank tea daily. Therefore, Chinese workers were less likely to get malaria.

第二部分 华工篇
Part Two　Chinese Workers

◎《见证历史的松树》　　　　　　　　　　　　　王彦博　画
　　*A Pine Tree Witnessing the History*　　　　　by Yanbo Wang

**见证历史的松树**

　　在华工建造的隧道上方，百年来一直挺立着一棵松树。如今它却垂下了90度，就像在给华工鞠躬致敬一样。

**A Pine Tree Witnessing the History**

　　On the top of the tunnel Chinese workers have built, there stands a pine tree over a hundred years old. It recently bent over about 90 degrees, which seems like bending and showing respect to those Chinese workers.

100 Years of Chinese Immigration in the United States and Canada

◉《手凿隧道贯通》　　　　　　　　　　　　　　　王彦博　画
　*Hand Chiseled Tunnel Penetration*　　　　　　　　by Yanbo Wang

**手凿隧道贯通**

1867年8月，6号隧道贯通。在没有任何电力、蒸汽动力的情况下，华工用手工凿出长1659英尺的隧道，最深处达124英尺，洞口误差仅2英寸。

**Hand Chiseled Tunnel Penetration**

Tunnel 6 was completed on August 1867. Without any electricity and steaming power, Chinese workers used hand chisels to dig a tunnel of 1,659 feet. The highest part of the tunnel reached up to 124 feet with a margin error of two inches.

第二部分　华工篇
Part Two　Chinese Workers

◎《打通 15 条隧道》　　　　　　　　　　　　　陈子杰　画
*15 Chiseled Tunnels*　　　　　　　　　　　　 by Alex Chen

## 打通 15 条隧道

1867 年秋,华工在内华达山脉的高海拔地区打通了 15 条隧道,总长度 1894 米。

## 15 Chiseled Tunnels

In the fall of 1867, Chinese workers completed 15 tunnels at the high elevation area of Sierra Nevada Mountain ranges with a total length of 1,894 meters.

◉《大罢工》  韩赫颐 画
*General Strike*  by Helen Han

**大罢工**

1867年6月，铁路沿线的华工默默地进行了一次长达6天的罢工。他们希望月工资从35美元增加到40美元，跟白人劳工一样；希望每天工作时间不超过10小时，希望在隧道里换班的时间能缩短到8小时；还希望有离开铁路工地去寻找其他工作的自由。

对此，资本家切断了工地上华工的食品、肉类等的日常供应，并警告说，不会涨工资，而且罢工的一切损失均由华工自己承担。饥饿难耐的华工，不得不恢复工作。

第二部分 华工篇
Part Two  Chinese Workers

**General Strike**

Chinese workers at the railroad construction sites peacefully went on strike for six days on June 1867. They requested the same salaries as white workers and raising monthly salary from $35 to $40. They also didn't want to work more than ten hours every day, hoped the shifting time of working in the tunnel was shortened to 8 hours, and were permitted to leave the railroad project freely to search for other working opportunities.

The companies suspended providing Chinese workers food, meat and other living supplies. They also warned that they would not raise salaries and that Chinese workers would be responsible for all the losses due to the strike. Chinese workers could not tolerate being famished and had to return to work.

◎《自豪的华工》　　　　　　　　　　　　　　　　　　　　　　胡锦海　画
　　*The Proud Chinese Workers*　　　　　　　　　　　　　　　　by Elmer Hu

## 自豪的华工

1868年6月18日，中央太平洋铁路公司的第一辆旅客列车驶过6号隧道。

## The Proud Chinese Workers

The first passenger train of Central Pacific Railroad Company rolled through Tunnel 6 on June 18, 1868.

第二部分　华工篇
Part Two　Chinese Workers

◎《进入沙漠地带》　　　　　　　　　　　　　　黄子恬　画
　Into the Desert　　　　　　　　　　　　　　by Alita Huang

## 进入沙漠地带

1869年4月28日，负责修西线的中央太平洋铁路公司和负责修东线的联合太平洋铁路公司都接近铁路合龙点普罗蒙特里。

## Into the Desert

The Central Pacific Railroad Company from the west and the Union Pacific Railroad Company from the east were all getting closer to the meeting point at the Promontory Summit on April 28, 1869.

100 Years of Chinese Immigration in the United States and Canada

◉ 《漠土之工》 　　　　　　　　　　　　　　　陈睿斌　画
　　*Working in the Desolation*　　　　　　　　　by Ruibin Chen

第二部分　华工篇
Part Two　Chinese Workers

◉《一万美元赌注》　　　　　　　　　　　　　　　　　马铭浩　画
　$10,000 Bet　　　　　　　　　　　　　　　　　　　　by Mario Ma

**一万美元赌注**

在还剩最后 14 英里的地方，双方工程师下赌注一万美元，看谁能够创下超过一天铺轨 7 英里的纪录。

中央太平洋铁路公司挑选了一批华工和爱尔兰劳工，许诺如果完成任务，工资将是平时的 4 倍。结果这些工人在一天工作了 12 个小时，铺轨总长度超过 10 英里。

**$10,000 Bet**

At the point of the last 14 miles to the meeting place, the engineers from the two railroad companies bet on $10,000 to see who could hit the record by laying seven-mile tracks per day.

The Central Pacific Railroad Company picked a group of Chinese and Irish workers and promised them to raise the salaries by four times if they completed the task. Eventually these workers worked 12 hours a day and laid a track of more than ten miles.

97

◉《比赛纪念牌》　　　　　　　　　　　　　　张云想　画
　Competition Commemorative Plaque　　　　by Yunxiang Zhang

## 比赛纪念牌

1869年4月28日，中央太平洋铁路公司的团队创造了在一天之内铺设10英里铁路的纪录。

## Competition Commemorative Plaque

On April 28, 1869, the Central Pacific Railroad Company crews laid a record of 10 miles of track in a single day.

第二部分　华工篇
Part Two　Chinese Workers

◉《赢得比赛》  
*To Win the Race*

张蕴涵　画  
by Yunhan Zhang

## 赢得比赛

中央太平洋铁路公司赢得了这场赌赛，然而只有 8 个当时干活的爱尔兰劳工的名字被记录了下来，所有华工的姓名都被隐去了。

## To Win the Race

The Central Pacific Railroad Company won the bet. However, only eight Irish workers' names were recorded in history. All the Chinese workers' names were ignored.

◉《他们是贡献者》  吴雨芮　画
*They Are Contributors*　　by Sherry Wu

# 第二部分　华工篇
# Part Two　Chinese Workers

**他们是贡献者**

　　华工与爱尔兰劳工是横贯大陆铁路最主要的建设群体，华工做出了最大的牺牲。许多人认为华工创造了工程奇迹，但中央太平洋铁路公司没有记录铁路上任何工人的死亡情况。据史料记载，有2000多名华工因铁路建设过程中雪崩、山体滑坡、爆炸、坠落、疾病和其他事故而死亡。

　　华工建设了铁路，铁路成就了美国。

**They Are Contributors**

　　Chinese workers and Irish workers were the main construction groups of the transcontinental railway, and Chinese workers made the greatest sacrifice. Many people think Chinese workers created a construction miracle. However, the Central Pacific Railroad Company did not record any accidental deaths during the construction of the railroads. Based on historical documents, approximately two thousand Chinese workers died from avalanches, landslides, explosions, falls, diseases and other accidents during the railroad construction.

　　Chinese workers built the railroad, connecting the United States from the west to the east.

◎《就要说再见》　　　　　　　　　　　　　　　　　　　陈乃仪　画
　Say Goodbye　　　　　　　　　　　　　　　　　　　　by Nia Chen

## 就要说再见

　　图为铁路修建工作完成，中央太平洋铁路公司的施工监督与一名华工合影。

## Say Goodbye

The Central Pacific Railroad Company construction supervisor and a Chinese worker took a picture together after the railroad was completed.

第二部分　华工篇
Part Two　Chinese Workers

◉《提前完工》　　　　　　　　　　　　　　　　　张馨雅　画
　　*Early Completion*　　　　　　　　　　　　　　by Xinya Zhang

## 提前完工

　　1863年1月太平洋铁路动工时，两家铁路公司计划用至少14年完工。然而，由于华工的努力，仅用了7年时间便贯通了美国东西大陆。

## Early Completion

At the onset of Pacific Railroad construction in January of 1863, two railroad companies had expected to complete the project at least 14 years. However, with the tremendous efforts of Chinese workers, the east and west railroads were connected within seven years.

◉《东西铁路终于合龙》 肖禹睿 画
East-west Railway Close by James Xiao

**东西铁路终于合龙**

1869年5月10日，经过2313天的奋斗和流血牺牲，在犹他州的普罗蒙特里高地，中央太平洋铁路公司完成了690英里的铁路建设，和联合太平洋铁路公司铺设的轨道合龙了。但在记录最后一个道钉被敲下的完工庆祝仪式照片中，没有一个华人的面孔。

图为中央太平洋铁路公司和联合太平洋铁路公司的总工程师握手庆祝。

**East-west Railway Close**

After 2,313 days of hard work, the Central Pacific Railroad Company completed construction of a railroad of 690 miles and met with the tracks built by the Union Pacific Railroad Company at the Promontory Summit, Utah, on May 10, 1869. However, no Chinese face could be found in the picture of the completion celebration ceremony that announced the last spike hammered down on the railroad.

The picture shows the Central Pacific Railroad Company and Union Pacific Railroad Company shaking hands to celebrate the completion of the transcontinental railroads.

第二部分　华工篇
Part Two　Chinese Workers

◉《美国欢庆》　　　　　　　　　　　　　　　　　陈睿斌　画
　 US National Celebration　　　　　　　　　　　　by Ruibin Chen

## 美国欢庆

1869 年 5 月 10 日上午，8 名华工被挑选出来，铺设最后一段铁轨。历史学家 J. N. Bowman 称：最后一颗铁质道钉可能是由中央太平洋铁路公司的某个华工打入的。

第一条横贯东西的大铁路合龙仪式在普罗蒙特里举行，中央太平洋铁路公司董事长斯坦福敲下最后一根金钉。电报发送到华盛顿，全美庆祝。

## US National Celebration

Eight Chinese workers were chosen to lay the last piece of track on the railroad in the morning of May 10, 1869. Historian J. N. Bowman stated that the last spike on the railroad was very likely to be tapped by a Chinese worker from the Central Pacific Railroad Company.

The celebration ceremony for the completion of the transcontinental railroad lines was held at the Promontory Summit in Utah. The Director of the Board of Central Pacific Railroad Company, Stanford, tapped the last golden spike on it. When the telegram was sent to Washington, D.C, the whole country celebrated it.

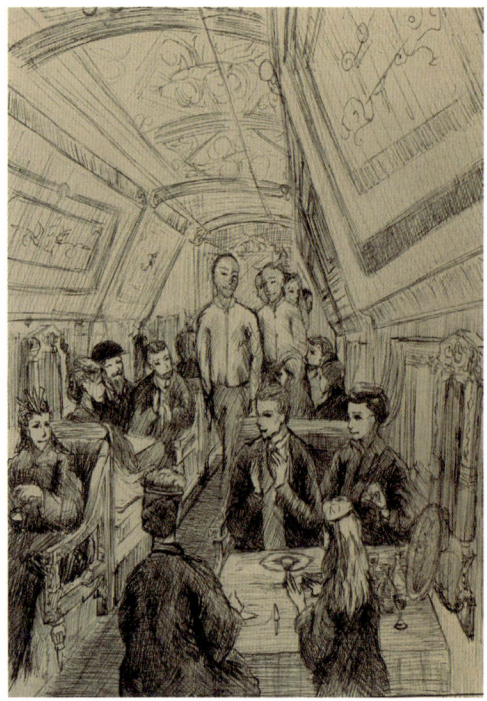

◎《华工代表受到尊重》
*Honored Chinese Worker Representatives*

祝云姝　画
by Maggie Zhu

**华工代表受到尊重**

8名华工代表被邀请到工程监督的车厢去庆祝。

当华工代表进入车厢的瞬间，所有在场的宾客都为他们欢呼，仿佛他们是一场比赛的胜利者。

**Honored Chinese Worker Representatives**

Eight Chinese worker representatives were invited in the cargo for the construction supervisor for the celebration.

When the Chinese workers walked into the cargo, all the guests applauded for them. They looked as if they were the winners of a race.

第二部分　华工篇
Part Two　Chinese Workers

◎《华工创造了奇迹》　　　　　　　　　　　　　　　胡锦海　画
　 *Chinese Workers Created a Miracle*　　　　　　　by Elmer Hu

## 华工创造了奇迹

中央太平洋铁路公司工程负责人在庆祝活动上发言：感谢勤劳的华工，没有他们，就没有这条伟大铁路。

## Chinese Workers Created a Miracle

The Director of the Central Pacific Railroad Company expressed thanks to the diligent Chinese workers during the celebration event. He also stated that this exceptional railroad would not be possible without those Chinese workers.

◉《通车》　　　　　　　　　　　　　　　　　　　郑好　画
　*The Railroad Opening*　　　　　　　　　　　　　by Eric Zheng

## 通车

横贯美国东西大陆的铁路提前通车了!

## The Railroad Opening

The transcontinental railroads linking the west and east of the United States were open to traffic before the planned date.

第二部分　华工篇
Part Two　Chinese Workers

◉《多么幸福的乘客们》
*Happy Passengers*

陈子鉴　画
by Kent Chen

## 多么幸福的乘客们

据中央太平洋铁路公司的铁路工人工资单记录显示，华工比例在工程后期曾高达 95%。

图为华工养路工向通过的列车挥手。

## Happy Passengers

According to Central Pacific Railroad Company's payroll records of the railroad worker, the proportion of Chinese workers was as high as 95 percent in the later stages of the project.

The picture shows the Chinese road maintenance workers waving to the passing train.

109

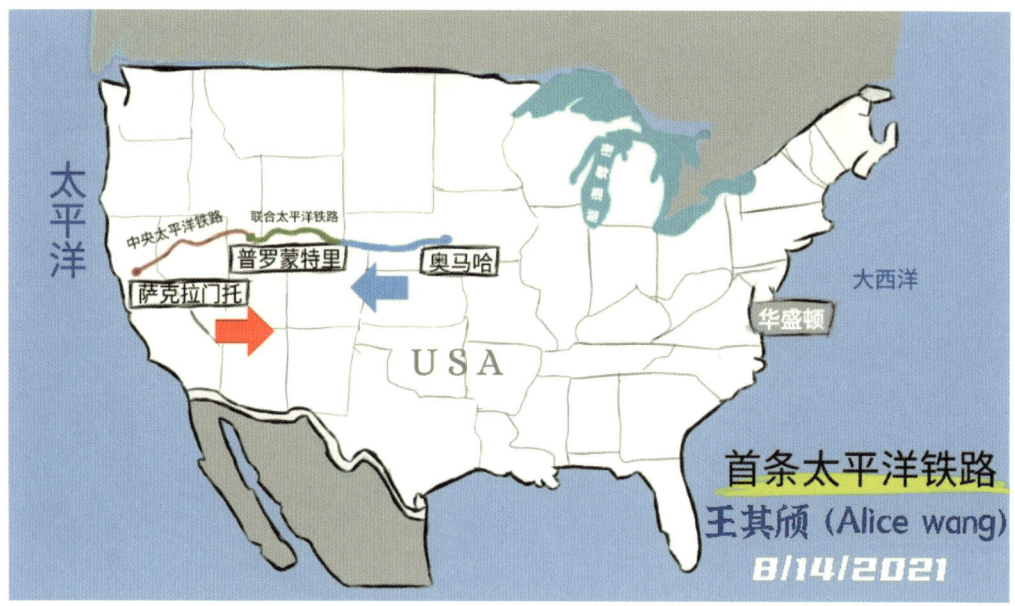

◉《支撑美国经济腾飞》　　　　　　　　　　　　王其颀　画
　　 A Support to the US Economy　　　　　　　　by Alice Wang

**支撑美国经济腾飞**

　　东西完整的铁路线连通后，从纽约到旧金山，乘火车只需 7 天时间。从此，这个强大的基础设施成为美国经济腾飞的支撑！

**A Support to the US Economy**

　　When the railroad was completed, it took only seven days to go from New York to San Francisco. This powerful infrastructure has become a support for the economic take-off of the United States!

（译文／宿佳博 编辑／李立峰）

# 第七章　华工生活

## Chapter 7　Life of Chinese Workers

100 Years of Chinese Immigration in the United States and Canada

◉ 《华工的帐篷》  
*Chinese Worker's Tent*

黄子恬　画  
by Alita Huang

**华工的帐篷**

华工最初来到工地时，每人月工资为 27 美元，而白人劳工工资为每月 35 美元。随着工程难度增加，华工的工资略有增长。但华工住在自己搭的简易帐篷里，白人劳工则住在公司为他们提供的车厢里。

**Chinese Worker's Tent**

When the Chinese workers first came to the construction site, each person could make only $27 monthly. The White workers, however, made $35 monthly. With the increased difficulty of construction, there was a slight increase in the Chinese workers salary. Chinese workers lived in simple tents that they set up themselves. Meanwhile, white workers, however, lived in the cargos provided by the company.

第二部分　华工篇
Part Two　Chinese Workers

◎《发工资》　　　　　　　　　　　　　　　　　　　　　祝云姝　画
　Payroll　　　　　　　　　　　　　　　　　　　　　　by Maggie Zhu

## 发工资

在铁路工地，华工通常 20～30 人作为一个小组，每组推选一人领工资。钱多半放在一个草帽里，附上一张写有中文的对账单。平均每个华工每月往家里寄 13～20 美元。

## Payroll

On the railroad construction site, Chinese workers usually worked in teams, twenty to thirty people in a team. Every team selected one person to get the salaries for the whole group. They often put the money in a straw hat, along with an invoice written in Chinese. On average, each Chinese worker could send $13—$20 back home each month.

● 《华工生活节俭》　　　　　　　　　　　　　　　　胡锦海　画
　 *Living Frugally*　　　　　　　　　　　　　　　　by Elmer Hu

## 华工生活节俭

　　华工从日出干到日落，每周 6 天，通常每天工作时间在 10 小时以上。华工对生活条件的要求非常低，为了减少花销，他们会在小溪流的旁边用木料搭一个简单的棚屋。

　　在辛勤工作的同时，华工也在生活中保持了极其节俭、朴素的习惯。

## Living Frugally

　　Chinese workers worked from sunrise to sunset, six days per week. They usually spent more than ten hours in working each workday. Chinese workers managed to adapt to the poor living conditions of the working place. In order to reduce the spending, they set up simple huts with timber besides the rivers.

　　Working diligently, Chinese workers kept the habits of living a very frugal and simple life.

第二部分　华工篇
Part Two　Chinese Workers

◉《杂货店》　　　　　　　　　　　　　　　　　　　　　　贾佳茵　画
　*Chinese Grocery*　　　　　　　　　　　　　　　　　　by Kaela Jia

**杂货店**

　　图为一名华裔铁路工程承包商开的杂货店。店员们从早上7点一直工作到夜里12点，吃住都在店里，挣钱、存钱、寄钱回家，是他们生活的目标。

　　华工可以通过这些杂货店往家里寄信寄钱，了解社区消息和朋友见面。

**Chinese Grocery**

　　The image shows a grocery store opened by a Chinese railroad construction contractor. The store clerks worked from seven o'clock in the morning until midnight. They ate and slept in the store. Their personal goal was to make money, save them and send the money back home.

　　Chinese workers could send letters and money to their families through these stores. They could also learn the news about the community and meet their friends there.

100 Years of Chinese Immigration in the United States and Canada

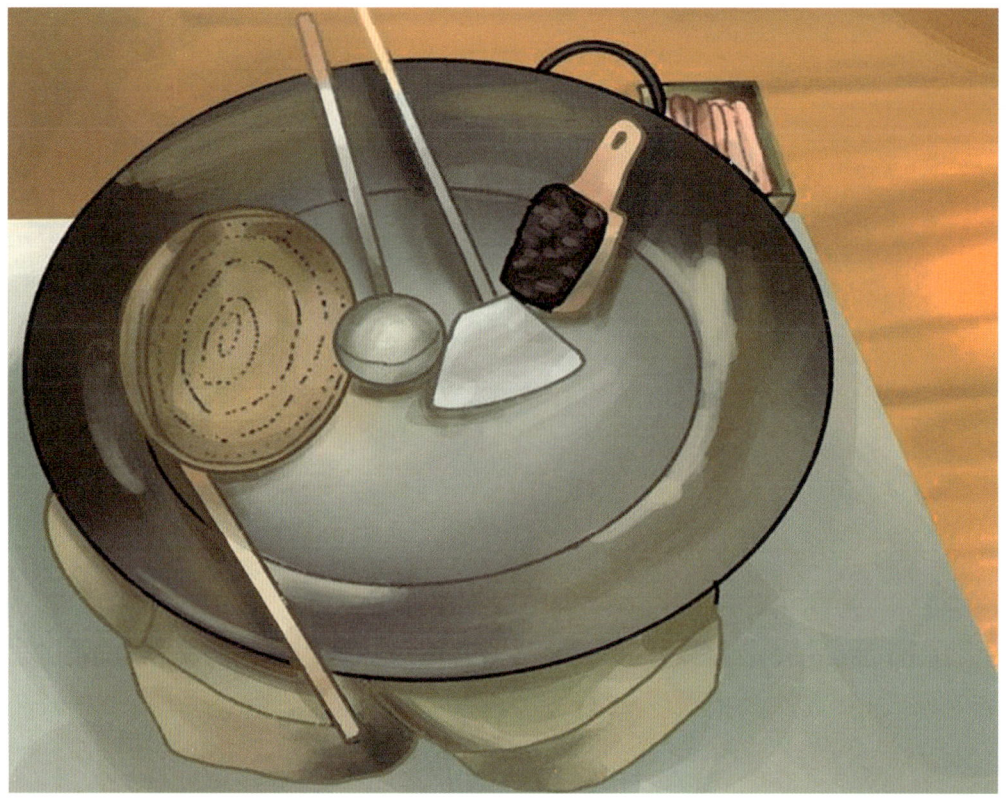

◎《厨房用具》　　　　　　　　　　　　　　　　　　吴雨芮　画
　*Kitchenware*　　　　　　　　　　　　　　　　　　by Sherry Wu

**厨房用具**

　　每组华工都有一个厨师，他们自己购买中国菜、食物、炊具和帐篷。厨师的薪水由中央太平洋铁路公司支付。华工坚持要求附近必须有中医。

　　图为华工用的厨具。

**Kitchenware**

　　Each team of Chinese workers had a cook. The cooks purchased Chinese food, ingredients, cooking utensils, and tents. The cooks' salaries were paid by the Central Pacific Railroad of California. Chinese workers insisted that traditional Chinese medicine practitioners work nearby.

　　The image shows the cooking utensils once used by Chinese workers.

第二部分　华工篇
Part Two　Chinese Workers

◉《厨师》
*The Cook*

吴雨芮　画
by Sherry Wu

**厨师**

　　图为厨师去镇上买菜。厨师通常用紫菜、金针菇、枸杞、鱿鱼干、干蔬菜、干蚝、红枣干等各种食材为华工烹制菜肴，相比白人劳工的牛肉、面包、土豆和黄油，华工吃得更丰富。

**The Cook**

　　This image shows a Chinese chef going to buy foods in town. Commonly purchased food and ingredients included shitaki mushrooms, seaweed, enoki mushrooms, goji berries, dried squid, dried vegetables, dried oysters and dried dates. Compared to the limited options, such as beef, bread, potato and butter on white workers' menu, the Chinese workers ate a richer variety of food.

◎《陶罐》
The Clay Pot

陈子杰　画
by Alex Chen

**陶罐**

各种盛放食物的容器，成为华工重要的财产。

**The Clay Pot**

All kinds of food containers became important properties of Chinese workers.

◎《斗笠》
Chinese Straw Hat

宿佳博　画
by Angeli Su

**斗笠**

图为华工戴着斗笠施工，既能通风透气，也能防晒挡雨。

**Chinese Straw Hat**

The picture shows that the Chinese workers were wearing a bamboo hat during construction, which can easily let the cool air in while protecting them from sun and rain.

第二部分　华工篇
Part Two　Chinese Workers

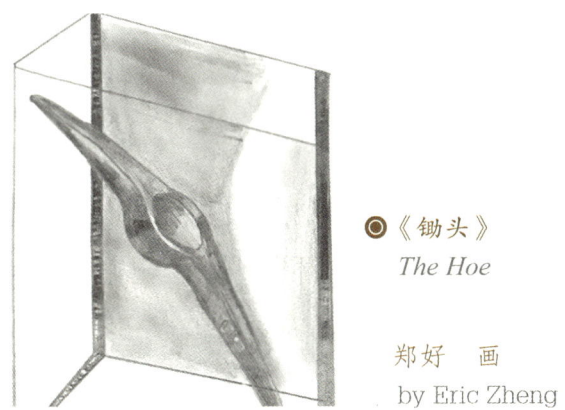

◎《锄头》
The Hoe

郑好　画
by Eric Zheng

**锄头**

图为华工用过的锄头。

**The Hoe**

This image shows the hoe that Chinese workers once used.

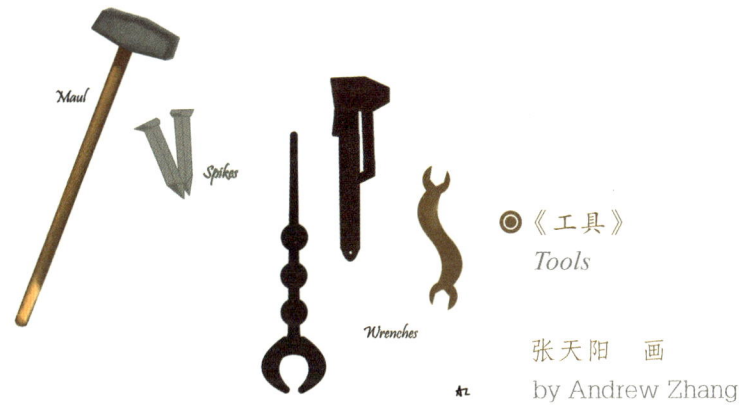

◎《工具》
Tools

张天阳　画
by Andrew Zhang

**工具**

图为华工修铁路时用过的简陋工具。

**Tools**

The image shows the simple tools used by the Chinese workers when they built the railways.

119

◉《华工的生活痕迹》　　　　　　　　　　　　　　　　　宿佳博　画
　　The Traces of Chinese Workers' Life　　　　　　　　by Angeli Su

### 华工的生活痕迹

在纽约美国华人博物馆里的一个展厅里陈列着从美国各地唐人街老店收集来的东西。比如华工用过的油灯、熏香、香烟、酒瓶、骰子等物件。

### The Traces of Chinese Workers' Life

The Museum of Chinese Americans in New York has an exhibition called "Grocery Store". It displayed the items that had been used by Chinese workers before. They were collected from the old stores in Chinatowns nationwide in the US, including oil lamps, incense, cigarettes, wine bottles, dice and other articles.

第二部分 华工篇
Part Two  Chinese Workers

◎《休息日》  韩赫颐 画
Day-off  by Helen Han

## 休息日

图为华工在周日放假时的活动。他们有时洗洗衣服，有时用骰子小赌几局，放松身心。

## Day-Off

This image shows what Chinese workers' activities during their leisure time on Sunday. They did laundries and sometimes they gambled with dice.

121

◉ 《遗骨》　　　　　　　　　　　　　　　　　　　　韩赫颐　画
　　The Remains　　　　　　　　　　　　　　　　　　by Helen Han

## 遗骨

　　一些华人组织会派人到内华达山脉铁路沿途收殓死去的同胞的遗骸。这些人小心翼翼地把这些遗骨收殓起来，待日后送回中国安葬。

## The Remains

Some Chinese organizations sent people to pick up the remains of the Chinese workers who died during the Nevada mountain range railroad construction. They carefully collected the remains and later sent them to China for burial.

（译文 / 宿佳博 编辑 / 李立峰）

# 第八章　排华浪潮

## Chapter 8　The Chinese Exclusion Tide

◉《排华潮》　　　　　　　　　　　　　　　　　　　　周子婷　画
　*Exclusion Tide*　　　　　　　　　　　　　　　　　by Helen Zhou

**排华潮**

　　太平洋铁路建成后，华工名声外传，很多铁路公司都开始招收华工，随着华人数量越来越多，到1870年，美国的很多行业都有华人劳工的身影。于是，很多美国人便惊呼，华人抢了他们的饭碗。19世纪70年代，美国西部爆发了大规模的排华浪潮，白人多次武装攻打华人居住区。另外，其他族裔如黑人也很不喜欢华人。就是在这样的历史背景下，美国人便开始讨论如何限制、打压华人。图为1878年，反华移民丹尼斯·科尔尼在加州演讲时鼓动白人让"中国人离开"，而华人王清福却拿着算盘与筷子，要跟丹尼斯公开辩论！

第二部分 华工篇
Part Two　Chinese Workers

**Exclusion Tide**

After the completion of the Pacific Railway, the good reputation of Chinese workers spread. At that time, many railroad companies wanted to recruit laborers. With the increasing number of Chinese, by 1870, many industries in the United States had Chinese laborers. As a result, many Americans exclaimed that the Chinese had robbed them of the jobs. In the 1870s, a large-scale wave of the Chinese exclusion broke out in the western United States, and many Americans repeatedly attacked Chinese residential areas with force. In addition, other ethnic groups such as African Americans, also disliked Chinese. It was in this historical context that Americans began to discuss how to restrict and suppress the Chinese. The image shows in 1878, there was an anti-Chinese immigrant by the name of Dennis. During his speech in California, Kearney encouraged Americans to let "Chinese leave!" Wang Qingfu, a Chinese, is holding an abacus and chopsticks to have an open debate with Dennis!

100 Years of Chinese Immigration in the United States and Canada

◎《洗衣店》 张蕴涵 画
*Laundromats* by Yunhan Zhang

## 洗衣店

1850—1860 年的淘金时期，已有 6 万名华人在旧金山生活。图为华人在唐人街经营的洗衣店和杂货店。

## Laundromats

During the gold rush years from 1850 to 1860, there were sixty thousand Chinese Americans living in San Francisco, California. The image above displays the laundromat and grocery store operated by the Chinese on Renjie Street.

126

第二部分 华工篇
Part Two　Chinese Workers

◉《华人遭劫》
The Robbery of the Chinese People

应心玥　画
by Betty Ying

## 华人遭劫

　　华人遭受越来越多的歧视和暴力，却得不到白人警察的保护。图为1871年10月24日，大约500个白人冲入洛杉矶的唐人街，大肆抢劫，拳打脚踢，甚至打死了18个华人（包括一名12岁的男孩和一名医生，其中14个人是被活活吊死的）。

## The Robbery of the Chinese People

　　The image shows that on October 24, 1871, about 500 white people rushed into Chinatown in Los Angeles, looted, punched, kicked, and even killed 18 Chinese (including a 12-year-old boy and a doctor, 14 of whom were killed by being hanged alive).

◉《大规模排华》　　　　　　　　　　　　　　　　　林昀晖　画
　*Mass Chinese Exclusion*　　　　　　　　　　　　by Kenny Lin

第二部分 华工篇
Part Two  Chinese Workers

**大规模排华**

1877年7月,旧金山发生大规模的排华骚乱,白人暴徒打砸抢华人开的商铺,火烧华人的居所,射杀街上的华人。加州政府派来国民卫队和数百名志愿者都不能阻止,最后依靠联邦政府派遣美国海军出兵支援,才控制了局势。

**Mass Chinese Exclusion**

In July 1877, a large-scale anti-Chinese riot occurred in San Francisco. White rioters smashed, destroyed, and looted Chinese-owned shops, set fire to Chinese residences, and shot Chinese people on the street. The California government sent the National Guard and hundreds of volunteers to stop it. Finally, the federal government sent troops from the US Navy to control the situation.

# 100年北美华人移民史
100 Years of Chinese Immigration in the United States and Canada

◉ 《排华法案》  王彦博　画
　*The Chinese Exclusion Act*　by Yanbo Wang

# 第二部分　华工篇
# Part Two　Chinese Workers

## 《排华法案》

1882年，美国国会受理了共和党参议员约翰·米勒提交的《排华法案》，就此美国国会展开了辩论。主张排华的人认为，华人抢了美国人的工作机会，而且不接受基督教伦理，还有诸多恶习。反对排华的人认为，出台这样一部法案，违背了美国"自由、平等"的立国原则，不符合中美《蒲安臣条约》中的自由移民政策。最终，1882年5月6日，《排华法案》在美国国会以多数票通过。法案规定，10年内不准华人入境、不得准许华人归化为美国公民等。

图为白人劳工聚集在旧金山广场游行，让华工离开！

### The Chinese Exclusion Act

In 1882, the United States Congress accepted the *Chinese Exclusion Act* submitted by Republican Senator John Miller, and the United States Congress launched a debate on this. Those who advocated Chinese exclusion believed that the Chinese had robbed Americans of job opportunities, that the Chinese did not accept Christian ethics, and that the Chinese had many vices. Opponents of Chinese exclusion believed that the introduction of such a bill went against the founding principles of "freedom and equality" in the United States and did not conform to the free immigration policy in the *Burlingame Treaty* between China and the United States. Finally, on May 6, 1882, with a majority vote the *Chinese Exclusion Act* passed the US Congress. The bill commanded that Chinese people not be allowed to enter the country for ten years and Chinese not be allowed to identify as US citizens.

The image shows the white laborers gathered in the San Francisco square to march, demanding to ask the Chinese workers to leave!

◉《石泉惨案》　　　　　　　　　　　　　　　　　　　　　韩赫颐　画
　　*The Shiquan Massacre*　　　　　　　　　　　　　　　by Helen Han

## 石泉惨案

　　1885 年 9 月 2 日上午，十余名石泉矿的白人矿工冲到 6 号矿区，与华人矿工发生冲突，三名华工受伤，冲突被矿主暂时平息。不久，百余名武装的和非武装的白人矿工集结起来，袭击 6 号矿区。他们还包围华工聚居区，洗劫财物，并纵火焚烧华工的住处。

## The Shiquan Massacre

　　On the morning of September 2, 1885, more than ten white miners from Shiquan Mine rushed to the No. 6 mining area and clashed with the Chinese miners. Three Chinese workers were injured, and the conflict was temporarily quelled by the mine owner. Before long, more than a hundred armed and unarmed white miners assembled and attacked the No. 6 mine. They also surrounded the settlement of Chinese workers, looted property, and set fire to the residences of Chinese workers.

## 第二部分 华工篇
## Part Two  Chinese Workers

◉ 《逃生》
  *Escape*

肖禹睿　画
by James Xiao

### 逃生

数百名华工对突袭毫无防备，本能地四散逃命，暴徒则在他们身后追击和射击。而围观的白人却拍手叫好，甚至参与抢劫华工及其住宅。

华工有的当场中弹身亡，有的被截住殴打受伤，有的则被大火活活烧死。根据事后统计，总共有 28 名华工死亡，15 人重伤。而华人被袭的理由是，拒绝与白人劳工一起罢工。

### Escape

Unprepared for the raid, hundreds of Chinese workers instinctively fled for their lives, with the thugs chasing and shooting behind them. The white people onlookers applauded and even participated in the robbery of Chinese workers and their houses.

Some Chinese workers were shot to death on the spot, some were intercepted, beaten, and injured, and some were burned to death by the fire. According to the statistics after the incident, a total of 28 Chinese workers were killed and 15 were seriously injured. The Chinese were attacked because they refused to go on strike with white laborers.

◉《公平何在？》　　　　　　　　　　　　　　宋毕昕　画
　　*Where is the Equity?*　　　　　　　　　　　by Anthony Song

第二部分 华工篇
Part Two  Chinese Workers

**公平何在？**

1892年,《排华法案》延长10年。1904年，美国国会通过将《排华法案》无限期延长的议案。

为美国的铁路建设做出贡献的华工，却没有一个落脚的地方。

**Where is the Equity?**

In 1892, the *Chinese Exclusion Act* was extended for 10 years, and in 1904, the US Congress passed a motion to extend the *Chinese Exclusion Act* indefinitely.

The Chinese workers who contributed to the construction of the American railways had nowhere to go.

◎《加华人头税》  马倩芸 画
　*Canadian Poll Tax*　by Annissa Ma

## 加华人头税

1880年，加拿大政府为修建太平洋铁路需要大量华工，于是1.5万名华工参与到从温哥华到蒙特利尔近5000千米的铁路线上。其间，5000余名华工付出生命的代价。然而，铁路提前完工后，加拿大华工也开始遭受排挤。1885年，加拿大政府通过了华人移民法案，对华人移民开始征收人头税。政府向抵加的华人收取每人50加元。1923年7月1日，加拿大排华法案生效，直到1947年5月14日才被加拿大政府废除。

## Canadian Poll Tax

In 1880, the Canadian government needed many Chinese laborers to build the Pacific Railway. As a result, 15,000 Chinese workers participated in the nearly 5,000-kilometer railway line from Vancouver to Montreal, during which more than 5,000 Chinese workers sacrificed their lives. However, after the railway was completed ahead of schedule, Canadian Chinese workers also began to be crowded out. In 1885, the Canadian government passed the Chinese Immigration Act, which started to levy a poll tax on Chinese immigrants. The government charges C$50 for each to Chinese arriving in Canada. The Canadian Chinese Exclusion Act came into effect on July 1, 1923 and was repealed by the Canadian government on May 14, 1947.

100 Years of Chinese Immigration in the United States and Canada

◎《黄金德案》  钟骐励 画
*Kim Huang's Case*  by Qili Zhong

第二部分　华工篇
Part Two　Chinese Workers

**黄金德案**

　　黄金德的父母是第一代移民。黄金德于 1871 年出生于美国。1894 年，在他 23 岁时回中国探亲，第二年 8 月回来时被拒绝入境。他勇敢地打官司，最终美国最高法院判决黄金德胜诉。从此，所有美国境内出生者都是美国公民的事实被认可。

**Kim Huang's Case**

　　Kim's parents are first-generation immigrants. He was born in the United States in the year of 1871. In 1894, when he was 23 years old, he returned to China to visit relatives and was refused entry when he returned in August of following year. He fought bravely, and the US Supreme Court ruled: He had won. Since then, the fact that all US-born people are US citizens has been recognized.

◉《天使岛移民站》 胡锦海 画
*Angel Island Immigration Station* by Elmer Hu

第二部分 华工篇
Part Two  Chinese Workers

**天使岛移民站**

1906 年，旧金山发生大火，大量移民档案被毁。许多华人声称自己是出生在美国的公民，而召集海外子女来美。为甄选来美的大量移民，加州于 1910 年设立天使岛移民站。

许多移民被拘禁在岛上，接受审查和询问的时间从几天到两年以上不等。其中 30% 的华人移民被直接遣返回中国。

图为排华期间的天使岛移民站。1940 年，该站因发生大火而弃用。

**Angel Island Immigration Station**

In 1906, a fire broke out in San Francisco, destroying many immigration files. Many Chinese claimed to be US-born citizens and recruited their children from overseas to come to the US To admit immigrants to the United States, California established the Angel Island Immigration Station in 1910.

Many immigrants were detained on the island, subject to scrutiny and questioning ranging from a few days to more than two years. 30% of Chinese immigrants were expelled back to China.

The image shows the Angel Island immigration station during the Chinese Exclusion period. In 1940, the station was abandoned due to a fire.

# 第九章 华工去向

## Chapter 9　The Next Direction of Chinese Workers

◉《四处谋生》　　　　　　　　　　　　　　　　宿佳博　画
　Make a Living　　　　　　　　　　　　　　　　by Angeli Su

## 四处谋生

　　横贯北美大陆的铁路修建完成后，一部分华工留在美国西部各州继续修建铁路。一部分华工则改行四处谋生，他们成为加州中部和萨克拉门托河汇流地带的三角洲的垦荒者，在三角洲开出一片片良田，帮着开垦出美国的粮仓。另有一批华人改行到内华达雪山当森林伐木工；一部分去往南方种植园；还有一批转入服务业，开洗衣店、餐馆，或到白人家里当佣工。此外，还有一部分华工回到了家乡。

第二部分　华工篇
Part Two　Chinese Workers

**Make a Living**

After the railway construction across North America was completed, some Chinese workers stayed in the western states to continue building the railway. Others changed their careers to make a living, and they became the pioneers of the Delta in the confluence of central California and the Sacramento River and helped open an American granary. Another group of Chinese diverted to work as forest loggers in the Snowy Mountains of Nevada, some went to plantations in the South, others transferred to the service industry, opened laundries, and restaurants, and worked as family servants in white homes. Other people portion returned to their motherland.

◉《威士忌与热茶》　　　　　　　　　　　　　　　　贾佳茵　画
　*Whiskey and Hot Tea*　　　　　　　　　　　　　　by Kaela Jia

## 威士忌与热茶

由于华人喜欢喝茶，爱尔兰劳工喜欢喝威士忌，所以有学者称，横贯大陆铁路是由茶和威士忌建成的。其实，主要是由茶建成的。图为铁路工地的白人劳工。

## Whiskey and Hot Tea

Since the Chinese like to drink tea and the Irish workers like to drink whiskey. Some scholars claim that the transcontinental railway was built from tea and whisky, mainly made by tea. The image shows the hard-working white laborers.

第二部分　华工篇
Part Two　Chinese Workers

**种植园里的华工**

1869 年夏，3 万名华工被带到南方种植园，替代已经自由的黑奴在棉田劳作。

**Chinese Workers in Plantations**

In the summer of 1869, 30,000 Chinese workers were brought to the southern plantations to replace the freed black slaves in cotton fields.

◉ 《跨过冰河》　　　　　　　　　　　　　　　　　　　贾佳茵　画
　　*Cross the Glacier*　　　　　　　　　　　　　　　　　by Kaela Jia

## 跨过冰河

图为1870年1月，250名华工从加州辗转去得州修铁路，他们在布拉斯卡州的奥马哈下车，跨过密苏里河。那时密苏里河已经结冰，衣着单薄的华工只好挑着扁担从冰面上提心吊胆地走过去。

## Cross the Glacier

The image shows that in January 1870, 250 Chinese workers traveled from California to Texas to build the railroad. They got off the train in Omaha, Brasca, and crossed the Missouri River. At that time, the Missouri River was frozen. The thinly dressed Chinese, carrying a shoulder pole nerves frayed and legs shaking, carefully walked across.

第二部分　华工篇
Part Two　Chinese Workers

◉《中央太平洋铁路公司养路华工》　　　　　　　　　　陈睿斌　画
　Road Maintenance Workers at Central Pacific Railroad Company　　by Ruibin Chen

**中央太平洋铁路公司养路华工**

　　建完铁路，中央太平洋铁路公司留下少量华工作为养路工，解雇了大部分华工。

**Road Maintenance Workers at Central Pacific Railroad Company**

　　After the railway was closed, the Central Pacific Railroad Company left a small number of Chinese workers as road maintenance workers and laid off most of the Chinese workers.

◎《联合太平洋铁路公司养路华工》　　　　　　　　　　张馨雅　画
　Road Maintenance Workers at Union Pacific　　　　　by Xinya Zhang

第二部分　华工篇

Part Two　Chinese Workers

**联合太平洋铁路公司养路华工**

1870年6月,联合太平洋铁路公司也雇用了一批华人养路工。

**Road Maintenance Workers at Union Pacific**

In June 1870, the Union Pacific Railroad Company hired a group of Chinese road maintenance workers.

◎《东岸修路》　　　　　　　　　　　　　　　　　　　郑好　画
　*East Coast Road Construction*　　　　　　　　　　　　by Oscar Zheng

### 东岸修路

1870年9月，150名华工来到东岸，修建新泽西和纽约之间的铁路。

### East Coast Road Construction

In September 1870, 150 Chinese workers came to the East Coast to build a railroad between New Jersey and New York.

第二部分　华工篇
Part Two　Chinese Workers

◉《庆祝中国年》　　　　　　　　　　　　　　　　　　　　胡锦海　画
　 *Celebrate Chinese New Year*　　　　　　　　　　　　　　by Elmer Hu

## 庆祝中国年

1870 年，300 名华工来到新泽西贝尔维尔镇蒸汽洗衣厂工作。1871 年 2 月，他们首次隆重庆祝中国新年。图为华工乐队过年期间唱大戏。

## Celebrate Chinese New Year

In 1870, 300 Chinese workers came to work at a steam laundry in Belleville, New Jersey. In February 1871, they celebrated Chinese New Year grandly for the first time.

The image shows they celebrated with a Chinese workers' band performance during Chinese New Year.

153

◎《华工在得州》　　　　　　　　　　　　　　　陈睿斌　画
　Chinese Workers in Texas　　　　　　　　　　by Ruibin Chen

## 华工在得州

1879 年，6000 名华工在得克萨斯州太平洋铁路公司工作。

## Chinese Workers in Texas

In 1879, 6,000 Chinese workers worked for the Texas Pacific Railroad Company.

第二部分　华工篇
Part Two　Chinese Workers

◎《50 周年纪念活动》　　　　　　　　　　　　　　祝云姝　画
　 *50th Anniversary Event*　　　　　　　　　　　　by Maggie Zhu

## 50 周年纪念活动

1919 年 5 月 10 日，8 位铺设最后一根铁轨的华工中的 3 名幸存者，在犹他州奥格登金色道钉 50 周年纪念活动中，被邀请站在平板彩车上，接受市民们的赞誉。

## 50th Anniversary Event

On May 10, 1919, three survivors of the eight Chinese workers who laid the last railroad track were invited to stand on a float and receive praise from citizens during the 50th anniversary of the Golden Spike in Ogden, Utah.

◎《北赴加拿大》 邹安琪 画
Heading to Canada in Texas by Angela Zou

## 北赴加拿大

1880年，加拿大太平洋铁路公司决定修建从温哥华到蒙特利尔的全长4667千米的铁路线。于是，一批美国中央太平洋铁路公司的华工来到加拿大铁路工地，同时该公司从广东招募了大批华工。1881—1885年，15000名华工来到加拿大卑诗省落基山区艰险地带修铁路。

## Heading to Canada

In 1880, the Canadian Pacific Railroad Company decided to build a 4,667-kilometer rail line from Vancouver to Montreal. Therefore, a group of Chinese workers from the American Central Pacific Railroad Company traveled to the Canadian railway construction site, and in the meantime, the company recruited a large number of Chinese workers from Guangdong. From 1881 to 1885, 15,000 Chinese workers built railways in the difficult and dangerous areas of the Rocky Mountains in British Columbia, Canada.

第二部分　华工篇
Part Two　Chinese Workers

◉《加拿大华工》　　　　　　　　　　　　　　　　黄子恬　画
　 Chinese Workers in Canada　　　　　　　　　　by Alita Huang

## 加拿大华工

温哥华、卡尔加里等城市是华工早期到达的地方，他们从事着最艰苦、最危险的土石工程作业。华工曾经冒着零下40℃的严寒，每天工作12个小时以上，而每天的劳动报酬仅有一美元。

## Chinese Workers in Canada

Cities such as Vancouver and Calgary were most challenging where Chinese workers arrived at the beginning of their journey. They worked in the most challenging and most dangerous earthwork conditions. Once, they worked in freezing temperatures of −40°C, and for more than 12 hours a day. However, they only got paid one dollar a day.

100 Years of Chinese Immigration in the United States and Canada

◉《加拿大华工在劳作》  张馨雅 画
  *Canadian Chinese workers at Work*  by Xinya Zhang

## 加拿大华工在劳作

1881年5月，3000名华工参与加拿大太平洋铁路段修建。

## Canadian Chinese workers at Work

In May 1881, 3,000 Chinese workers participated in the construction of the Canadian Pacific Railroad.

第二部分　华工篇
Part Two　Chinese Workers

◎《荒山修路》　　　　　　　　　　　　　　　　　　　周子婷　画
　Road Construction in Barren Hills　　　　　　　　　by Helen Zhou

**荒山修路**

　　加拿大华工在荒山野岭劳作，忍受着缺医少药的艰苦的原始生活条件。

　　加拿大太平洋铁路完成后，大多数华工转做其他工作，比如在矿场、农场、牧场工作或做家仆。

**Road Construction in Barren Hills**

　　Canadian Chinese workers worked in barren mountains and endured the harsh primitive living conditions with a lack of medicine and medical care.

　　After completing Canadian Pacific Railroad, most Chinese workers changed to other jobs, such as working in mines, ranches and farms; or becoming family servants.

◎《入土为安》  张云想 画
Reburied and at Rest  by Yunxiang Zhang

第二部分　华工篇
Part Two　Chinese Workers

**入土为安**

1996年，内华达州卡林镇发现13具华工遗骨。中餐馆老板王丽珠女士经过数年奔波，坚持让华工再次入土为安。图为该镇居民为华工举行再葬仪式。

**Reburied and at Rest**

In 1996, the remains of 13 Chinese workers were found in Carlin, Nevada. After few years of tireless efforts, Ms. Liju Chin, an owner of a Chinese restaurant, buried the Chinese workers with full honors in their final resting place. This picture is the burial ceremony conducted by the town residents for the Chinese workers.

◎《长青公墓》 张馨雅 画
*Evergreen Cemetery* by Xinya Zhang

## 长青公墓

2005年6月,洛杉矶发现一处华工墓地。当地官员伊薇特·拉波塞说:"我们着手带头纠正那段错误,将华工重新葬入'长青公墓'这个一度拒绝他们的地方。"

## Evergreen Cemetery

In June 2005, a Chinese worker cemetery was discovered in Los Angeles. "We are taking the lead in correcting a mistake and reburied the Chinese workers in the 'Evergreen Cemetery', a place that once rejected them," said a local official Yvette Rapose.

第二部分 华工篇
Part Two  Chinese Workers

◎《祭拜先辈》
Worship Ancestors

祝云姝　画
by Maggie Zhu

## 祭拜先辈

2015年秋，美国新泽西州贝尔维尔镇的荷兰归正教堂地下室发现了华工遗骸。3年后，华人社团在教会墓地举办了纪念先辈的祭拜仪式。林洁辉女士两次向该教会捐赠了3.5万美元。她感谢了教会和当地居民对华工先辈的善待。

## Worship Ancestors

In the fall of 2015, the remains of Chinese workers were found in the basement of the Dutch Reformed Church in Belleville, New Jersey. Three years later, the Chinese community held a monument dedication ceremony in the church cemetery. Ms. Jiehui Lin donated $35,000 to the church twice. She thanked the church and residents for their kind treatment of the Chinese ancestors.

◎《劳工部荣誉堂》　　　　　　　　　　　　　胡锦海　画
*Department of Labor Hall of Fame*　　　　　　by Elmer Hu

**劳工部荣誉堂**

2014年5月9日，铁路华工入选美国劳工部荣誉堂，以纪念在修建太平洋铁路中做出巨大贡献的铁路华工。

**Department of Labor Hall of Fame**

On May 9, 2014, Chinese railway workers were inducted into the US Department of Labor's Hall of Fame to remember the Chinese railway workers who made great contributions to the construction of the Pacific Railway.

（译文/王小龙 责编/许静）

# 第三部分　战争篇
## PART THREE
## THE WARS

# 第十章　美国南北战争中的华人
## Chapter 10　Chinese in the American Civil War

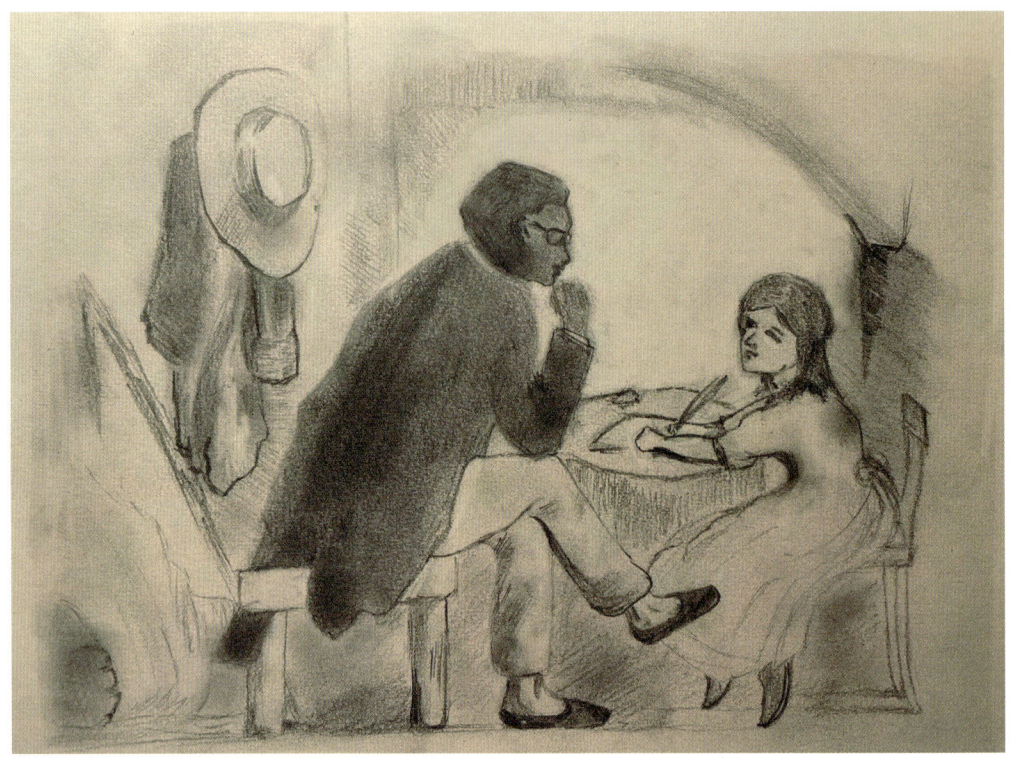

◉《南北战争》　　　　　　　　　　　　　　　　　　　　宋毕昕　画
　*American Civil War*　　　　　　　　　　　　　　　　by Anthony Song

**南北战争**

　　1861—1865 年，美国爆发了历史上一场规模最大的内战，参战双方为北方的美利坚合众国和南方的美利坚联盟国。战争以南方联盟炮击萨姆特要塞为起点，350 万人参战，最终以北方联邦胜利告终。大约 10% 的北方青壮年与 30% 的南方青壮年死于这场内战。

　　加州"淘金潮"末期，美国 19 世纪最畅销的小说《汤姆叔叔的小屋》出版，这本反奴隶制小说，让北方人知道奴隶们的辛酸血泪，也加速了《废奴令》的颁布，某种程度上激化并导致了内战爆发。

第三部分　战争篇
Part Three　The Wars

## American Civil War

From 1861 to 1865, the largest civil war in American history broke out between the United States of America in the north and the Confederate States of America in the south. The war began with the Confederate bombardment of Fort Sumter, 3.5 million men fought, and ended in a Confederate victory. About 10 percent in the north and 30 percent of young adults in the south died in this civil war.

At the end of the California Gold Rush, the best-selling novel "Uncle Tom's Cabin" in the 19$^{th}$ century in the United States was published. This anti-slavery novel made the northerners aware of the bitter blood and tears of slave. Also, it accelerated the promulgation of the "Abolition Order," to some extent intensified and led to the outbreak of civil war.

◉《华人卷入美国内战》　　　　　　　　　　　　　　　祝云姝　画
　　*Chinese Involved in American Civil War*　　　　　　by Maggie Zhu

## 华人卷入美国内战

　　据记载，在 1861—1865 年的四年美国内战中，超过 100 名华人在（陆、海）军中服役。其中大部分是海军，他们承担的基本上是地勤人员、厨师和舰舱服务等非战斗性职能。而在陆军中，南北双方则都有中国军人参与战斗，但数量很少。目前已知正面和直接参加前线军事战斗的，有入伍参加美国南北战争的李叶维，有随联邦军参加葛底斯堡战役中"皮克特冲锋"的约瑟夫·皮尔斯，有为南方军作战的"邦克"两兄弟，还有包括查尔斯·张及爱德华·科霍特在内的 5 人。

　　这些华裔士兵分别从纽约、康州、宾州、新泽西、北卡及乔治亚甚至西岸加州等地登记入伍。而当时南北战争主战场——密西西比河以东的美国东部华人总数仅 200 余人。与当时美国的其他族裔相比，他们的入伍比率是罕见的高。但他们之中，只有少数人在后来的生活里享受到抚恤金、福利和入籍等待遇。

第三部分　战争篇
Part Three　The Wars

**Chinese Involved in the American Civil War**

According to historical records, more than a hundred Chinese served in the army and the navy during the four-year American Civil War from 1861 to 1865. Most of them served in the navy performing non-combat functions such as ground crew, cooks and cabin service. In the army, Chinese soldiers also fought for the north and the south on the battlefields, though the number was very small. Today we know that among those who fought on the battlefields, Lee Yewei (Thomas Silvanus ) was the first Chinese who served in the Civil War, Joseph Pierce was in the "Pickett's Charge" with the Union Army in the Battle of Gettysburg, the "Bunker" brothers fought for the Confederate Army, and five others included Charles Zhang and Edward Cohort.

These Chinese soldiers were registered in New York, Connecticut, Pennsylvania, New Jersey, North Carolina, Georgia, and even West Coast California. At that time, the number of Chinese who lived in the east of the Mississippi River, the main battlefield of the Civil War, was estimated to be fewer than 200. Their enlistment rate was unusually high compared to other ethnic groups in the United States at the time. However, only a few of the Chinese soldiers received pensions, benefits, and naturalization when the war ended.

●《托玛斯·西尔韦纳斯》
*Thomas Sylvanus*

韩赫颐　画
by Helen Han

## 托玛斯·西尔韦纳斯

　　托玛斯·西尔韦纳斯的中文名为"李清"或"李叶维"。他青少年时来到美国。在巴尔的摩生活期间，正值美国南北战争爆发。1861年8月31日，他到费城加入了联邦军的宾夕法尼亚州第81志愿团，用名托玛斯·西尔韦纳斯。他是第一位入伍参加美国南北战争的中国人。

　　1862年6月底，李叶维以17岁的低龄随联邦军队与南方军战斗。

　　1862年12月10日，他因为视力原因被迫退伍。

　　1863年9月11日，李叶维又报名入伍纽约第42志愿团，随军开往前线，参加了在维吉尼亚的系列著名战斗。

　　1864年5月，南北战争最惨烈的阶段，他担任"有色卫队"下士，指挥作战。他率领的"有色卫队"最后只剩他一人，却仍顽强撑起军团战旗！

　　1864年6月22日，他在"彼得斯堡战役"中受伤，并被南方军俘虏。他被南方军移送到乔治亚州的安德森维尔监狱，直到战争结束后，他才获释。在安德森维尔关押期间，李叶维视力严重下降，近乎失明。战后他因视力问题无法找到工作。

　　1870年，在一位朋友的推荐下，他来到位于宾州偏远中西部的印第安纳小镇，在一家小酒店找了份工作。李叶维后来与一名爱尔兰女人结婚，并育有三名子女。但不久婚姻破裂。李叶维曾两度经营洗衣店，也因视力问题无法经营下去。

　　1891年6月15日，李叶维在印第安纳镇去世，终年46岁。他长眠的奥克兰

第三部分　战争篇
Part Three　The Wars

墓园最初建设于南北战争期间的 1863 年，现在有超过 3 万名逝者安葬于此。他是第一位被美国政府授予公民权的中国人，也是第一位从美国政府领取养老金的华人。美国当代的历史学者称这个群体为"华裔洋基"。

**Thomas Sylvanus**

　　Ching Lee or "Lee Yewei" came to America as a teenager. When he was living in Baltimore, the American Civil War broke out. On August 31, 1861, he went to Philadelphia to join the 81$^{st}$ Pennsylvania Volunteer Infantry of the Union Army under the name of Thomas Silvanus. He was the first Chinese to enlist in the American Civil War.

　　At the end of June 1862, Lee Yewei fought with the Union Army and the Confederate Army at the age of 17. On December 10, 1862, he was discharged from the army for vision reasons. On September 11, 1863, Li Yewei joined the 42$^{nd}$ Volunteer Infantry in New York, and went to the front lines of a series of famous battles in Virginia. In May 1864, during the most tragic phase of the Civil War, he served as a corporal of the colored troop, commanding operations. The "colored troop" he led was wiped out, and he was the only one left, but he still held up the battle flag of the legion tenaciously!

　　On June 22, 1864, he was wounded at the "Battle of Petersburg" and captured by the Confederates. The Confederate Army transferred him to Andersonville Prison in Georgia, where he was not released until after the war. In Andersonville Prison, Li Yewei suffered severe vision loss and was almost blind. After the war, he was unable to find work due to vision problems.

　　In 1870, referred by a friend, Lee came to the town of Indiana in the remote Midwest of Pennsylvania and found a job in a small hotel. Lee Yewei later married an Irish woman and had three children. But the marriage soon broke down. Lee Yewei tried to open a laundromat twice, but he could not run the business because of his vision problems.

　　On June 15, 1891, Li Yewei died in Indiana, PA at the age of 46. The Oakland Cemetery where he now rests was first established in 1863 during the Civil War, housing more than 30,000 dead. He was the first Chinese to be granted citizenship by the US government, and the first Chinese to receive a pension from the government. Today American historians call this group the "Chinese Yankee".

◉《约瑟夫·皮尔斯》
*Joseph L. Pierce*

李涵融　画
by Elaine Li

**约瑟夫·皮尔斯**

　　4岁的约瑟夫·皮尔斯被"康涅狄格号"的船长阿莫斯·派克（Amos Peck）从中国广东带到美国，船长成为他的养父。

　　1861年7月26日，约瑟夫·皮尔斯刚满21岁，身高5.5英尺、黑头发黑眼睛的他加入了第14康涅狄格步兵团，并服役3年。他参加了内战时期最著名的葛底斯堡战役。

　　他于1863年11月1日晋升为下士。为当时联邦军所有华裔美国人中军衔最高者。他的照片成为葛底斯堡博物馆馆藏。

　　2007年，美国众议员通过一项决议，表彰皮尔斯和其他亚太裔军人在南北战争中的表现。他也是第一位有影像资料可考的华裔美国军人。

第三部分　战争篇
Part Three　The Wars

◎《约瑟夫·皮尔斯》
*Joseph L. Pierce*

林之雅　画
by Candice Lin

**Joseph L. Pierce**

At four years old, Joseph L. Pierce was brought to the United States from Guangdong, China, by Captain Amos Peck of the Connecticut. The captain became his adoptive father.

On July 26, 1861, Joseph Pierce, who had just turned 21, was 5.5 feet tall, with black hair and black eyes, joined the 14th Connecticut Infantry and served for three years. He participated in the most famous Battle of Gettysburg during the Civil War. He was promoted to corporal on November 1, 1863. He was the highest ranked Chinese-Americans in the Union Army at that time. His picture is in the collection of the Gettysburg Museum.

In 2007, the US House of Representatives passed a resolution honoring Pierce and other Asian Pacific American service members in the Civil War. He is also the first Chinese-American soldier with video materials available.

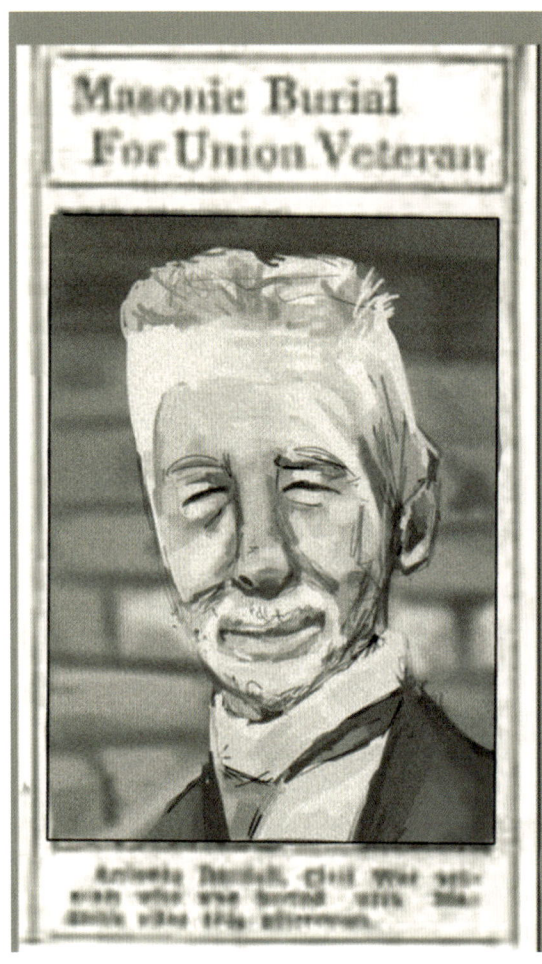

◎《安东尼奥·达德尔》
*Antonio Dardelle*

吴雨芮　画
by Sherry Wu

**安东尼奥·达德尔**

他出生于广东，7岁时沦为孤儿，美国船长大卫·怀特把他带到康涅狄格，并收养了他。安东尼奥·达德尔在康州克林顿学院接受了教育。

1862年10月，安东尼奥·达德尔18岁时，在纽黑文报名入伍康州第27步兵志愿团的A连。在华盛顿，他所在的第27志愿团被编入到著名的"波多马克军团"。在玛丽高地，第27团参战人员伤亡率近三分之一，达德尔右肩膀受了重伤，他被转回纽黑文的医院治疗。出院后，他又返回军中，一直作战到最后。

根据康州政府记录，安东尼奥·达德尔及其第27团的其他官兵一起"光荣退役"。依照规定，只有"光荣退役"的军人，未来才有资格享受政府的退伍兵福利。

第三部分　战争篇
Part Three　The Wars

**Antonio Dardelle**

Born in Guangdong, he was orphaned at the age of 7. Captain David White brought him to Connecticut and adopted him. Antonio Dardelle was educated at the Clinton Academy in Connecticut.

In October 1862, at the age of 18, Antonio Dardelle enlisted in Company A of the 27th Connecticut Volunteer Infantry in New Haven. The 27th Volunteer Regiment was mustered into the famous "Army of the Potomac" in Washington. At Mary Heights, where the 27th Infantry had a casualty rate of nearly one-third, Dardelle suffered a severe injury to his right shoulder and was transferred back to New Haven hospital for treatment. After being discharged from the hospital, he returned to the army and fought until the end.

According to Connecticut state records, Antonio Duddle and the rest of the 27th Regiment were "honorably discharged." Soldiers who were "honorably retired" were eligible for pensions.

◉《下士约翰·汤米》　　　　　　　　　　　　　　　　　林昀晖　画
　*Corporal John Tomney*　　　　　　　　　　　　　　by Kenny Lin

## 下士约翰·汤米

　　1861年，18岁的约翰·汤米加入北方军队。1862年3月，他因掉队被俘。在被释放后，他又一次加入了北方军精锐军团（The Excelsior Brigade），这个军团是北方军最勇敢的军团，而汤米是这个军团最勇敢的士兵。

　　他因为聪明、机智、勇敢而曾被《亚当斯哨兵报》《波士顿每日广告商》《斯普林菲尔德共和党人》《太阳报》《特洛伊日报》《纽约时报》《波士顿晚报》《每日公民和新闻》《哈特福德日报》《纽约先驱论坛报》《罗马公民》《纽约哈瓦那日报》《旧金山公报》《葛底斯堡时报》《每日宪政》等20余家媒体在1863年7—10月报道和称赞。他们称他为最勇敢的精锐旅中最勇敢的士兵之一，所有战友们都喜爱他。他于1863年7月2日在葛茨堡战役中失去双臂和双腿，并于1863年10月19日因伤去世。他在痛苦中度过了3个月零17天。

第三部分　战争篇
Part Three    The Wars

**Corporal John Tomney**

John Tomney joined the Union Army at the age of 18 in 1861. In March 1862, he was captured and as a prisoner. After he was released, he joined the Union Army again, and this time the Excelsior Brigade. Excelsier Brigate has taken part in eighteen engagements, and was known as "the bravest of brigades" of the Union. John Tomney was "one of the bravest soldiers."

Because of his cleverness, wit and bravery, he has been featured by *Adams Sentinel, Boston Daily Advertiser, Springfield Republican, Sun, Troy Daily, New York Times, Boston Evening News, Daily Citizen and News, Hartford Journal  New York Herald Tribune, Rome Citizen, New York Havana Daily, San Francisco Gazette, Gettysburg Times, Daily Constitution* and more than 20 media outlets between July and October, 1863. They called him one of the bravest soldiers of the bravest elite brigade, and all his comrades loved him. He lost both arms and legs at the Battle of Gettysburg on July 2, 1863, and died of his wounds on October 19, 1863. He spent three months and 17 days in pain.

- 《约翰·韩》
  *Tong Neok Woo*

  黄子恬　画
  by Alita Huang

**约翰·韩**

　　学者郭代伟将其名字译为"吴弘诺"。他于1841年生于中国浙江宁波。另一份资料则显示他于1839年生于广东。大约在1857年,他搭乘"无畏号"轮船来

第三部分 战争篇
Part Three　The Wars

到美国。他以前的职业是厨师。他于 1860 年 9 月 22 日加入了美国国籍。在 1863 年 7 月 24 日，他 22 岁时，登记加入为期两年的美国海军地勤部队，成为第一位在美国海军服役的华裔，并参加了南北战争。

1890 年 3 月 20 日，他成立了纽约州的第一家华人慈善协会，目的是改善纽约市华人贫困人口的状况。他一直被称为"唐人街市长"。《纽约时报》1904 年 8 月 17 日报道，他与另外两名富裕华人因投票给议员而被捕，称他们为非法入籍。根据入籍法，他们在法律上没有投票权。尽管他提供了一份完整的由印第安纳州里士满县法院于 1892 年 10 月 6 日授予他的入籍证明，但他还是在交纳了 500 美元保释金后才被放出。

1923 年 12 月，他去世于纽约史坦顿岛（其他资料说他是在上海去世的）。

## Tong Neok Woo

Historian Guo Daiwei translated his name in Chinese as "Wu Hongnuo". Tong Neok Woo was born in Ningbo, Zhejiang, China in 1841. Another source shows that he was born in Guangdong in 1839. Around 1857, he came to the United States on the steamship Intrepid. His previous occupation was as a chef. On September 22, 1860, he became a naturalized citizen. On July 24, 1863, in the year of 22, he enrolled in the US Navy Ground Service. He served it for two years, becoming the first Chinese American to serve in the US Navy and to participate in the Civil War.

On March 20, 1890, he established New York State's first Chinese charitable association with the aim to improve the living conditions of the Chinese poor in New York City. He had always been known as the "Mayor of Chinatown." According to the *New York Times* on August 17, 1904, he and two other wealthy Chinese were arrested for voting in the Congressional election, because under the charge of illegal naturalization and the naturalization law, they had no legal rights to vote. He was released after posting $500 bail. Although he provided a full certificate of naturalization, granted to him on October 6, 1892 by the Richmond County Court of Indiana.

He died in Staten Island, New York, in December 1923. Other document said he had died in Shanghai.

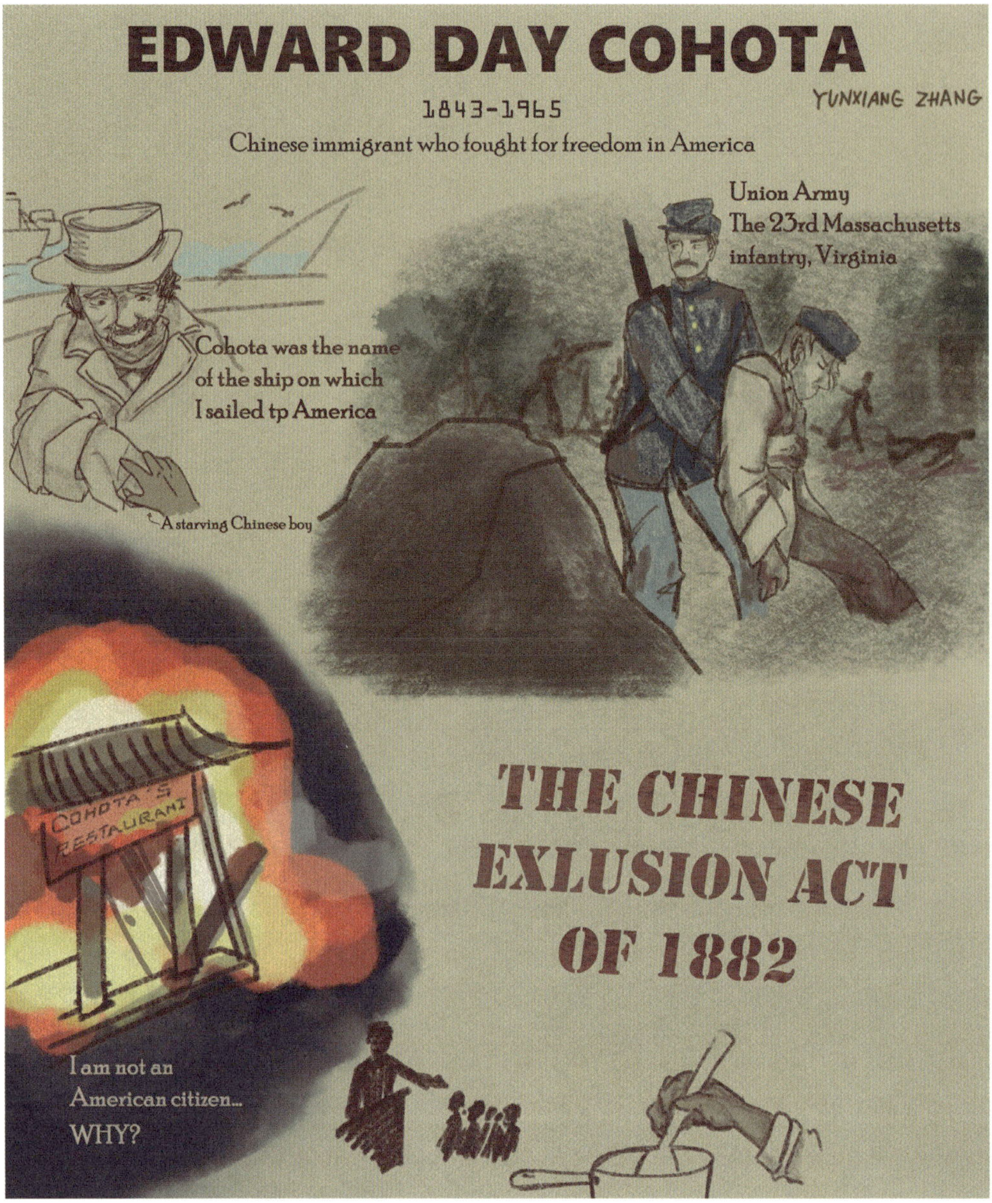

◉《爱德华·戴·考霍塔》
*Edward Day Cohota*

张云想 画
by Yunxiang Zhang

第三部分　战争篇
Part Three　The Wars

**爱德华·戴·考霍塔**

　　1845年冬，美国轮船"考霍塔号"从上海启程回美国马萨诸塞州。戴船长在甲板上发现一名快要饿死的四岁男孩，于是收留他为养子，并取名爱德华·戴·考霍塔（Cohota）。爱德华长大后参加了南北战争，战后在美国军队服役长达二十余年并且以南北战争军人的身份光荣退休。他在1882年《排华法案》之前就已经取得公民身份，但是他的公民权一再被否决并因此得不到光荣退役金。他始终以共和党人身份投票并一直没有停止抗争。直到1926年82岁时，他才领到了南北战争军人的退休金。

**Edward Day Cohota**

　　In the winter of 1845, the American steamship Cohota set off from Shanghai to return to Massachusetts. Captain Day found a starving four-year-old boy on deck and took him in as his adopted son. He gave him the name Edward Day Cohota. Edward grew up and fought in the Civil War, served in the US Army for more than two decades after the war and was honorably discharged. He became a naturalized citizen before the *Chinese Exclusion Act* of 1882, but later his citizenship had been repeatedly denied and a result, he couldn't get his Civil War pension. He had never stopped fighting for his right. He filed several multiple lawsuits. During the time, he had voted as a Republican. It was until 1926, at the age of 82, that he finally received his Civil War Pension.

（译文／茉莉　责编／陆颖）

# 第十一章　美墨边境战中的华人
## Chapter 11　Chinese in the Mexican-American War

◎《潘兴华人》  张蕴涵　画
*Pershing Chinese*  by Yunhan Zhang

**潘兴华人**

约翰·潘兴（John J. Pershing）是华盛顿之后的美军第二位五星级将军。1916年，他率军远征墨西哥，当时墨西哥北部的许多华人冒着被绞死的危险，选择在战争中协助美军工作。

1917年战争结束时，虽然排华仍在继续，但潘兴将军等人游说美国国会，将527位华人带回美国重新安置，他们大多定居在得克萨斯中部的安东尼奥，也被称为"潘兴华人"。

图为潘兴华人在山姆·休斯敦堡美军军营劳动。

第三部分　战争篇
Part Three　The Wars

**Pershing Chinese**

John J. Pershing was the second five-star general in the US military after Washington. In 1916, he led an expedition to Mexico. At that time, many Chinese in northern Mexico risked being hanged to choose to assist the US military in the war.

At the end of the war in 1917, although the Chinese exclusion continued, General Pershing and others lobbied the US Congress to bring 527 Chinese back to the United States for resettlement. Most of these Chinese settled in Antonio in Central Texas, known as the "Pershing Chinese."

The picture shows the "Pershing Chinese" working in the Fort Sam Houston US Army base.

（译文 / 林之雅 责编 / 朱国荣）

# 第十二章 "一战"中的美国华人
## Chapter 12　American Chinese in World War Ⅰ

100 Years of Chinese Immigration in the United States and Canada

◎《上士刘成基》　　　　　　　　　　　　　　　　　　　　　　　　　曹奕佳　画
　*Senior Sergeant Lau Sing Kee*　　　　　　　　　　　　　　　　　　by Christina Cao

第三部分　战争篇
Part Three　The Wars

## 上士刘成基

1917 年，美国加入第一次世界大战。1896 年，刘成基出生于加州。1917 年，他从加州搬到纽约，同年报名参加第 77 步兵师，成为通信兵。

1918 年 8 月，刘成基所在部队在法国北部一个村庄与德国部队交火，与他同在阵地上的 20 名通信兵全部倒下，仅他一人连续三天三夜坚守火线，独自撑起阵地通信，四次往返于阵地与指挥部之间。

"一战"结束，刘成基从中士被提升为上士，潘兴将军签发证书，授予刘成基"杰出服役勋章"（Distinguished Service Cross），同时，他还被授予"紫心勋章"和"法国英勇十字勋章"，成为首位获得美国战斗勋章的华裔美国人。

## Senior Sergeant Lau Sing Kee

In 1917, the United States entered World War Ⅰ. Lau Sing Kee was born in California in 1896. In 1917, he moved to New York and enlisted in the Signal Corps at the 77th Infantry Division.

In August 1918, Lau Sing Kee's troop exchanged fire with German troops in a village in northern France. All 20 signal soldiers on the same front with him fell in the battle. He was the only one who stayed in the battle line for three consecutive days and nights, keeping the communication alive. He went back and forth between the front line and the command center four times.

At the end of World War Ⅰ, Lau Sing Kee was promoted from sergeant to senior sergeant. General Pershing issued a certificate to award Lau Sing Kee the "Distinguished Service Cross". At the same time, he was also awarded the "Purple Heart" and " Croix de Guerre". He became the first Chinese-American to receive the US military medals.

◉《英雄举旗手》
*A Hero Flagbearer*

贾佳茵 画
by Kaela Jia

### 英雄举旗手

1919年,第一次世界大战宣告结束。欧美各大城市纷纷举行隆重的胜利大游行。据美华史记载,当时纽约市特意在曼哈顿第五大道与24街交界处建造了一个凯旋门。

1919年5月6日,护旗中士刘成基所在的美军第77步兵师在潘兴将军率领下,穿过精美的凯旋门,沿着著名的第五大道阔步前行,当时纽约民众万人空巷,欢呼声震天。图中右二举旗者就是"一战"中的美国英雄刘成基中士。

### A Hero Flagbearer

In 1919, World War Ⅰ came to an end. Major cities in Europe and the United States held grand victory parades. To celebrate the victory of World War Ⅰ, New York City deliberately built a triumphal arch at the junction of Fifth Avenue and 24th Street in Manhattan.

On May 6, 1919, the 77th Infantry Division of the US Army, led by General Pershing, passed through the exquisite Arc de Triomphe and strode along the famous Fifth Avenue. At that time, all New Yorkers turned out cheering along the avenue. In the image, Senior Sergeant Lau Sing Kee was second from the right, holding the flag. He was an American hero in World War Ⅰ.

第三部分　战争篇
Part Three　The Wars

◉《花车游行》　　　　　　　　　　　　　　　　　曹奕佳　画
　*Parade on Flower Floats*　　　　　　　　　　　by Christina Cao

## 花车游行

1919年6月13日，刘成基回到加州，和父母一起参加圣何塞市的庆祝"一战"胜利游行，他们一家三口坐在花车上接受市民致敬！

## Parade on Flower Floats

On June 13, 1919, Lau Sing Kee returned to California to join his parents in a parade celebrating the victory of World War Ⅰ in San Jose. The family of three sat on the flower float to receive the respect of the citizens!

193

◉《炊事兵关崇琼》
*Cooking Soldier Dea Hong Toy*

韩赫颐　画
by Helen Han

## 炊事兵关崇琼

第一次世界大战时，住在亚利桑那州的 24 岁的关崇琼应征入伍，之前他在餐馆打工。他在纽约与爱尔兰人的战斗师接受训练，之后被派往欧洲战场，他是美国远征军第 164 步兵团的炊事员。20 个月后，他受伤了。1919 年，他从法国返回，并收到退役通知。

## Cooking Soldier Dea Hong Toy

Dea Hong Toy, a 24-year-old living in Arizona, was drafted into the army during World War Ⅰ after working in restaurants. He trained with the Irish combat division in New York before being sent to the European theater of war. He served as a cook for the 164th Infantry Regiment of the US Expeditionary Force. Twenty months later, he was injured. In 1919, he returned from France with a retirement letter from the military.

（译文 / 林之雅　责编 / 朱国荣）

# 第十三章 "一战"中的加拿大华人
## Chapter 13　Canadian Chinese in World War Ⅰ

◉《费德瑞克·李》
Frederick Lee

胡锦海　画
by Elmer Hu

◉《骑兵营机枪队合影》
The Rocky Mountain Cavalry Machine Gun Team

李炳毅　画
by Bingyi Li

第三部分　战争篇
Part Three　The Wars

**费德瑞克·李**

第一次世界大战期间，约有 300 名华裔加入加拿大军队。

加拿大裔华人费德瑞克·李志愿加入落基山骑兵队。之后，他被派往欧洲战场，被安排做了机枪手。

然而战争无情，1917 年 8 月，在法国北部朗斯小镇郊外的一场战役中，年仅 21 岁的费德瑞克牺牲了，遗体至今未找到。

落基山骑兵营机枪队合影中费德瑞克坐在前排正中。

**Frederick Lee**

During the First World War, about 300 Chinese joined the Canadian army.

Frederick Lee, a Chinese Canadian young man joined the Rocky Mountain Ranger as a volunteer. He was stationed on the European battlefield and was appointed as a machine gunner.

Unfortunately, the war was relentless. In August 1917, a war occurred on the outskirts of the small town of Lens in northern France. During this battle, Frederick died heroically when he was only 21 years old. His remains were not found yet.

In the image of the Rocky Mountain Cavalry Machine Gun Team, Federek sat in the middle of the front row.

◎《纪念碑》 胡锦海 画
*The Monument* by Elmer Hu

第三部分　战争篇
Part Three　The Wars

## 纪念碑

温哥华华裔企业家甄硕明（Jack Gin）在参与山峰–70纪念项目时，发现了费德瑞克的华裔身份。在他的呼吁下，加拿大华裔社区对山峰–70纪念项目给予了极大支持。特别是得益于前加拿大参议员利德蕙（Vivienne Poy）博士及知名慈善家何鸿毅（Robert H. N. Ho）等人的慷慨资助，"一战"胜利101年后的2019年10月，当年的战场阵地上终于竖立起一座纪念碑，并修建了相关纪念设施，包括一条以费德瑞克·李命名的走道和长椅等。

图为加拿大多位军政界要员出席纪念碑揭幕仪式。

## The Monument

When Vancouver Chinese entrepreneur Jack Gin participated in the Hill-70 Memorial Project, he discovered Frederik's Chinese identity. Under his appeal, the Chinese Canadian community expressed concern for the Hill-70. The commemorative project gave great support. Especially thanks to the generous funding of a former Canadian Senator, Dr. Vivienne Poy and a well-known philanthropist Robert H. N. Ho, etc, in October 2019, 101 years later after the victory of World War I, a monument was erected on the battlefield. Other memorial facilities were also built, including a walkway and benches named after Frederick Liang. Many Canadian military and political figures attended the unveiling ceremony of the monument.

（译文/胡锦海　责编/陈丽）

# 第十四章 欧洲战场
Chapter 14  European Battlefield

100 Years of Chinese Immigration in the United States and Canada

◉《华人积极参加"二战"》　　　　　　　　　　　　张天阳　画
　　*Chinese Soldiers Sent to the European Battlefield*　　by Andrew Zhang

## 第三部分　战争篇
Part Three　The Wars

### 华人积极参加"二战"

据美国征兵总局统计,"二战"期间,超 1.3 万名华人在美国陆军服役,占当时美国华人男性的 22%。他们中的 70% 在陆军,25% 服役于陆军航空军,是美国各族裔参军人数百分比最高的族裔之一。他们中近 20% 的人在海外阵亡,40% 的人没有美国国籍。

华人积极参战的主要原因:

1. 1937 年日军全面侵华以后,许多在美华人的亲人仍在故土,他们受到的战争影响是巨大的。华人在西方战场参加"二战",是华人士兵们对抗日本侵略的另一种方式。

2.《排华法案》实施之后,美国社会对华人的不信任和排斥无处不在。而大部分华裔实际上拥有和其他美国人对这个国家一样的爱国热情。积极加入美军参加"二战",就是最好的证明。

### Chinese Soldiers Sent to the European Battlefield

According to statistics from the General Administration of Recruitment of the United States, more than 13,000 Chinese served in the US Army, during World War II, accounting for 22% of the Chinese men in the United States at that time. 70% of them served in the Army and 25% in the Army Air Forces, one of the highest percentages of any ethnic group in the United States. Nearly 20% of them were killed overseas and 40% had no US citizenship.

The main reasons why the Chinese actively participated in the war are:

1. After the Japanese invasion of China in 1937, many relatives of the Chinese in the United States still lived in China, the impact of the war those Chinese Americans was huge. Chinese participation in World War II on the Western battlefield was another way for the Chinese to fight against Japanese aggression.

2. After the implementation of the *Chinese Exclusion Act*, distrust and rejection of Chinese people in American society existed everywhere. Most Chinese Americans had the same patriotic enthusiasm for the country as other Americans. Actively joining the US military to participate in World War II was the best proof for that.

◉《华人士兵参加诺曼底登陆》　　　　　　　　　　　　　　林昀晖　画
　　*Chinese Soldiers Took Part in the Normandy Landings*　　by Kenny Lin

## 华人士兵参加诺曼底登陆

经过培训，华人士兵们被派往欧洲战场、亚洲战场和太平洋战场，他们英勇作战，用生命为代价，为华裔后代赢得了在美国这个国家的尊重，并获得平等权益。

诺曼底登陆战役中，在奥马哈滩头向内陆推进的同盟国军队士兵中不乏华裔士兵。

## Chinese Soldiers Took Part in the Normandy Landings

After training, the Chinese soldiers were sent to the European battlefield, the Asian battlefield and the Pacific battlefield. They fought bravely and at the cost of their lives. They won the respect of the Chinese descendants in this country and gained equal rights and interests with the whites.

The image shows the Confederate Army soldiers advancing inland on the beachhead of Omaha during the Battle of D-Day in Normandy. Among them were Chinese soldiers.

第三部分　战争篇
Part Three　The Wars

◉《华人在美英商船服务》　　　　　　　　　　　　　　　龙可为　画
　Chinese Serving in the US and UK Merchant Ships　　　by Claire Fillon

## 华人在美英商船服务

"二战"期间，有1.5万华人海员在美国和英国的商船上做后勤服务工作。

图为华人海员在为美军修船——在船上起螺丝和螺杆。

## Chinese Serving in the US and UK Merchant Ships

During World War Ⅱ, 15,000 Chinese mariners in the US navy performed administrative services on the US and UK merchant ships.

The image shows Chinese mariners repairing ships for the US army, such as tightening screws on the deck.

○《炮兵指挥官罗伯特·伊莱·汉姆》
*Artillery Commander Robert E. Ham*

杨彬鑫　画
by Misty Yang

## 炮兵指挥官罗伯特·伊莱·汉姆

他1921年出生于亚利桑那，有三个兄弟一个姐姐。"二战"爆发后，他入伍参加了美国陆军，全程参加"二战"。他跟随部队到过英国、法国、德国、比利时等多个欧洲国家，参加过包括诺曼底战役等多个重大战役。由于战功突出，他被升任中校炮兵指挥官职务，也获得了8枚勋章奖牌。

## Artillery Commander Robert E. Ham

He was born in Arizona in 1921, and had three brothers and one sister. After the outbreak of World War Ⅱ, he joined the US Army and participated in World War Ⅱ throughout. He followed the troops to the United Kingdom, northern France, Germany, Belgium and many other European countries. He participated in many major battles including the Battle of Normandy. Due to his outstanding military exploits, he was promoted to the post of Lieutenant Colonel Artillery Commander and won 8 medals.

第三部分　战争篇
Part Three　The Wars

◉《机师龚丹坤》
*Maintenance Pilot Kun Dan Gong*

高大牛　画
by Daniel Gao

**机师龚丹坤**

　　他出生于亚利桑那，"二战"爆发后入伍。经过培训，他成为一名 B-24 重型轰炸机的维修机师，并奔赴欧洲战场，曾在英国、加拿大蒙特利尔、冰岛等盟军基地维修战机，并参加过诺曼底登陆战役以及意大利西西里岛的战役。

　　图左为龚丹坤。

**Maintenance Pilot Kun Dan Gong**

　　He was born in Arizona and joined US Army after the outbreak of World War Ⅱ. After training, he became a maintenance pilot of a B-24 heavy bomber, and went to the European battlefield. He maintained fighter planes in the United Kingdom, Montreal of Canada, Iceland and other Allied bases and participated in the battles of Normandy landing and the Italian island of Sicily.

◉《海军厨师陈来妹》  宋波菲 画
*Navy Chef Laimei Chen*  by Sophia Song

第三部分　战争篇

Part Three　The Wars

**海军厨师陈来妹**

他生于福建长乐。12 岁时，他就在香港的英国船上当海员。

1939 年，陈来妹所在的船队到达美国纽约时，正赶上"二战"爆发，所有人都无法回香港。有些人下船找工作，有些人去了别的国家，但陈来妹选择参加"二战"。他被分配到在纽约的美国海军后勤部队，在那里当了一名厨师，一直到 1944 年"二战"结束前夕，他才回到家乡。

为了给家里挣更多的生活费，1946 年他又返回美国，在纽约和新泽西打工，每隔两年回家一次，这样的生活持续到 20 世纪 70 年代。他的子女们办理美国入籍手续时被告之，无论生在哪里都是美国公民，因为他们的父亲曾在"二战"期间为美国海军服役。

图为陈来妹 24 岁回到家乡时的结婚纪念照。

**Navy Chef Laimei Chen**

Born in Changle, Fujian, he was a sailor on a British ship in Hong Kong at the age of 12.

In 1939, when Laimei Chen's fleet arrived in New York, USA, it was just in time for the outbreak of World War II. No one could return to Hong Kong. Some people left the ships to look for job, some went to other countries, while Laimei Chen chose to participate in World War II. He was assigned to the US Navy Logistics Unit in New York, where he became a chef. It was until the end of World War II in 1944 when he finally returned home.

To earn more money for his family, he returned to the United States in 1946 and worked in New York and New Jersey. He returned home every two years, and continued to do this until the 1970s. When his children went through the US naturalization process, they were told they were US citizens already no matter where they were born, because their father served in the US Navy during World War II.

The picture shows the wedding ceremony photo of Laimei Chen when he returned to his hometown at the age of 24.

◉《江华九——欧洲战场的华裔飞行员》
*Wau Kau Kong—Chinese Pilots on the European Battlefield*

林昀晖 画
by Kenny Lin

## 江华九——欧洲战场的华裔飞行员

他是美国华裔中的第一位战斗机飞行员，少尉军衔。他生于夏威夷的檀香山。1941年加入美国陆军航空兵团，1943年10月23日被派驻英国，服役于第354飞行大队的第353飞行中队，在欧洲战场作战。

## Wau Kau Kong—Chinese Pilots on the European Battlefield

He was the first Chinese-American fighter pilot with the rank of second lieutenant. He was born in Honolulu, Hawaii. In 1941, he joined the United States Army Air Corps. On October 23, 1943, he was sent to the United Kingdom. He served in the 353rd Squadron of the 354th Flying Group and fought in the European battlefield.

第三部分　战争篇
Part Three　The Wars

◉《华人的机会》
*Chinaman Chance*

林昀晖　画
by Kenny Lin

## 华人的机会

江华九把他驾驶的 P-51 野马式战斗机命名为"华人的机会"（Chinaman Chance）。1944 年 2 月，江华九在护送轰炸机回法兰克福途中，击落一架德国 FW-190 战斗机，这是他的第 12 次任务。他第一次击落敌机的事迹曾被刊登在《时代》杂志。

## Chinaman Chance

Wau Kau Kong named the P-51 Mustang fighter he piloted as "Chinaman Chance"! In February 1944, Wau Kau Kong shot down a German FW190 fighter jet while escorting the bomber back to Frankfurt. This was his 12th mission. The story of his first shooting down of an enemy plane was published in *Time* magazine.

◉《江华九》
*Wau Kau Kong*

田芯语　画
by Melody Tian

**牺牲在欧洲战场**

1944年2月22日，江华九在执行第14次任务时被德军飞机击落，牺牲时年仅25岁。

1941年美国加入"二战"时，他正在夏威夷大学攻读化学硕士学位。作为化学研究人员，他本可以避免从军。但他对父母说，当被需要去战斗的时候，却在一旁欢呼，让他于心不安，他希望自己的世界中，有一部分充满激情、探险和刺激。

这两幅图片是江华九和他不同种族的飞行战友。

第三部分　战争篇
Part Three　The Wars

◎《飞行战友》　　　　　　　　　　　　　　　　　　　　　田芯语　画
　*Airmen*　　　　　　　　　　　　　　　　　　　　　by Melody Tian

**Sacrifice on the European Battlefield**

On February 22, 1944, Wau Kau Kong was shot down by a German aircraft during his 14th mission. He was only 25 years old when he died.

When the United States participated in the World War Ⅱ in 1941, he was studying for a master's degree in chemistry at the University of Hawaii. As a chemistry researcher, he could have avoided joining the military. But he told his parents that he was cheering in heart when he was called upon to fight. This made him uneasy. He wanted his world full of passion, adventure and excitement.

These two images show Wau Kau Kong and his airmen of different races.

◉《黄门赞》
*Mun Charn Wong*

石啸天　画
by Ian Bryant

**黄门赞**

　　他是江华九儿时好友、高中及大学同学，1940年获得理学学士学位。受江华九影响，他加入了美国空军，当时也在欧洲战场执行任务，后来晋升为中校。当他获知江华九牺牲的消息，发誓要找到朋友的遗骸。1945年8月德国投降，在等待回夏威夷期间，他征得指挥官同意，开着吉普车并携带一名翻译前往博朗贝克江华九飞机爆炸的地点，经过多方探访，询问现场证人，他终于寻获江华九的遗骨，送回檀香山埋葬。

　　战后，黄门赞成为一名成功的人寿保险高管。

**Mun Charn Wong**

　　He was a childhood friend, high school and college classmate of Wau Kau Kong. He received a Bachelor of Science degree in 1940. Influenced by Wau Kau Kong, he joined the US Air Force and was also on missions in the European battlefield at that time. He was later promoted to lieutenant colonel. When he heard about the death of Wau Kau Kong, he swore to find the remains of his friend. In August 1945. Germany surrendered unconditionally. While waiting to return to Hawaii, after getting the commander's permission, he drove a jeep with an interpreter to the aircrash site of Wau Kau Kong. After several visits and questioning of witnesses at the scene, he finally found Wau Kau Kong's remains and sent them back to Honolulu for burial.

　　After the war, Mun Charn Wong became a successful life insurance executive.

第三部分　战争篇
Part Three　The Wars

◉《亚瑟·黄》
*Arthur Wong*

李可欣　画
by Maggie Li

## 亚瑟·黄

他生于加州的奥克兰市，在美国陆军航空军的第 359 战斗大队服役，被派驻欧洲战场作战，最高军衔至少尉。他于 1944 年圣诞节前夕，因飞机在德国的科布伦茨 (Koblenz) 坠毁沦为战俘。

当时，亚瑟·黄所在的大队驻扎在英国诺福克附近的空军基地，曾获得杰出部队的褒奖令。在与敌军激战中，该大队共损失 121 名飞行员。

## Arthur Wong

Born in Oakland California, he served in the 359th Combat Group of the US Army Air Forces. He was sent to the European battlefield with the highest rank to second lieutenant. He became a prisoner of war after his plane crashed in Koblenz, Germany, on Christmas Eve, 1944.

At that time, Arthur Wong's brigade was stationed at the Air Force Base near Norfolk, United Kingdom. He was awarded as Outstanding Troop. In fierce battles with the enemy, a total of 121 pilots died.

◎《洪波》
*Bock Hong*

殷思齐 画
by Iris Yin

## 洪波

　　他出生于中国，小时候来到美国，在家里的杂货店工作。他擅长摄影，"二战"期间，他加入了盟军第九陆空兵团第 13 照片技术部门。作为美军下士，他辗转于英国、法国和德国等各个战场。

　　"二战"结束后，洪波回到了美国，得到《退伍军人法》的基金支持，上了大学，后来成为休斯敦有名的艺术家。但他为"二战"做出的贡献，一直没有受到嘉奖。

## Bock Hong

　　He was born in China, and came to the United States as a child. He worked for the grocery store owned by his family. He was good at photography. During World War II, he joined the 13th Photographic Technical Department of the Ninth Army and Air Corps of the Allied Forces. As a corporal in the US military, he traveled to various battlefields such as Britain, France and Germany.

　　After the World War II, Bock Hong returned to the United States. With the funding from the *Veterans Act*, he went to college, and later became a well-known artist in Houston. But his contribution to World War II has not been rewarded.

第三部分　战争篇
Part Three　The Wars

◉《黄君裕》
*Junyu Huang*

张薇薇　画
by Vivian Zhang

**黄君裕**

　　1938 年，15 岁的黄君裕从广东台山移民到美国波士顿。

　　1943 年他报名参军，成为陆军第一军团第五军第 28 步兵师第 110 团三营 A 连侦察兵。1944 年 6 月 6 日作为先头部队参加举世闻名的诺曼底登陆战役，后转战法国、比利时、卢森堡、德国。

　　他所在的连队出征时 187 人，凯旋时只剩下 5 人。

　　"二战"结束后，黄君裕于 1947 年回到家乡结婚，然后携妻回美，在大波士顿地区的布鲁克莱恩 (Brookline) 养育了五个孩子。

　　黄君裕的事迹长期被埋没，直到 2009 年美国政府才给其颁发紫心勋章、铜星勋章等荣誉勋章。

　　2020 年 4 月 26 日黄君裕离世，享寿 96 岁。

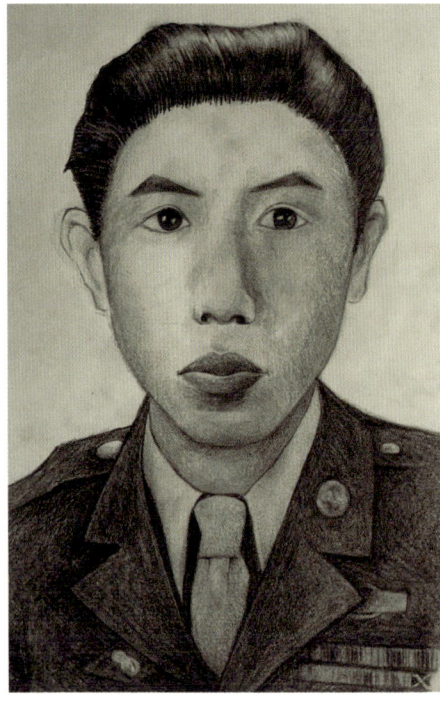

◎《黄君裕》
*Junyu Huang*

刘娜娜　画
by Kalina Liu

## Junyu Huang

In 1938, 15-year-old Junyu Huang immigrated to Boston, USA from Taishan, Guangdong.

In 1943, he joined the army and became a scout for Company A, 3rd Battalion, 110th Regiment, 28th Infantry Division, 5th Army, 1st Army Corps. On June 6, 1944, it participated in the world-famous D-Day invasion as the vanguard and then moved to France, Belgium, Luxembourg, and Germany.

His company had 187 men at the time of the expedition and only 5 men left at the time of the triumph.

After World War II, Junyu Huang returned to his hometown to get married in 1947. He returned to the United States with his wife to raise five children in Brookline, in the Greater Boston area.

Junyu Huang's deeds have been buried for a long time. It was until 2009 that the US government awarded him the Purple Heart, Bronze Star and other honorary medals.

On April 26, 2020, Junyu Huang passed away at the age of 96.

第三部分　战争篇
Part Three　The Wars

◉《弗朗西斯·B. 魏上尉》
*Captain Francis Brown Wai*

龙可为　画
by Claire Fillon

**弗朗西斯·B. 魏上尉**

1917 年，他出生于夏威夷，父亲年轻时来到美国，母亲是有白人血统的夏威夷人，他在中学时喜欢冲浪、美式足球与棒球。他毕业于加州大学洛杉矶分校金融专业。

1940 年他加入国民警卫队。1941 年他参军入伍，并在美军第 34 步兵师服役，先赴欧洲战场，后调亚洲，1944 年 10 月在菲律宾战死。

他获得了美军最高荣誉勋章"国会荣誉勋章"。

**Captain Francis Brown Wai**

He was born in Hawaii in 1917. His father came to the United States when he was young. His mother was a Hawaiian of white descent. He enjoyed surfing, American football and baseball in middle school. He graduated from UCLA in Finance major.

In 1940 he joined the National Guard. He enlisted in the Army in 1941 and served in the 34th Infantry Division of the US Army, first in Europe, then in Asia. He died in Philippines in October 1944.

He received the US military's highest honor, the Congressional Medal of Honor.

◎《关荣业》
*Wing Yip Quan*

茉 莉　画
by Moli

**关荣业**

他出生于1907年,"二战"时加入美军。

1944年6月5日夜,关荣业所属的第101空降师伞兵部队投入战斗,在位于卡昂和瑟堡半岛之间的诺曼底海岸跳伞降落,他们的任务是确保桥梁安全,切断德国军队通信及补给。

6月6日清晨,近300万盟军士兵横渡英吉利海峡,历史上规模最大的海上登陆作战在法国诺曼底地区展开。

关荣业在第101空降师是一名一等兵。"二战"胜利后,他获得包括欧洲－非洲战役奖章等四枚奖章。

第三部分　战争篇
Part Three　The Wars

**Wing Yip Quan**

Born in 1907, he served in the US Army during World War II.

On the night of June 5, 1944, the paratroopers of the 101$^{st}$ Airborne Division that Wing Yip Quan belonged to went into battle. They parachuted down the coast of Normandy between Caten and Cherbourg peninsula. Their task was to ensure the safety of bridges and cut German army communications and supplies.

In the early morning of June 6, nearly three million Allied soldiers crossed the English Channel, and the largest naval landing operation in history was launched in Normandy, France.

Wing Yip Quan was a first-class soldier in the 101$^{st}$ Airborne Division. After his victory in World War II, he received four medals, including the Euro-African Campaign Medal.

◉《空军中尉弗雷德·龚》
*Fred Gong, US Air Force Lieutenant*

殷思齐　画
by Iris Yin

**空军中尉弗雷德·龚**

1939年至1945年他报名参加了"二战",被派往地中海战区服役,担任一架B-17空中堡垒的首席投弹员。

他获得了"二战"国会金牌、杰出飞行勋章等四次航空勋章。

**Fred Gong, US Air Force Lieutenant**

He participated in World War II from 1939 to 1945 and was sent to serve in the Mediterranean battlefield as a chief bombardier of a B17 Flying Fortress. He received four aviation medals, including the Congressional Gold Medal in World War II and the Distinguished Flying Medal.

第三部分　战争篇
Part Three　The Wars

◎《伞兵 Leon Yee》
*Paratrooper Leon Yee*

杨咏志　画
by Robert Yang

## 伞兵 Leon Yee

1944 年 6 月 6 日午夜过后，超过 13000 名美国伞兵进入战备状态，他们将前往法国参加诺曼底战役。

Leon Yee 生于旧金山唐人街。他在美国的陆军训练基地班宁堡受训后，成为一名拆弹和爆破专家，1942 年，他被指派到第 507 伞兵团。

当载着 Yee 和他的战友们的飞机飞往法国海岸的时候，德军的地面防空高射炮开火了，火光照亮了整个黑夜，他们的飞机也被炮弹击中。Yee 背上 100 多磅的武器设备，在凌晨两点的法国上空，从 1000 多尺的高空一跃而下。

## Paratrooper Leon Yee

After midnight on June 6, 1944, more than 13,000 US paratroopers entered combat readiness for the Battle of Normandy in France.

Leon Yee was born in San Francisco's Chinatown. After training at Fort Benning, the US Army training base, he became a bomb disposal and demolition specialist, and in 1942 he was assigned to the 507$^{th}$ Parachute Regiment.

As the plane taking Yee and his comrades to the French coast, German anti-aircraft guns on the ground opened fire, illuminating the night. Yee's plane was hit by the shells. At two o'clock in the morning, more than 100 pounds of weapons and equipment on his back, Yee jumped from more than 1,000 feet above France.

◉《肯尼斯·杨》
*Kenneth Wah Leong Young*

穆烊昕 画
by Emily Mu

**肯尼斯·杨**

　　1919 年,他生于夏威夷檀香山,是家中的第二个儿子。他在圣路易斯高中毕业后,乘坐轮船离开檀香山前往芝加哥上大学,并顺利从伊利诺伊理工学院 (IIT) 毕业。

　　1942 年,他被任命为陆军第二中尉,但他拒绝了,转而去新泽西州的一家电子公司 Belmar 工作。然而半年后,他还是加入了军队,服役于陆军第 3 步兵师。他的军衔是第 216 防空炮营 D 连队 4 级技术员。

　　他被派往欧洲战场,曾在安齐奥的滩头、那不勒斯到福贾、罗马、阿诺、法国南部、莱茵兰和中欧等阵地参战。为此,他获得了总统级别的嘉奖,获得紫心勋章、胜利勋章和战斗步兵徽章。

第三部分　战争篇
Part Three　The Wars

◎《肯尼斯·杨和战友》　　　　　　　　　　　　　　　穆烊昕　画
　Kenneth Wah Leong Young and Comrades　　　　　　by Emily Mu

## Kenneth Wah Leong Young

He was born in Honolulu, Hawaii, in 1919, as the second son in the family. After graduating from St. Louis High School, he left Honolulu by boat for college in Chicago. He successfully graduated from the Illinois Institute of Technology (IIT).

In 1942, he was appointed second lieutenant in the Army, but he declined and went to work for Belmar, an electronics company in New Jersey. But half a year later, he joined the army and served in the Army's 3$^{rd}$ Infantry Division. His rank was Technician 4$^{th}$, Company D, 216$^{th}$ Anti-Aircraft Artillery Battalion.

He was sent to the battlefields of Europe and fought from the beachheads of Anzio, Naples to Foggia, Rome, Arnold, southern France, the Rhineland and Central Europe. Therefore, he was honored at the presidential level with the Purple Heart, the Victory Medal and the Combat Infantry Badge.

◉《英尚汉》
*Shang Hon Eng*

黄子恬　画
by Alita Huang

## 英尚汉

英尚汉出生于1937年，24岁时，他移民到美国芝加哥，在金雉餐厅担任服务员和调酒师。

1940年，他成为芝加哥征召的第一个华人，但直到1943年12月他才正式入伍。

1944年7月，他所在的第134步兵团（第35师的一部分）从诺曼底出发，经过比利时和荷兰，到达德国的汉诺威。为表彰他作为一等兵的杰出兵役，英尚汉被授予铜星勋章、良好行为勋章、欧洲-非洲-中东战役勋章、"二战"胜利勋章、占领军勋章和战斗步兵徽章。

"二战"后，英尚汉回到芝加哥继续在金雉餐厅工作。根据1945年《战争新娘法案》的规定，他提交了文件，将他的妻女从香港接到美国。1947年，在他移民到美国10年后，一家人终于团聚。

他的四个在美国出生的孩子都就读于加州大学伯克利分校并获得学位，英尚汉于1995年去世。

第三部分　战争篇
Part Three　The Wars

**Shang Hon Eng**

Born in 1937, at the age of 24, Shang Hon Eng immigrated to Chicago, USA as a son. He worked as a waiter and bartender at the Golden Pheasant Restaurant.

In 1940, he became the first Chinese conscript in Chicago, but did not officially enlist in the army until December 1943.

In July 1944, his 134$^{th}$ Infantry Regiment (part of the 35$^{th}$ Division) set out from Normandy through Belgium and the Netherlands to Hanover, Germany. In recognition of his outstanding military service as a First Class, Shang Hon Eng was awarded the Bronze Star, Good Conduct Medal, Europe-Africa-Middle East Campaign Medal, World War II Victory Medal, Occupation Army Medal and Combat Infantry Badge.

After World War II, Shang Hon Eng returned to Chicago and continued to work at the Golden Pheasant Restaurant. Under the terms of the War Brides Act of 1945, he filed papers to bring his wife and daughter back to the United States from Hong Kong. In 1947, ten years after he immigrated to the United States, the family was finally reunited.

All four of his US-born children attended and earned degrees from the University of California, Berkeley. Shang Hon Eng passed away in 1995.

◉《秦远道》
*Randall Ching*

李涵融　画
by Elaine Li

**秦远道**

　　秦远道 1924 年生于旧金山唐人街。1930 年，为了逃避大萧条，他和父母回到中国。但 1941 年日本突袭珍珠港之前，他的父母敦促他回到美国参加"二战"。入伍之后，军队本来让他当厨师，但他却想当步兵，而且他的枪法很准，八次有七次命中靶心，于是他报名当了一名游骑兵。他使用自己的武术功夫，虽然身高只有 5.4 英尺，却在欧洲战场消灭了一支德国巡逻队，因此获得一枚铜星勋章。

　　1944 年，他作为美国的 6000 名游骑兵的一员，参加诺曼底海滩登陆。他希望外界把他看作一个可以与游骑兵中最好的士兵站在一起的中国人。

　　"二战"结束后，他回到唐人街亲戚的杂货店做存货经理。后来去夜校，获得电子技术员认证，并成为一名维修经理，直到 1990 年退休。

第三部分　战争篇
Part Three　The Wars

**Randall Ching**

　　Randall Ching was born in San Francisco's Chinatown in 1924. In 1930, to escape the Great Depression, he and his parents returned to China. Before the Japanese attacked Pearl Harbor in 1941, his parents urged him to return to the United States to fight in World War Ⅱ. After enlisting, the army wanted him to be a cook, but he wanted to be an infantryman. His marksmanship was very accurate. He could hit the bullseye seven times out of eight shots. So he decided to sign up to be a ranger. Although he was only 5-foot-4 tall, with his martial arts, he eliminated a German patrol in Europe, for which he was awarded a Bronze Star.

　　In 1944, he participated in the Normandy Beach landings as a member of the 6,000 US Rangers. He wanted to be considered as a Chinese, who could stand with the best soldiers in the Rangers.

　　After World War Ⅱ, he returned to work as an inventory manager at a relative's grocery store in Chinatown. Later he went to night school, got certified as an electronic technician, and became a maintenance manager until his retirement in 1990.

◎《雷建廷》
*Gain Thyn Lui*

叶子思　画
by Alice Ye

**雷建廷**

雷建廷又名雷奥（Sonny Leo）。他的爷爷和父亲都是铁路华工。1925年，他出生于广东台山，13岁随父母来到旧金山，后搬到怀俄明州的罗克斯普林斯。

1885年9月2日，28名华人矿工在石泉矿镇被杀害。28座华人房屋被烧毁，这些人中大多是雷奥的家族亲戚。

雷奥在石泉矿读完七年级后，在咖啡馆工作，他白天做中餐，晚上继续读私立学校。

1944年，他应征入伍，并在犹他州道格拉斯堡服役。他被分配到第20装甲步兵营，参与了阿登、莱茵兰和中欧的战斗和战役。

由于他的英勇表现，他被授予银星奖章、胜利勋章、欧洲－非洲－中东地区三颗战斗之星服役勋章、良好行为勋章和战斗步兵徽章。

"二战"后，他退役了，并于1959年成为美国公民。

2006年，雷奥去世。

第三部分　战争篇
Part Three　The Wars

## Gain Thyn Lui

Gain Thyn Lui was also known as Sonny Leo. His grandfather and father were both Chinese railway laborers. Born in Taishan, Guangdong Province in 1925, he moved with his parents to San Francisco 13 and later moved to Rock Springs, Wyoming.

On September 2, 1885, 28 Chinese miners were killed in Rock Springs Mining Town. Twenty-eight Chinese houses were burned, most whom were family relatives of Leo.

After finishing seventh grade at Rock Springs, Leo worked in a cafe, cooked Chinese food during the day and continued to attend private school at night.

In 1944, he was drafted into the Army and served at Fort Douglas, Utah. Assigned to the 20th Armoured Infantry Battalion, he participated in battles and campaigns in the Ardennes, Rhineland and Central Europe.

He was awarded the Silver Star, Victory Medal, Eurasian-African-Middle East Three Battle Star Service Medal, Good Conduct Medal and Combat Infantry Badge for his gallantry.

After World War Ⅱ, he left the Army, and became a US citizen in 1959.

Leo passed way in 2006.

（译文 / 赵汉黎　责编 / 胡辉）

# 第十五章　亚洲战场
## Chapter 15　Asian Battlefield

◎《在诺克斯堡训练》
*Training at Fort Knox*

林昀晖 画
by Kenny Lin

**在诺克斯堡训练**

"二战"期间,很多华裔美国士兵来到美国肯塔基州的诺克斯堡陆军基地,接受训练。培训机构有美国陆军征兵司令部、美国预备役军队训练团、美国陆军装甲学校和其他机构。

图为在诺克斯堡训练的华裔美国士兵。

**Training at Fort Knox**

During World War Ⅱ, most Chinese American soldiers came to Fort Knox, the US Army base in Kentucky, for training. There were US Army Recruiting Command, US Army Reserve Officers Training Corps, US Army Armored School and other institutions.

The image shows Chinese American soldier training at Fort Knox.

第三部分　战争篇
Part Three　The Wars

◉ 《招募海报》　　　　　　　　　　　张天阳　画
　　*Flying Cadets Recruitment*　　　by Andrew Zhang

## 招募海报

1940 年美国空军招募航空学员的海报。

## Flying Cadets Recruitment

A flying cadets recruitment poster from the United States Army Air Corps in 1940.

235

⊙《冲绳岛航空母舰战斗群》
*Okinawa Aircraft Carrier Strike Group*

张天阳　画
by Andrew Zhang

### 戈顿·派伊亚·钟云

戈顿·派伊亚·钟云的祖父来自广东韶山，年轻时他跟随美国商船移民到夏威夷，开了一家糖厂。他的父亲是小威廉·钟云，是中英混血儿——华英裔夏威夷人，是当地有钱有势的望族，他的母亲阿格尼斯·普纳纳，是夏威夷人。

钟云1910年在夏威夷檀香山出生，后就读于马里兰州海军预备学校并于1934年毕业，是该学院第一位华裔美国人。该学院的学生都有准尉军衔，毕业后，晋升为少校后的他们还需至少服役5年。学生时代的钟云是一个能跑、能踢、能传球的中卫和射门员，1933年成为海军学校的头号橄榄球明星，1934年，他带领海军代表队击败陆军橄榄球队，终结了海军11年连败的纪录。

1945年4月14日，"西格斯比"号被编入一支航母编队参加攻占日本冲绳岛的战役，行军途中，"西格斯比"号突然遭到"神风特攻队"的劫击。其中一架敌机在突破战舰防空火力网后直接撞向"西格斯比"号，舰上23名水兵当场死亡。

此时，年仅35岁的钟云并没有慌乱，他一面命令高炮部队还击日本战机，一面指挥士兵抢修战舰。经过数小时激战，钟云指挥击落了共20架日军战机，击退了"神风特攻队"，并驾驶几乎完全瘫痪的战舰安全返航。由于此役战功卓著，钟云随后获颁美国海军十字及银星勋章，并晋升为少将。

戈顿·派伊亚·钟云是美国海军首位华裔军官。

他从海军退役后返回老家夏威夷定居，被任命为夏威夷州农业厅厅长，于1979年5月去世。

第三部分　战争篇
Part Three　The Wars

## Gordon Pai'ea Chung-Hoon

Gordon Pai'ea Chung-Hoon's grandfather was from Guandong, Zhongshan, who immigrated to Hawaii with an American merchant ship when he was young. He started a sugar factory. His father, William Chung-Hoon Jr., a Chinese-English-Hawaiian, was a county treasurer and his mother Agnes Punana, a Hawaiian.

He was born in Honolulu, Hawaii in 1910. Chung-Hoon attended the United State Naval Academy and graduated in May 1934 in Maryland. He became the first Asian American graduate from the academy. In the Academy, all students have the rank of warrant officer. After graduation, they were promoted to second lieutenant, then they had to serve at least five years. While a student he gained national prominence as the football team's halfback and punter, and in 1934 starred on the team that broke an 11-year winless streak against the Army team. Chung-Hoon was featured as one of football stars of 1933.

On the evening of the April 14, 1945, Chung-Hoon was commanding the USS Sigsbee, a Fletcher Class destroyer. He was part of the large naval fleet involved in the Battle for Okinawa. The USS Sigsbee came under attack from Japanese Kamikaze aircraft, when struck by an enemy plane, all power was lost and 23 of the crews died.

While Chung-Hoon directed damage control efforts to keep the USS Sigsbee afloat, at the same time he was coolly directing his crew's anti-aircraft fire against the Japanese planes. They fought so hard and with such accuracy that they were accredited with shooting down 20 Kamikaze planes. Later, Chung-Hoon supervised damage control procedures (to return his ships) to port under its own restored power. For his actions in this battle at Okinawa, Chung-Hoon received the Navy Cross and the Silver Star for conspicuous gallantry and extraordinary heroism at the age of 35.

Gordon Pai'ea Chung-Hoon was the first Chinese American flag officer of the United States Navy.

After retiring from the military, Chung-Hoon became the director of the Hawaii Department of Agriculture. He passed away in July 1979.

◉ 《威尔伯·卡尔·斯》  张天阳　画
　 *Wilbur Carl Sze*  by Andrew Zhang

## 威尔伯·卡尔·斯

威尔伯·卡尔·斯是第一位在海军陆战队服役的华裔美国军官，珍珠港事件发生时，他还是一名高中生。1944年，他18岁，在大学学习采矿工程。他个子虽小，但很强壮。毕业后被分配到圣地亚哥海军陆战队新兵仓库。

"二战"结束时，他成为一名中士。

## Wilbur Carl Sze

Wilbur Carl Sze was the first Chinese American officer commissioned in the Marine Corps.

He was a high school student when Pearl Harbor happened. In 1944, when he was 18 and studied mining engineering in college. Although he was short and quite strong. He was assigned to the San Diego Marine Corps Recruit Depot.

Upon the end of World War II, he was a sergeant.

第三部分　战争篇
Part Three　The Wars

◎《爱德华·殷》　　　钱书涵　画
　　Edward Yin Ong　　by Justin Qian

龙可为　画
by Claire Fillon

**爱德华·殷**

　　爱德华·殷于1942年加入美国陆军航空兵，之后成为一名飞行员。1943年，他被派往太平洋战区，加入了菲律宾的第375航空服务中队第55运输部队。他执行了多次任务并获得6枚奖牌。1945年3月26日，他在一次执行任务中不幸离世。

**Edward Yin Ong**

　　Edward Yin Ong joined the US Army Air Forces in 1942 and became a pilot after training. In 1943, he was sent to the Pacific Theater and joined the 375th Air Services Squadron's 55th Transportation Unit in the Philippines. He performed several missions and won 6 medals. Unfortunately, he died during a mission on March 26, 1945.

◉《托马斯·唐》
*Thomas Tang*

潘洁筱　画
by Jieling Pan

## 托马斯·唐

1922年，托马斯·唐出生于菲尼克斯，1942年，他通过预备役军官训练营参军，后成为美国陆军中尉。

入伍期间，被驻派到中国帮助改进中缅边境、云南、广西等地的军事装备，同时他还要从日本军队手中收回相关武器。1952年，唐从军队离职，经历了一段短暂的私人训练。之后他担任亚利桑那州马里科帕县的副县检察官。1977年，吉米·卡特总统任命唐为美国第九巡回法院巡回法官。因他卓越的贡献，，他加入了亚利桑那州退伍军人名人堂协会。

## Thomas Tang

Thomas Tang was born in Phoenix in 1922. He joined the military through ROTC in 1942 and became a First Lieutenant in the United States Army. He was sent to China to help China improve military equipment in the China-Myanmar border, Yunnan, Guangxi and other places. His other responsibility was to recover relevant facilities from the Japanese army. In 1952, Tang resigned from the Army and after a brief stint of private practice. He served as Deputy County Attorney of Maricopa County, Arizona. In 1977, President Jimmy Carter appointed Tang as a United States Circuit Judge for the Ninth Circuit. To honor his outstanding contribution, he entered the Arizona veteran hall of fame society.

第三部分　战争篇
Part Three　The Wars

◉《詹姆斯·余》
*James Sing*

龙可为　画
by Claire Fillon

## 詹姆斯·余

詹姆斯·余于1942年6月加入美国陆军航空兵。他首先接受了得克萨斯州北美航空学校B-52轰炸机的技术培训。4个月之后，他和机组人员前往加利福尼亚州进行飞行训练。1943年，他的部队被派往南太平洋。1944年11月，在菲律宾的莱特岛，当时日本人的"神风突击队"驾驶零式战斗机攻击了他的部队，他英勇牺牲。

## James Sing

James Sing joined United States Army Aviation in June 1942. He first received technical training for the B-52 bomber at the North American Aviation School in Texas. Four months later, he and the flight crew went to California for training. In 1943, his unit was sent to the South Pacific. In November 1944, on Leyte Island in the Philippines, when the Japanese "Kamikaze Commando" drove the Zeros to attack his unit, he sacrificed his young life.

●《余毓铨》
*Jack N. Yee*

高大牛　画
by Daniel Gao

**余敏铨**

余敏铨于 1942 年 2 月加入美国陆军。经过培训，他成为一名食品物流员中士。1944 年 7 月，他和 400 名华裔美国士兵被派往密苏里州的克劳德营，接受信号通信培训。之后作为通信员被派往印度和中国，然而，当他在印度等待命令时，"二战"结束了。"二战"期间，他获得了 3 枚奖牌，并于战后退役。

**Jack N. Yee**

Jack N. Yee joined the US Army in February 1942. After training, he became a food logistics sergeant. In July 1944, 400 Chinese American soldiers including himself were sent to Camp Crowder, Missouri, to receive signal communications training. Then they were sent to India and China as correspondents. While he waited for orders in India, World War II ended. During World War II, he won 3 medals and retired from the military after the war.

第三部分 战争篇
Part Three  The Wars

◉《董武》
*Dong Woo*

叶子捷　画
by Jenny Ye

**董武**

　　董武于 1943 年参军，担任陆军航空和机械工程师。同年被派往澳大利亚，随后又被派往菲律宾。他协助本国军队击落了日本零式战斗机，并获得了铜星勋章。

**Dong Woo**

　　Dong Woo joined the army in 1943 as an Army Aviation and Mechanical Engineer. He was dispatched to Australia in the same year and then to the Philippines. He assisted the troops in shooting down the Japanese Zero and won the Bronze Star Medal.

◉《董明浩》
*Dong M. Hom*

邵奕霏　画
by Sophia Shao

**董明浩**

董明浩于1944年2月加入美国海军并在新兵训练营训练了八周,之后在爱达荷州服役于导航信号部队。接着,他去了太平洋战场,参加了中途岛战役和硫磺岛战役。他的主要职责是为作战舰队提供燃料。

**Dong M. Hom**

Dong M. Hom joined the US Navy in February 1944 and trained for eight weeks at boot camp in Idaho as a Navigation Signal Corps. Then he went to the Pacific battlefield, where he participated in the Battles of Midway and Iwo Jima. His main responsibility was to supply fuel to the battle fleet.

第三部分　战争篇
Part Three　The Wars

◉《乔·权》
*Joe Quan*

叶子捷　画
by Jenny Ye

## 乔·权

乔·权是一名上士。"二战"期间，他作为第一骑兵团第8军骑兵队骑兵驻扎日本。

## Joe Quan

Joe Quan is a staff sergeant. During World War Ⅱ. He was stationed in Japan as the 8th Cavalry Regiment of the 1st Cavalry Division.

◉《冯坤》
*Kun Fung*

贾诗涵　画
by Cara Jia

## 冯坤

冯坤是一名上士。"二战"期间，他驻扎在日本神户。

## Kun Fung

Kun Fung is a staff sergeant. During World War Ⅱ, he was stationed in Kobe, Japan.

245

◉《吉米·唐》
*Jimmy C. Tang*

叶子思　画
by Alice Ye

## 吉米·唐

　　吉米·唐在"二战"期间，被派往日本大阪的第 65 战斗工兵营中工作。

## Jimmy C. Tang

During World War Ⅱ, Jimmy C. Tang was posted to Osaka, Japan as the 65th Combat Engineering Battalion.

第三部分　战争篇
Part Three　The Wars

◎《本杰明·陈》
*Benjamin Chan*

茉莉　画
by Moli

## 本杰明·陈

1923年，本杰明·陈出生于加利福尼亚州萨克拉门托，高中毕业后在加利福尼亚州的信号部队学校完成了一系列课程。"二战"期间，他曾在美国陆军队担任中士，然后在马瑟空军基地担任电子安装工。他又在两所技术学院接受继续教育，获得了电子安装学位和文学辅修学位。战后，他在萨克拉门托陆军仓库担任电子检查员，工作了41年。

## Benjamin Chan

Born in Sacramento, California, in 1923, Benjamin Chan completed a series of courses at the Signal Corps School in California after high school. During World War II, he served as a sergeant in the US Army, then as an electronics installer at Mather Air Force Base. He continued his education at two technical colleges, earning a degree in electronics installation and a minor in Literature. After the war, he worked for 41 years at the Sacramento Army Depot as an electronics inspector.

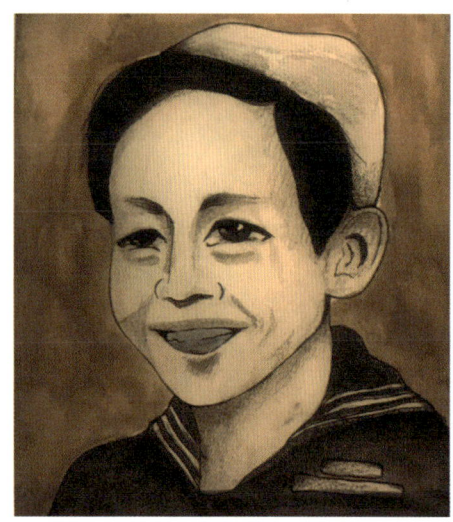

◉《乔治·庞》
*George Pong*

韩赫颐　画
by Helen Han

## 乔治·庞

乔治·庞在俄亥俄州洛兰出生并长大，是勤劳的中国移民父母所生的8个孩子之一。"二战"期间乔治兄弟四人均在军队服役，分别是海军2人，陆军2人，而他的服役期为1942年12月29日到1946年3月15日。服役期间，他获得了海军品行优秀奖章、"二战"胜利勋章、美国战役勋章、带有1颗银星和1颗铜星的亚太战役勋章、海军部队表彰丝带、战斗行动地带、1颗铜星的菲律宾解放勋章和菲律宾总统表彰丝带。1944年10月24日，乔治·庞在美国海军驱逐舰阿尔伯特·W.格兰特DD649服役，期间在菲律宾苏里高海峡战役战斗中受伤，格兰特号船在美国和日本的交火中受到了来自两方的攻击，分别是7枚日本4.7英寸炮弹和11枚美国6英寸穿甲弹。38人死亡，104人受伤。

乔治·庞就读于加利福尼亚州格伦代尔的加州航空技术学院，并作为世纪工程师公司的航空航天设计工程师，开始了漫长的职业生涯。闲暇时，他与终身女友贝蒂·布雷德洛夫一起环游世界。乔治·庞于2016年去世，享年91岁。

第三部分　战争篇
Part Three　The Wars

## George Pong

George Pong was born and raised in Lorain, Ohio, one of 8 children born to hard-working immigrant Chinese parents whose 4 sons served concurrently in the military during World War Ⅱ, 2 in the Navy and 2 in the Army. George served our country Dec 29, 1942—March 15, 1946. While in service, he received the Navy Good Conduct Medal, WWII Victory Medal, American Campaign Medal, Asiatic Pacific Campaign Medal with 1 Silver Star and 1 Bronze Star, Navy Unit Commendation Ribbon, Combat Action Ribbon, Philippine Liberation Medal with 1 Bronze Star, and the Philippine Presidential Unit Citation Ribbon. He sustained wounds in battle while serving on the destroyer USS Albert W. Grant DD649. On October 24, 1944 in the Battle of Surigao Straits, Philippine Islands, the Grant was caught between US and Japanese crossfire receiving hits from both Japanese and American fleets–seven Japanese 4.7-inch projectiles and eleven American 6-inch armor-piercing shells. 38 men were killed and 104 wounded.

George Pong attended Cal-Aero Technical Institute in Glendale, CA and began a long career as an aerospace design engineer for Century Engineers. In leisure, he traveled the world with his lifelong girlfriend, Betty Breedlove. George Pong passed at the age of 91 in 2016.

◎《江井》
*Jing "Thomas" Quock*

钱书涵　画
by Justin Qian

## 江井

江井 1917 年出生于中国，14 岁时来到旧金山。在天使岛待了一个月后，他和叔叔一起在唐人街待了一段时间并在那里学会了理发。之后，他毕业于加利福尼亚州伯克利的阿姆斯特朗学院，并取得商业学位。

"二战"爆发后，他加入了海军，并在奥德堡经过培训成为一名厨房服务员。后来被分配到科约特角的一个单位。在"二战"期间，他在唐人街 YMCA 认识了内莉·汤姆，后来与她结婚。江井和内莉后来在旧金山唐人街开了一家商店，并抚养了三个儿子。江井一直在旧金山工作，直到退休，并住在旧金山，直到 2015 年去世。江井的生活以辛勤工作、周游世界、通过捐赠对家乡村庄的持续支持以及与孙子相处为主。直到去世前，他都还在跟孙子们分享他的"二战"故事。

第三部分　战争篇
Part Three　The Wars

**Jing "Thomas" Quock**

　　Jing "Thomas" Quock was born in 1917 in China and came to San Francisco when he was 14. After spending a month on Angel Island, he spent time with his uncle in Chinatown where he went to school and learned to be a barber. He later graduated from Armstrong College in Berkeley, California with a degree in business.

　　Upon the start of World War II, he joined the Navy, where he was trained as a mess attendant at Fort Ord and was later assigned to a unit at Coyote Point. During World War II, he met Nellie Tom, whom he later married, at the Chinatown YMCA. Thomas and Nellie later opened a store in San Francisco Chinatown and raised three sons.

　　Thomas continued to work in San Francisco until his retirement and would continue to live in San Francisco until his passing in 2015. Thomas' life was defined by hard work, traveling the world, continuous support to his home village in China through donations, and spending time with his grandchildren. In the years before his passing, he could share his story of World War II with his grandchildren.

◎《爱德华·江》
*Edward Kong*

林之雅　画
by Candice Lin

**爱德华·江**

爱德华·江在亚利桑那州凤凰城和旧金山长大。"二战"爆发后，他应征入伍。他曾在第14装甲师和第45步兵师服役。虽然他是步兵，但被分配到航空部队服役。他获得了铜星勋章。战后，他以美国海军预备役人员的身份签约，在海军航空兵处继续工作。

**Edward Kong**

Edward Kong grew up in Phoenix and San Francisco, Arizona. When World War II broke out, he joined the army. He served in the 14th Armored Division and the 45th Infantry Division. Although he was an infantryman, he was assigned to serve in the aviation unit. He was awarded the Bronze Star. After the war, he signed on as a US Navy reservist and continued to serve in the Naval Air Force.

第三部分　战争篇
Part Three　The Wars

◉《托尼·唐·莫伊》
*Tony Tun Moy*

穆烊昕　画
by Emily Mu

## 托尼·唐·莫伊

托尼·唐·莫伊在"二战"期间加入美国海军。他在太平洋战区担任炮手，在"匹兹堡号"航空母舰轰炸冲绳岛和硫磺岛时担任炮手。

## Tony Tun Moy

Tony Tun Moy joined the US Navy during World War II. He served as a gunner in the Pacific Theater and participated in the USS Pittsburgh attacking Okinawa and Iwo Jima.

◎《劳伦·罗》
*Loren Low*

林之雅　画
by Candice Lin

## 劳伦·罗

　　劳伦·罗是第三代华裔美国人，1917年出生于俄勒冈州塞勒姆。他的爷爷是铁路华工，奶奶是旧金山唐人街的一名获救童奴。罗于1941年入伍，被分配到位于檀香山的第7陆军航空队第804工程航空营，跟随部队在整个南太平洋建造机场。1944年6月15日，美军占领南太平洋塞班岛。1944年10月7日第7期《空军杂志》上的文章介绍他"用推土机踏板战胜敌军"的英勇行为。

## Loren Low

　　Loren Low is a third-generation Chinese American born in Salem, Oregon, in 1917. His grandfather was a Chinese railway worker, and his grandmother was a rescued child slave in San Francisco's Chinatown. Low enlisted in 1941 and was assigned to the 804th Engineering Aviation Battalion, 7th Army Air Forces, in Honolulu, where he followed the unit to build airfields throughout the South Pacific. On June 15, 1944, the US military occupied Saipan in the South Pacific. He was in *Air Force Magazine,* Issue 7, October 7, 1944. The article described his heroic action during the war as follows, "Using bulldozer pedals to defeat the enemy."

第三部分　战争篇
Part Three　The Wars

◎《钱永祥》
*Neil Y.H Chin*

叶子捷　画
by Jenny Ye

## 钱永祥

　　钱永祥1918年生于台山，1923年定居波士顿。"二战"期间，他加入美国海军，退伍后，在波士顿唐人街美国军团邮报328担任创始成员。他是一位公民领袖和社区活动家。他在马萨诸塞州联邦保险委员会担任执行秘书，直至1985年退休。他也是中国租客协会的领导者，一生都是经济适用房的倡导者。

## Neil Y.H Chin

　　Mr. Chin was born in Taishan in 1918 and settled in Boston in 1923. Served in the US Navy during World War Ⅱ. After being discharged from the U.S Navy, the veteran was a founding member and past commander of Boston Chinatown's American Legion Post 328. Mr. Chin was a civic leader and community activist. Mr. Chin worked for the Commonwealth of Massachusetts Group Insurance Commission, where he rose to the position of Executive Secretary until his retirement in 1985. He was a leader in the creation of the Chinese Tenants Association and had been an advocate for affordable housing throughout his life.

◉《陈文宽》
*Moon Fun Chin*

刘阅辰　画
by Scarlett Liu

## 陈文宽

陈文宽随父亲从西雅图搬到巴尔的摩。高中毕业后就读柯蒂斯赖特飞行学校，并获得商业飞行员执照。"二战"期间，陈文宽积极参加频繁的军事救援任务，挽救了许多美军人员的生命。其中就有率领美国空军中队轰炸东京的詹姆斯·杜立德中校，他将其从昆明运送到缅甸北部城市密支那。他还用他的飞机运送许多美国海军人员往返于美国海军设有气象站的戈壁沙漠。

## Moon Fun Chin

Moon's father, took the young Moon from Seattle to Baltimore where he later completed his high school education. He decided to enroll in Curtiss Wright Flying School and graduated with a Commercial Pilot License. During World War II, even though Moon was only a civilian aviation pilot, he volunteered actively in frequent military rescue missions and secured many American soldiers' lives. Among those military personnel, Lt Col James Dolittle who led the USAF squadron in the bombed Tokyo. He transported him from Kunming to Myitkyina, a city in northern Burma. Moon also carried in his aircraft many American navy personnel to and fro the gobi desert where the American Navy had a weather station.

第三部分　战争篇
Part Three　The Wars

◉《容兆珍》
*John C. Young*

祝云姝　画
by Maggie Zhu

## 容兆珍

　　容兆珍1912年出生于美国，高中毕业后被斯坦福大学录取并于1935年获得学士学位。1937年，他获得了该校的工程硕士学位，毕业后成为一名工程师。之后，他作为预备役少尉接受了军事训练。1942年初，容兆珍加入了美国陆军。他曾在中缅印服役作为中美军队之间的联络官，支持中国抵抗日本的入侵。

　　战后，容兆珍回到旧金山经营自己的制造业，并在中国商会任职。

## John C. Young

　　Born in the United States in 1912, Young was admitted to Stanford University after graduating from high school and received a bachelor's degree from Stanford University in 1935. He received a master's degree in engineering from the school in 1937 and became an engineer after graduation. He underwent military training as a reserve second lieutenant officer during his college years. In early 1942, he joined the US Army. Young served in the China Burma India Theater as a liaison officer between Chinese and American Troops to support China's resistance to Japan.

　　Young returned to San Francisco to run his own manufacturing business and to serve on the Chinese Chamber of Commerce.

100 Years of Chinese Immigration in the United States and Canada

◎《凯旋》
*Triumphal Return*

祝云姝　画
by Maggie Zhu

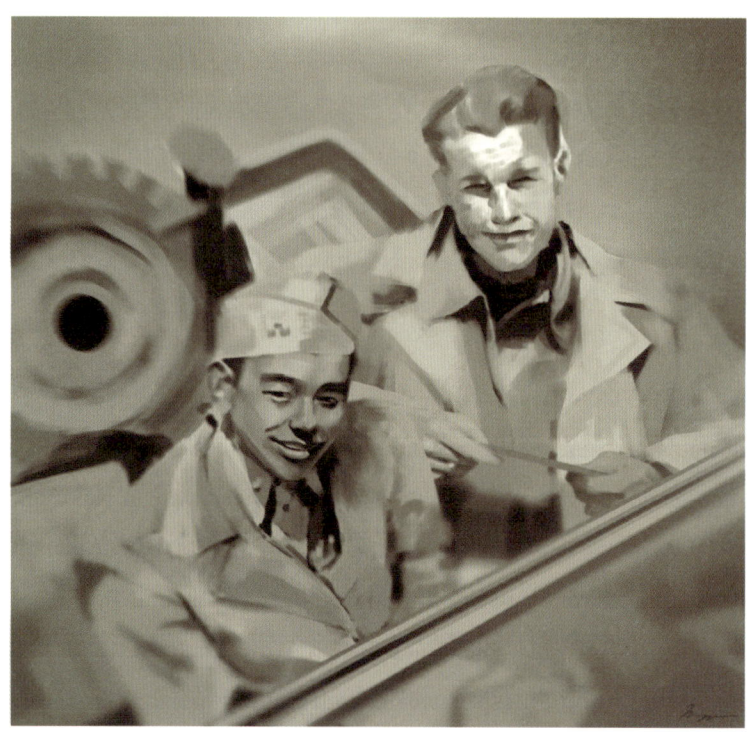

祝云姝　画
by Maggie Zhu

第三部分　战争篇
Part Three　The Wars

### 战后华裔族群壮大

图为胜利后从战场上归来的华裔士兵。

因为华人对美国的巨大贡献，加上中美两国在"二战"中的盟友关系，《排华法案》终于在实施61年后被废除，在美华人终于得到了公民身份。大批华人男青年回到中国相亲、结婚，把新娘带回美国。

美国华人族群在战后终于得到新生和壮大。

### The Chinese American Community Grew After WW II

The image shows Chinese American soldiers returning from the battlefield after the victory.

Because of the significant great contributions of the Chinese Americans to the United States and the alliance between China and the United States in World War II, the "Chinese Exclusion Act" was finally repealed after 61 years. Chinese in the United States finally obtained citizenship. A large number of young Chinese Americans returned to China for blind dates, marriages and brought their brides back to the United States.

The Chinese community in the United States finally got a new life and expanded after World War II.

（译文/钱书潭 责编/赵京燕）

# 第十六章　华裔飞虎队

## Chapter 16　Chinese Flying Tigers

◉《飞虎队》  张天阳 画
*Flying Tigers*  by Andrew Zhang

# 第三部分　战争篇
Part Three　The Wars

## 飞虎队

"飞虎队"严格来讲仅指1941年8月到1942年7月来华助战的美国第一志愿队。后来，随着战事推进和战略需要，美国第一志愿队进行过多次改编，"飞虎队"作为一个非官方的民间代称，泛泛地把美国陆军第10航空队的美国驻华空军特遣队、美国陆军第14航空队、中美空军混合联队、驼峰空运队以及中国航空公司等均含盖在内。

## Fly Tigers

Strictly speaking, the "Flying Tigers" only refers to the First American Volunteer Team that came to China to help from August 1941 to July 1942. Later, with the advancement of the war and the changing strategic needs, the First Volunteer Team of the United States undergone many adaptations. "Flying Tigers", formally an unofficial nickname, became a general name, referring to the US Air Force in China of the US Army 10th Air Force, the US Army 14th Air Force, the Sino-US Air Force Mixed Wing, the Hump Airlift and China Airlines.

◉ 《华裔飞虎队》　　　　　　　　　　　　　　　　　　　　　邹安琪　画
　　Chinese Flying Tigers　　　　　　　　　　　　　　　　　　by Angela Zou

## 华裔飞虎队

"二战"时期，美军中有两支部队全部由华裔组成，即407航空服务中队和987信号连，这两支部队隶属第14航空队，即泛称的飞虎队，其作战地区在中缅印战区。

"二战"中，部分华裔被调往中缅印战区的第14空勤大队（14$^{th}$ Air Service Group），以及中美混合团，剩下约70%的华裔军人分别在第3、第4、第6、第32和第77步兵师服役。

图为第14航空服务中队行进队列，大都是华裔面孔。

第三部分 战争篇
Part Three  The Wars

**Chinese Flying Tigers**

During World War II, two units in the US military were composed entirely of Chinese individuals, namely the 407th Air Service Squadron and the 987th Signal Company. They belonged to the 14th Air Force. They are commonly known as the Flying Tigers. Their combat area was in the China-Burma-India theater.

During World War II, some Chinese were transferred to the 14th Air Service Group of the 14th Air Service Group in the China-Myanmar-India Theater and the Sino-American Mixed Regiment. The remaining 70% of the Chinese soldiers were in the 3rd, 4th, 6th, 32nd and 77th Infantry Divisions service.

The image shows the marching queue of the 14th Air Service Squadron. Most of the pilots were Chinese.

◉《987 特别通信连》 林昀晖 画
The 987th Special Signal Company by Kenny Lin

## 987 特别通信连

987特别通信连是一支秘密部队，负责包括中国地面部队之间、中国和美国部队之间、野战或者后勤部队与盟军司令部之间，以及中国与渗透到日军占领区和国家的侦察特工人员等所有军用无线电通信联系。他们还要破译日军的电报，培训中国技术人员。这支特殊的部队由8名军官和176名士兵组成，除了连长等少数军官是美国人外，其余全部是在美国招募的华人。要求每一个士兵必须同时懂中英文，他们除了学习使用各种武器外，还要学习使用便携式和大型电台。

图为1943年，987特别通信连在密苏里州进行野外训练。

第三部分　战争篇
Part Three　The Wars

## The 987th Special Signal Company

The 987th Special Signal Company was a covert force responsible for the wireless communication among the Chinese ground forces, and between Chinese and US forces. It also worked between the field or the logistical forces and the Allied Commands, and worked for the Chinese reconnaissance agents that had infiltrated Japanese-occupied areas and for the spies and investigators. It also had to decipher Japanese telegrams and train Chinese technicians. This special unit consists of 8 officers and 176 soldiers. Except for a few officers, such as the company commander, who were Americans, the rest were all Chinese recruited in the United States. It was required that every soldier understand both Chinese and English. In addition to learning to use various weapons, the Chinese must also learn how to use portable or large radio station.

The picture shows the 987th Special Signal Company conducting field training in Missouri in 1943.

100 Years of Chinese Immigration in the United States and Canada

◉《甄崇运》　　　　　　　　　　　　　　　　　　　　　　　肖禹睿　画
　Chongyun Zhen　　　　　　　　　　　　　　　　　　　　　by James Xiao

第三部分　战争篇

Part Three　The Wars

**甄崇运**

  甄崇运 1922 年出生于广东台山四九镇，1932 年来美国。1942 年，他 20 岁时应征入伍，成为美国第 14 航空队 987 特别通信连一名通信兵。被派到密苏里军事基地受训 18 个月后，经过 60 天航行，他和战友们抵达昆明，穿上绣着"血符"的军装参加战斗。

**Chongyun Zhen**

  Born in Sijiu Town, Taishan, Guangdong, in 1922, Chongyun Zhen came to the United States in 1932. In 1942, he was drafted into the army at 20 and became a signal soldier of the 987th Special Signal Company of the 14th Air Force. He was sent to the Missouri military base to train for 18 months. After 60 days voyage, he and his comrades arrived in Kunming. Putting on military uniforms embroidered with "blood talismans", they began to participat in the battle.

◉《英雄电报员》
*Hero Telegraph Operator*

肖禹睿 画
by James Xiao

## 英雄电报员

图为甄崇运与队友在执行任务。他的连队的主要任务是负责所有军用无线电通信联系，破译敌军电报。为了保证电台安全，每部电台都安装了自行毁灭装置，只要发现日军进入电台方圆 15 英里的范围，他们就会启动电台的自爆装置。

因战绩突出，甄崇运荣获"二战"铜星英勇成就勋章。

战后甄崇运根据联邦军人安置法，进入高校读书。后来他被福特汽车公司录用，成为一名模具专家。

第三部分　战争篇
Part Three　The Wars

**Hero Telegraph Operator**

This image shows Chongyun Zhen and his teammates performing a mission. The task of his company was to oversee all military radio communications and to decipher enemy telegrams. To ensure the safety of the radio, each radio station was equipped with self-destruction devices, which would be activated whenever the Japanese army was found coming lose 15-mile the radio station.

Due to his outstanding achievements, Chongyun Zhen was awarded the Bronze Star Medal for Heroic Achievement in World War II.

After the war, under the federal military resettlement law, Chongyun Zhen in received college education. He was later hired by the Ford Motor Company as a tooling specialist.

◎《陈瑞钿——空战英雄》　　　　　　　　　　　吴雨芮　画
　*Arthur Chin—Air Combat Hero*　　　　　　　　by Sherry Wu

**陈瑞钿——空战英雄**

　　1913年秋,铁路华工后代陈瑞钿出生于美国波特兰市。父亲来自广东台山,母亲则是来自秘鲁的德裔白人。他早年就有志于飞行事业,所以在高中时期就靠打工挣钱学习飞行。在日本入侵中国时,他已取得美国的飞行执照。

　　1931年"九一八事变"发生后,波特兰市华人团体决定派志愿者回国参加抗日空战,当时陈瑞钿已从当地华人创办的美洲航空学校毕业,他与来自俄勒冈州、华盛顿州、加利弗尼亚州的13位(其中一位是女性)热血青年一起参加了志愿队伍。

　　图为临行前志愿飞行员们合影留念。

第三部分　战争篇
Part Three　The Wars

**Arthur Chin—Air Combat Hero**

In the autumn of 1913, Arthur Chin, a descendant of Chinese railway workers, was born in Portland, United States. His father is from Taishan, Guangdong, and his mother is a German from Peru. He was interested in flying in his early years, so in high school, he learned to fly with the money earned by working. He had obtained a US pilot's license by the time Japan invaded China.

After the "September 18" Incident in 1931, the Portland Chinese group decided to send volunteers to China to participate in the anti-Japanese air war. At that time, Arthur Chin had graduated from the American Aviation School, a school founded by the local Chinese. He volunteered to join the 13 young people from Oregon, Washington and California, including one woman.

The volunteer pilots took a group photo before leaving.

◉ 《参加中国抗战》　　　　　　　　　　　　　　祝云姝　画
　 *Participate in the Chinese Anti-Japanese War*　　　by Maggie Zhu

## 参加中国抗战

　　陈瑞钿一行乘船首先抵达上海，但当时的南京政府不信任这批广东籍的华侨，并未同意，于是他们转而加入了陈济棠的广东空军。不久便分配在广东空军第六飞行队，军衔少尉。

## Participate in the Chinese Anti-Japanese War

　　Arthur Chin and his party first arrived in Shanghai by boat, but the Nanjing government at that time did not trust the overseas Chinese from Guangdong. They did not agree to let them fight in war. So they joined Chen Jitang's Guangdong Air Force. Soon, they were assigned to the Sixth Air Force of Guangdong, under the rank of second lieutenant.

第三部分　战争篇
Part Three　The Wars

◉《晋升中尉》
*Promoted to Lieutenant*

韩赫颐　画
by Helen Han

**晋升中尉**

　　1935 年陈瑞钿被派往德国学习战斗机飞行和战术，他在纳粹空军的勒切费德基地进行驱逐战术的系统深造。回国后晋升为中尉。1936 年 7 月，因陈济棠投归南京政府，广东空军随之被中央收编，陈瑞钿则被分配在杭州笕桥中央航校任战斗机飞行教官。同年 10 月任驻广东空军第 3 大队第 17 中队中队长。

**Promoted to Lieutenant**

　　In 1935, Arthur Chin was sent to Germany to study fighter flight and tactics. He conducted advanced systematic studies in deportation tactics at the Lechfeld base of the Luftwaffe. After returning home, he was promoted to lieutenant. In July 1936, due to Jitang Chen's surrender to the Nanjing government, the Guangdong Air Force was subsequently incorporated by the central government, and Arthur Chin was assigned to serve as a fighter flight instructor at the Central Aviation School of Jianqiao, Hangzhou. In October, he served as the squadron commander of the 17th Squadron of the 3rd Brigade of the Guangdong Air Force.

◉ 《三次跳伞逃生》  王小龙 画
  *Three Skydive Escapes*  by Joy Wang

第三部分　战争篇
Part Three　The Wars

## 三次跳伞逃生

1937年8月16日，日军航空队突袭陈瑞钿所在的机场，他和战友们紧急起飞拦截。陈瑞钿追击日军的带队长机，并击破了日机的油箱，日机燃油漏尽后迫降时坠毁。而陈瑞钿的飞机发动机也被其他日机击中，他只得滑翔返航迫降。

1937—1939年，陈瑞钿骁勇善战，其座机曾三度被敌机击落，但都跳伞成功幸运生还。他因击毁5.5架敌机而荣获"王牌飞行员"称号。

## Three Skydive Escapes

On August 16, 1937, the Japanese Air Force raided the airport where Arthur Chin was. He and his comrades scrambled to stop them. Arthur Chin chased the leader place of the Japanese army and destroyed the fuel tank of it. Fuel out, the aircraft crashed before it could make an emergency landing. Arthur Chin's engine was also hit by the Japanese planes, and he had to glide back and make an emergency landing.

From 1937 to 1939, Arthur Chin fought bravely. His aircraft had been shot down by enemy planes three times, but he was lucky to survive by parachuting. He was awarded "Ace Pilot" title for destroying more than five aircrafts.

◉ 《撞机》  张天阳 画
　*Collider*  by Andrew Zhang

**撞机**

1938年7月，陈瑞钿所在中队11架战机参加武汉会战。不久，88架日机与陈瑞钿的中队在空中展开激战。他率先击伤1架日机，而另外3架日机对他进行了轮番攻击，他的战机身中数弹。但他驾驶着战机撞向一架准备俯冲下来开火的日机。结果日机被撞成碎片，陈瑞钿跳伞逃生。

**Collider**

In July 1938, 11 fighter planes in Arthur Chin's squadron participated in the battle of Wuhan. Soon, 88 Japanese aircrafts fought fiercely against Chin's squadron. He was the first to damage a Japanese plane. Meanwhile, three Japanese planes kept attacking him, his fighter plane was damaged several times. He raced his fighter towards a Japanese plane that was about to dive and fire at him. In the end, the Japanese plane was crashed into pieces. Arthur Chin escaped by parachuting.

第三部分　战争篇
Part Three　The Wars

◎《严重烧伤》
*Severe Burns*

祝云姝　画
by Maggie Zhu

**严重烧伤**

1939年12月，陈瑞钿率领3架战机和3架护航轰炸机，与日本海军的13架战机遭遇。陈瑞钿率先击落1架日机，自己也遭日机偷袭，飞机油箱被击中。他驾驶熊熊燃烧的战机，跳伞逃生，但其身上和面容多处被火严重烧伤。

**Severe Burns**

In December 1939, Arthur Chin led three fighters and three escort bombers to encounter 13 Japanese navy fighters. Arthur Chin was the first to shoot down a Japanese plane, but he also got shot. His fuel tank was damaged and he flew the flaming plane until he could parachute out. His body and face were severely injured by fire.

● 《陈瑞钿的连环画》　　　　　　　　　　　　　　　宿佳博　画
　*Comic of a flying hero*　　　　　　　　　　　　　　by Angeli Su

**再返中国战场**

　　在美国治愈烧伤后，陈瑞钿再次返回中国战场，进入美国陆军航空队第14中队，驾驶运输机飞越驼峰航线。直到1945年3月1日退役。

　　"二战"期间，他总计击落8.5架日机，3次跳伞成功逃生。

　　1997年10月，位于美国得克萨斯州的美国空军历史博物馆所属的美国空军战斗英雄馆举行仪式，表彰美国第二次世界大战的第一位空战英雄——陈瑞钿。

　　图为美国媒体在报上刊登的两幅连环画，赞扬陈瑞钿是飞行英雄。

## Back to the Chinese Battlefield

After being treated for burns in the United States, Arthur Chin returned to the Chinese battlefield and entered the 14$^{th}$ Squadron of the United States Army Air Forces, flying a transport plane over the hump route. He retired on March 1, 1945.

During World War II, he shot down 8.5 Japanese planes and successfully parachuted three times.

In October 1997, a ceremony was held at the US Air Force Combat Heroes Pavilion, US Air Force History Museum in Texas, USA, to honor Arthur Chin, the first air combat hero of World War II.

The picture shows a comic strip published by the American newspaper, praising Arthur Chin as a flying hero.

◉《黎荣福》
*Rongfu Li*

叶子思　画
by Alice Ye

## 黎荣福

他15岁时持一张假身份证，带着15美元从广东台山来到美国。19岁时，他应征入伍，先是被分配到伊利诺伊州的一所军校做无线电报务员，后成为美国第14航空队的一名航空无线电报务员，他曾38次飞越驼峰，执行运输任务。那时滇缅公路还未修好，前线需要武器弹药以及军需物资，都得用骡子驮运，有段时间，飞机往昆明运送骡子。

在执行驼峰航运任务过程中，许多飞机被击落，黎荣福也受过伤。他最终获得4枚勋章。

## Rongfu Li

15 years old, he came to the United States from Taishan, Guangdong, with a fake identity. At the age of 19, he was drafted into the military. He was first assigned to a military academy in Illinois as a radio operator, and later became an aviation radio operator for the 14th Air Force. He flew over the hump 38 times to perform transport missions. At that time, the Burma Road had not yet been completed. The front line needed weapons, ammunition and military supplies, but they had to be carried by mules. For some time, planes were used to transport mules to Kunming.

When carrying out the hump shipping mission, many planes were shot down, and Rongfu Li was injured. He ended up receiving four medals.

第三部分　战争篇
Part Three　The Wars

◉《战后开餐馆》
*Running a Restaurant After War*

茉莉　画
by Moli

**战后开餐馆**

"二战"结束后，黎荣福从零做起，他在中餐馆刷了几年盘子，然后自己开了一家中餐馆，儿女们都受到了良好教育。

黎荣福从事中餐业 30 余年，直到退休。

**Running a Restaurant After War**

After the World War Ⅱ, Rongfu Li started from scratch. He spent a few years working at a Chinese restaurant, and then opened a Chinese restaurant by himself. His sons and daughters were all well educated.

Rongfu Li worked in the Chinese restaurant industry for more than 30 years until his retirement.

### 哈里·林

他曾在"二战"期间被编入第14航空队407空中服务中队,为中国、印度、缅甸地区的空军提供飞机维护和设备支持。战争结束后,哈里在军用飞机公司中找到了一份工作,很少有人知道他光荣的战地经历。

### Harry Lim

Harry Lim was assigned to the 407th Air Service Squadron of the 14th Air Force during World War II. He provided aircraft maintenance and equipment support to the air forces of China, India and Myanmar. After the war, Harry took a job with a military aircraft company, and few people know about his glorious field experience.

### 易孔

他出生于中国,来到美国后,"二战"爆发,他应征入伍,成为第14航空队407空中服务中队的一员。战后,他从事建筑和机械工作,还开了一家洗衣店,活到近百岁。

### Kwong Y. Yee

Kwong Y. Yee was born in China and came to the United States when World War II broke out. He enlisted in the army and became a member of the 407th Air Service Squadron of the 14th Air Force. After the war, he worked in construction and mechanics, and also opened a laundromat. He lived to be nearly a hundred years old.

第三部分　战争篇
Part Three　The Wars

◉《朱安琪》
*Anqi Zhu*

刘阅辰　画

by Scarlett Liu

**朱安琪**

1923年出生于加州奥克兰，祖籍广东台山，是美国第二代华侨。他14岁便随父亲进入美洲中华航空学校学飞行。他从航校毕业才一周，适逢日军侵华，大家筹钱为他买了去中国的船票和机票，在父亲的安排下，1939年7月1日，年仅17岁的朱安琪就独自经夏威夷登上"柯立芝总统号"远洋轮船前往中国昆明。与他同届的28名飞行员及17名机械师乘船经由太平洋，辗转香港地区、越南到中国加入空军抗战。1939—1945年，他在中国西北战区和中南战区驾驶P-40战机，先后参加过数十场对日作战，3次往返飞越驼峰航线接P-40和P-51战斗机。后来他被授予上尉。

**Anqi Zhu**

Born in Oakland, California in 1923, his ancestral home is Taishan, Guangdong, and he is the second generation of overseas Chinese in the United States. At 14, he came with his father to the "Civil Aviation Flight University of China" to learn to fly. It was only a week after he graduated from aviation school when the Japanese army invaded China. The Chinese friends and relatives raised money and buy the ferry and air ticket for him to go to China. Under the father's arrangement, on July 1, 1939, Anqi Zhu, who was only 17 years old, boarded the ocean-going ship "President Coolidge" via Hawaii to Kunming, China alone. He and his fellows, including 28 pilots and 17 mechanics, sailed across the Pacific Ocean, traveled to Hong Kong and Vietnam and fimally reached China to join the Anti-Japanese Air Force. From 1939 to 1945, he flew P-40 fighter in China's Northwest and Central South Theaters, participating in dozens of operations against Japan. He also flew over the hump route three times to pick up P-40 and P-51 fighters. He was later awarded captain.

◎《战争中的爱情》  穆烊昕  画
　Love in War  by Emily Mu

第三部分　战争篇
Part Three　The Wars

**战争中的爱情**

朱安琪在飞虎队期间,认识了驻地附近当银行职员的太太,朱安琪跟她学会说中文,一年后求婚成功。

图为朱安琪和蒋有贤伉俪结婚照。

**Love in War**

When Anqi Zhu was in the Flying Tigers, he met his wife who was a bank clerk near the station. Anqi Zhu learned to speak Mandarin from her. One year later, they married.

The image shows the wedding photos of Anqi Zhu and Youxian Jiang.

◉《未能享受退伍军人待遇》　　　　　　　　　　　　　　　穆烊昕　画
　Not Eligible for Veterans Treatment　　　　　　　　　　by Emily Mu

第三部分 战争篇
Part Three　The Wars

## 未能享受退伍军人待遇

朱安琪从 1939 年去中国抗日，到 1948 年提交辞呈，多年冒死征战未获分文退役金，连回美国的路费还得给父亲写信请家人筹集。美国法律规定，朱安琪参加中国空军就丧失了美国国籍。美国参战后，这项规定得以修正，可是重办国籍手续十分烦琐。

朱安琪没有在美军中服役，他和其他华侨青年早在"珍珠港事件"爆发之前，志愿跑到中国去参加空军，不能享受任何美国退伍军人应有的待遇。

战后，他一切从零开始，为生活打拼，上大学全靠半工半读赚取学费。

## Not Eligible for Veterans Treatment

Anqi Zhu went to China to fight against Japan in 1939, and submitted his resignation letter in 1948. He fought for many years without receiving a penny for his retirement. He even had to write to his father to ask his family to raise money for the fee back to the United States. According to American law, Anqi Zhu had lost his American citizenship when he joined the Chinese Air Force. After the United States entered the war, this provision was amended, but the procedures for regaining the citizenship were very complicate.

Anqi Zhu did not serve in the US military. Before the "Pearl Harbor Incident", he and other overseas Chinese youth volunteered to go to China to join the Air Force. That's why they couldn't get the benefits that other veteraus had.

After the war, he started everything from scratch, working hard for a living, and went to college with the tuition that was earned through part-time work.

◉《陈熊文》
*Moon Chen*

张云想　画
by Yunxiang Zhang.

## 陈熊文

他的母亲死于 1918 年的瘟疫，父亲则在 1924 年去世。15 岁的陈熊文在中学毕业后进入密歇根大学学习航空工程，每周末都去华人餐厅打工。大学毕业后，他来到长岛的罗斯福飞行学校，驾驶美国邮政服务的开放式驾驶舱双翼飞机，往来全美各地。

1936 年，拿到商业飞行员证书的陈熊文来到上海，得到中国航空公司的飞行工作。

1939 年，他来到云南垒允的中央飞机制造厂工作，并于 1941 年 7 月参加美国志愿航空队驾驶 P-40 战斗机作战。

"珍珠港事件"发生后，陈熊文加入美国空军，参加了驻华航空特遣队，1943 年，他成为飞虎队"第 14 航空队"的中尉。

他曾 500 多次飞过驼峰航线。战后，陈熊文在波士顿生活，101 岁去世。

第三部分　战争篇
Part Three　The Wars

◉ 《飞过驼峰航线》  
　Flying over the Hump Route

张云想　画  
by Yunxiang Zhang

## Moon Chen

His mother died of the plague in 1918, and his father in 1924. 15-year-old Moon Chen entered the University of Michigan to study aerospace engineering after graduating from middle school and worked in a Chinese restaurant every weekend. After college, he went to Roosevelt Flight School on Long Island to fly the US Postal Service's open-cockpit biplane to and from the country.

In 1936, Moon Chen, who had obtained a commercial pilot certificate, came to Shanghai and got a flight job with China Airlines. In 1939, he came to work at the Central Aircraft Factory in Leiyun, Yunnan. In July 1941, he participated in the "American Volunteer Air Force" to fly P-40 fighter jets!

After the "Pearl Harbor Incident", Moon Chen joined the US Air Force and participated in the "Air Task Force in China". In 1943, he became a lieutenant of the "14th Air Force" of the Flying Tigers.

He has flown the Hump route more than five hundred times. After the war, Moon Chen retired to Boston and died at the age of 101.

◉ 《唐东》
*Don C. Tang*

王小龙　画
by Joy Wang

## 唐东

唐东1943年8月加入美国陆军航空兵，成为一名C-46运输机机组人员，在第13空军部队中执行任务，得过7枚勋章奖牌。1945年7月17日，"二战"胜利之前的1个月，他在执行任务过程中，因天气恶劣，飞机撞山，与其他4位华裔机组人员一起不幸遇难，牺牲时年仅20岁。

## Don C. Tang

Don C. Tang joined the US Army Air Force in August 1943 as a C-46 transport aircraft crew member. He performed missions in the 13th Air Force and won 7 medals. On July 17, 1945, a month before the victory in World War II, his plane crashed into the mountain due to bad weather during a mission. He died together with four other Chinese crew members. He was only 20 years old when he was sacrificed.

第三部分　战争篇
Part Three　The Wars

◉ 《邓桐臻》
*Albert Ong*

马嘉奇　画
by Jake Ma

**邓桐臻**

邓桐臻 1941 年当兵，1942 年前往战斗机械部学校学习。"二战"中他先被派往印度卡拉奇，后被派往中国，成为美国援华第 14 航空队飞虎队的情报参谋，转战昆明、湖南等地。由于他懂中文，便让他来培训中国军人学习军事战斗技术，打击日军。四年半的军旅生涯，让邓桐臻官至上尉，得过 8 枚勋章，包括崇高勋章、宝鼎勋章、抗战纪念勋章等。

**Albert Ong**

Albert Ong joined the army in 1941 and went to study at the School of Combat Machinery in 1942. During World War II, he was sent to Karachi, India, and then to China. He became part of the intelligence staff of the Flying Tigers of the 14th Air Force Aid China and he moved to Kunming, Hunan and other places. Because he knew Chinese language, he trained Chinese soldiers to learn military combat techniques and attack the Japanese army. Four and a half years into his military career, Deng Tongzhen was awarded eight medals, including the Noble Medal, the Baoding Medal and the Chinese War Memorial Medal.

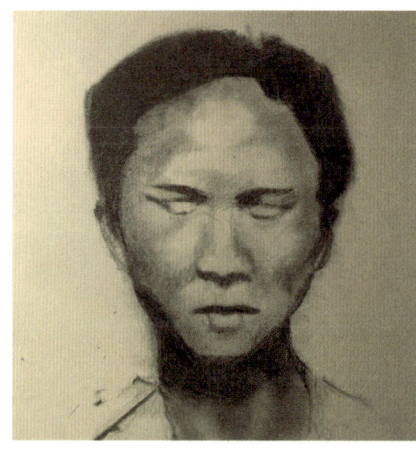

◎《邓作霖》
*Douglas L. Dong*

叶子思　画
by Alice Ye

## 邓作霖

1942年1月，邓作霖加入美国陆军，在加州基地受训两周后便奔赴前线。他进驻美国第14航空队，为前线话务接线员。10个月后，他先后被派往贵州贵阳、湖南衡阳前线，后来到重庆，直到战争结束。

1945年底，他光荣退伍。

## Douglas L. Dong

In January 1942, Douglas L. Dong joined the US Army and went to the front after two weeks of training at a base in California. He was stationed in the US 14th Air Force as a frontline operator. Ten months later, he was sent to the front lines in Guiyang, Guizhou, Hengyang, and Hunan, and later, he was deployed to Chongqing until the end of the war.

At the end of 1945, he was honorably discharged from the army.

第三部分　战争篇
Part Three　The Wars

◎《邓阿里》
*Harry Ong*

高大牛　画
by Daniel Gao

**邓阿里**

邓阿里1942年2月2日入伍，成为美国陆军航空兵，在得克萨斯州接受训练。1944年4月，他被派往昆明，加入第14航空队的驻华空军特遣队。后来他奔赴上海，在那里遇到了他未来的新娘Jean。

他曾获得6枚奖章。

**Harry Ong**

Harry Ong enlisted on February 2, 1942, as a US Army Airman and trained in Texas. In April 1944, he was sent to Kunming to join the 14th Air Force's Task Force in China. Later he went to Shanghai, where he met his future bride, Jean.

He had won 6 medals.

◎《陈贵东》
*Guy Gordon Chin*

刘闵辰　画
by Scarlett Liu

## 陈贵东

1924年，陈贵东生于旧金山。1942—1946年，他在克莱尔·陈纳德指挥的中缅印战区服役，是飞虎队14中队的一名飞机机械师。战后，他回到加州结婚，育有四个子女。2012年去世。

## Guy Gordon Chin

Guy Gordon Chin was born in San Francisco in 1924. From 1942 to 1946, he served in the China-Burma-India Theater under the command of Claire Chennault as an aircraft mechanic in the 14th Squadron of the Flying Tigers. After the war, he returned to California to marry and had four children. He died in 2012.

第三部分　战争篇
Part Three　The Wars

◉《陈泽硕》
W. C. Chin

贾诗涵　画
by Cara Jia

## 陈泽硕

陈泽硕是第三代华人。他的爷爷来自广东，1859 年来到美国修铁路，曾经担任中央太平洋铁路公司的工头劳务承包商。

"二战"期间，陈中尉在中缅印战区的飞虎队第 23 战斗机大队担任通信官。

## W. C. Chin

W. C. Chin, a third generation American-born Chinese. His grandfather was from Guangdong Province. When he immigrated to the United States in 1859, he served as a foreman labor contractor for the Central Pacific Railroad Company.

He was a communications officer during World War II with the 23rd Fighter Group, Flying Tigers in the China-Burma-India Theater.

◉《谭振瀛》　　　张云想　画
Jennings Hom　by Yunxiang Zhang

◉《谭振瀛》　　　穆烨昕　画
Jennings Hom　by Emily Mu

**谭振瀛**

1924年，谭振瀛出生于加州圣地亚哥。他自幼喜欢制作飞机模型，高中毕业后，他在职业学校学习焊接。"二战"爆发时他18岁，他主动参军，被编在美国陆军航空队，在第14航空服务大队第555航空服务中队担任飞机维修技师。他曾在一幅画中描绘了他的吉普车装载着圣地亚哥华裔美籍伙伴，他们穿越驼峰航线，将印度的物资通过缅甸运往中国。

战后，他在圣地亚哥州立大学获得工商管理学士学位，并成为唐人街家族商店 Woo Chee Chong 的经理，他的家族业务扩展到圣地亚哥。

晚年，他患帕金森综合征，《圣地亚哥联合论坛报》20世纪90年代对他的专访中，称他为社区领袖。他于2011年去世，享年87岁。

第三部分　战争篇
Part Three　The Wars

## Jennings Hom

Jennings Hom was born in San Diego, California, in 1924. He had loved making model airplanes since he was a child, and after graduating high school, he studied welding in a vocational school. At the age of 18 when World War II broke out, he volunteered to join the army and was assigned to the US Army Air Corps as an aircraft maintenance technician in the 555th Air Service Squadron, 14th Air Service Group. He was once depicted in a painting that he and his San Diego Chinese-American partners crossed the Hump Route in a jeep to transport the India supplies to China via Burma.

After the war, he earned a bachelor's degree in business administration from San Diego State University and became the manager of Woo Chee Chong, a family store in Chinatown. His family business eventually expanded to San Diego.

Later in life, he had Parkinson's disease. In an exclusive interview with the *San Diego Union-Tribune* in the 1990s, he was called a community leader. He died in 2011 at the age of 87.

100 Years of Chinese Immigration in the United States and Canada

◉ 《易岳汉》
*John H. Yee*

王小龙　画
by Joy Wang

## 易岳汉

易岳汉 1921 年生于云南昭通，两岁时被英国传教士收养。1940 年，他加入美国志愿援华航空队，作为情报翻译参与对日作战。

飞虎队解散后，他于 1944 年赴美学习，并留在美国。他在科罗拉多州的多所大学担任历史教授。2019 年，97 岁的"二战"飞虎队老兵易岳汉去世。

2021 年，时任科罗拉多州州长约翰·希肯卢珀签署法令，确定 7 月 17 日为该州的"易岳汉日"。

## John H. Yee

Born in Zhaotong, Yunnan, in 1921, John H. Yee was adopted by British missionaries at the age of two. In 1940, he joined the American Volunteer Air Force to China and participated in the war against Japan as an intelligence interpreter.

After the Flying Tigers disbanded, he went to the United States to study in 1944 and stayed in the United States. He is a professor of history at various universities in Colorado. In 2019, John H. Yee, a 97-year-old World War II Flying Tiger veteran, died.

In 2021, then Colorado Governor John Hickenlooper signed a decree to determine July 17 as the state's "Yi Yuehan Day".

（译文 / 王小龙　责编 / 许静）

# 第十七章 华裔女军人
## Chapter 17　Chinese Female Soldiers

　　1943年7月1日，美国女子陆军军团（Women's Army Corps，WAC）正式成立，超过2.5万名亚太裔女子报名，只有1830人被录取接受飞行训练。其中有1074人完成培训。之后，美国陆军航空军也开始招收华裔女性，其中的一小部分在后来以平民身份组成了女性航空军飞行员（Women Airforce Service Pilots）。两年时间里，这些飞行员几乎驾驶了所有类型的飞机。她们的主要工作是在基地之间运送飞机，还负责测试新飞机，培训男性飞行员，并将受损的飞机带回基地进行维修。她们在恶劣的天气下航行，夜间在没有照明的跑道上降落。其中38名女性在服役期间身亡。

　　从历史资料中，我们选出了几位美国华裔女军人以及加拿大"二战"女兵进行绘画，并讲述她们曾经为人类的和平做出的杰出贡献。

The U.S. Women's Army Corps was established officially on July 01, 1943. More than 25,000 Asian Pacific American women signed up, but only 1,830 were admitted to flight training. Among them, 1,074 completed the training. Later, the U.S. Army Air Force also began recruiting Chinese women, and a small number later formed the Women Airforce Service Pilots as civilians. For two years, these pilots flew nearly every type of aircraft. Their main task was to transport planes between bases, but they also tested new planes, trained male pilots and brought damaged planes back to the base for repairs. They sailed in bad weather and landed on unlit runways at night. Thirty-eight of the women died while serving.

From the historical data, we selected some Chinese American female soldiers and Canadian female soldiers of World War II to draw to describe their outstanding contributions to the peace of humanity.

第三部分　战争篇
Part Three　The Wars

◉《科学家朱美娇》
*Scientist Maggie Gee*

李涵融　画
by Elaine Li

## "二战"后的科学家

1944年12月，女子勤务航空大队被解散，朱美娇回到加州，在伯克利大学获得物理和数学学位后，在劳伦斯·利弗莫尔国家实验室工作30余年。她的研究领域包括癌症、核武器设计及聚变能源等。2010年她和所有在世的原女子航空大队飞行员一同获得国会金质奖章。

## Scientists After World War II

In December 1944, the Women's Service Aviation Brigade was ordered to disband. Zhu Meijiao returned to California, where she worked for more than 30 years at Lawrence Livermore National Laboratory after earning degrees in physics and mathematics from Berkeley University. Her research interests included cancer, nuclear weapon design, and fusion energy. In 2010 she was awarded the Congressional Gold Medal along with all remaining former Women's Air Force pilots.

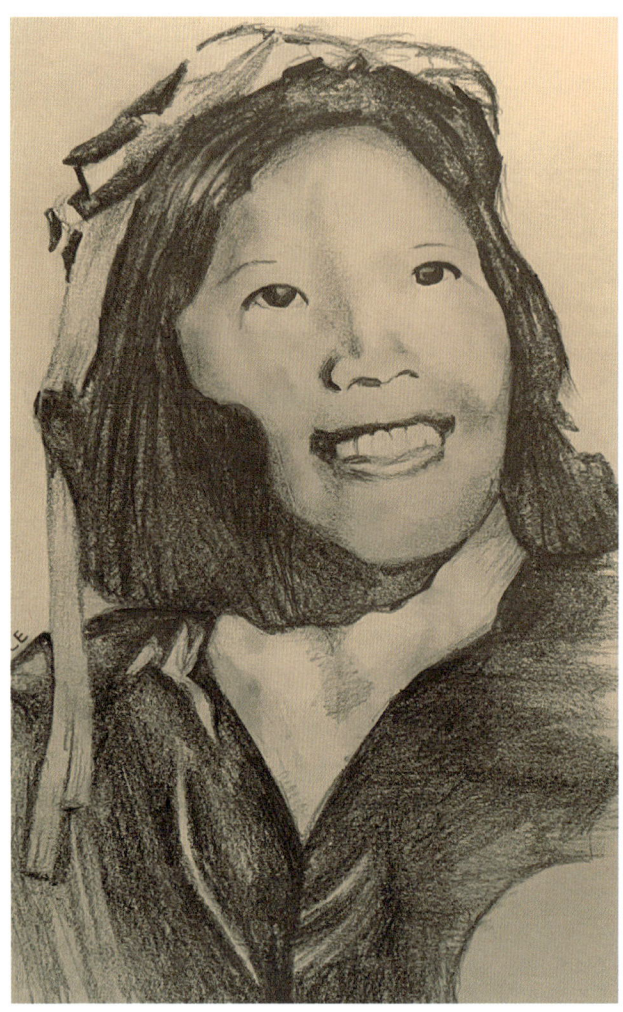

◎《飞行员朱美娇》
*Pilot Maggie Gee*

林之雅　画
by Candice Lin

## 美国女子飞行员、物理学家朱美娇

朱美娇1923年出生于加州伯克利市,她是第三代华裔美国人,在成长过程中,也曾因肤色而遭受种族歧视。"二战"爆发后,她听说内华达州的航空学校学费需要800美元,就开始节省每一分钱,立志学习飞行。

20岁时,她在航空学校受训两个月,随后接受女子飞行队面试,加入美国女子空军服务队。之后,她被分派到内华达州拉斯维加斯空军基地,接受飞行员军事训练,负责驾驶靶机,帮助男飞行员训练,并运输战斗机。

第三部分　战争篇
Part Three　The Wars

**American Female Pilot and Physicist, Maggie Gee**

　　Maggie Gee was born in Berkeley, California, in 1923. She is a third-generation Chinese-American. Growing up, she also suffered racial discrimination because of her skin color. When World War II broke out, she heard that aviation school tuition in Nevada cost $800, and she began saving every penny and was determined to learn how to fly.

　　At age 20, she was trained at an aviation school for two months, then was interviewed for the women's flying team to join the US Women's Air Service. Afterward, she was assigned to the Las Vegas Air Force Base in Nevada, where she received military pilot training, learning how to fly target drones, helping male pilots with training, and transporting fighter jets.

### 战斗机飞行员李月英

李月英 1912 年出生于俄勒冈州波特兰市，祖籍广东台山，父亲是一名商人，母亲是家庭主妇。1932 年高中毕业后，李月英在波特兰的华侨航空学校学习飞行，成为首位有飞行执照的美国华裔女飞行员。在飞行学校，她遇到了正在接受军事训练的中国学员雷炎均。

1933 年，李月英与华侨航空学校男同学一起回到中国，希望加入中国空军，但遭到拒绝，说女人不适合飞行。李月英转而留居广州，提任驾驶商业和私人航班飞行员。

1937 年，抗战全面爆发，李月英再度要求加入中国空军，仍遭拒绝。于是 1938 年 12 月回到美国纽约，任国民政府驻美采购员。

1943 年，李月英加入新成立的美国女子空军服务飞行队，她被编入第三运输大队，多次驾驶运输机飞越大西洋，前往英国，因其出色表现，美国空军授予她中尉军衔。10 月 9 日，她与雷炎均结婚，那时雷是一名中国空军少校。同年，她从女子飞行队员培训班毕业，并被派往密歇根州罗穆卢斯。

1944 年 11 月，李月英在执行任务时，由于塔台指挥出现通信系统故障，她驾驶的战斗机与另一架战机相撞发生爆炸，牺牲时，年仅 32 岁。三天后，她在美军装甲部队服役并正在法国战场作战的弟弟，也为美国捐躯。

当李家为姐弟俩安葬时，却遭到墓园反对，理由是有色人种不能葬在白人区墓地。最终，李家选了一处好墓地，为姐弟俩举行了一场非军人葬礼。

◉《战斗机飞行员李月英》
*Fighter Pilot Hazel Ying Lee*

田芯语　画
by Melody Tian

第三部分 战争篇
Part Three   The Wars

**Fighter Pilot Hazel Ying Lee**

Hazel Ying Lee was born in Portland, Oregon, in 1912. His ancestral home is Taishan, Guangdong. His father was a businessman, and his mother was a housewife. After graduating from high school in 1932, Hazel Ying Lee learned to fly at the Overseas Chinese Aviation School in Portland, and became the first Chinese-American female pilot with a pilot's license. At the flight school, she met Lei Yanjun, a Chinese cadet undergoing military training.

In 1933, Hazel Ying Lee returned to China with the male students of the Overseas Chinese Aviation School, hoping to join the Chinese Air Force. She was rejected, saying that women were not suitable for flying. Hazel Ying Lee moved to Guangzhou, where she was promoted to fly commercial and private airline planes.

When the Second Sino-Japanese War broke out in 1937, Hazel Ying Lee asked to join the Chinese Air Force but was rejected again. So, in December 1938, she returned to New York, USA, and served as a buyer of the National Government in the United States.

In 1943, Hazel Ying Lee joined the newly established US Women's Air Force Service Flying Team. She was incorporated into the Third Transport Brigade and flew over the Atlantic many times to the United Kingdom. Because of her outstanding performance, the US Air Force awarded her the rank of lieutenant. On October 9, 1943, she married Yanjun Lei, who was then a major in the Chinese Air Force. She graduated from the Women's Flight Crew Training Program in 1943 and was sent to Romulus, Michigan.

In November 1944, when Hazel Ying Lee was performing her mission, due to a communication system failure in the tower commander, the fighter she was piloting collided with another fighter. Her fighter exploded. When she died, she was only 32 years old. Three days later, her younger brother, who served in the US Armored Forces and was fighting in France, also died for the United States.

When the Lee family buried the siblings, they were opposed by the cemetery owner, claiming that people of color could not be buried in the white area cemetery. In the end, the Li family chose another cemetery and held a non-military funeral for the sister and brother.

●《华裔女上校海伦·潘·昂叶特》
*Chinese Female Colonel Helen Pon Onyett*

吴雨芮  画
by Sherry Wu

## 华裔女上校海伦·潘·昂叶特

海伦 1918 年生于康涅狄格州沃特伯利，她在沃特伯利医院护理学校接受培训。1942 年，她服役于陆军护士军团，去过地中海基地，也在美国本土服役。她在医疗船上巡回多次后，被派往北非的一所帐篷医院服务，并悉心护理伤兵，她用缴获的德国羊毛毯给伤兵保暖。当她和德国俘虏相处时，学会了他们的语言。她曾在弗吉尼亚州的帕特里克·亨利营工作，负责神经精神病、性病和传染性肝炎病房。她曾获得荣誉勋章。1971 年，她作为第一位华裔美国女性晋升为上校。

"二战"结束后，她退役，后来又参加后备队。1978 年，她从陆军退休，军旅生涯达 36 年。2005 年 5 月 18 日离世，享年 86 岁。

## Chinese Female Colonel Helen Pon Onyett

Born in Waterbury, Connecticut, in 1918, Helen was trained at the Waterbury Hospital School of Nursing. In 1942, she served in the Army Corps of Nurses, visited bases in the Mediterranean, and served on American soil. After several tours on the hospital ship, she was sent to serve in a tent hospital in North Africa, where she cared for the wounded and kept them warm with captured German wool blankets. While she was working with German captives, she learned their language. She worked at Camp Patrick Henry in Virginia, where she was in charge of the neuropsychiatric, venereal, and infectious hepatitis wards. She was awarded the Legion of Merit. In 1971, and was the first Chinese-American woman to be promoted to colonel.

After World War II, she retired and later joined the reserves. In 1978, she retired from the Army and served thirty-six years in the military. She died on May 18, 2005, at the age of 86.

第三部分 战争篇
Part Three　The Wars

◉《海军少尉玛丽特·琼·恩》
*Navy Second Lieutenant, Marietta Chong Eng*

张蕴涵　画
by Yunhan Zhang

## 海军少尉玛丽特·琼·恩

玛丽特·琼·恩出生于夏威夷檀香山。"二战"爆发后，因为弟弟当时已经在海军服役，她也加入了海军志愿紧急服务女子队。

她在海军接受培训后，被分派到加利福尼亚州马累岛美国海军医院工作。她负责护理在战争中失去手脚的伤兵们，帮助他们恢复生活自理能力和信心。

她喜欢军装，甚至在自己的婚礼上，也穿着军装。战后，她定居加州奥克兰，生育抚养了三个孩子。

## Navy Second Lieutenant, Marietta Chong Eng

Marietta Chong Eng was born in Honolulu, Hawaii. After the outbreak of World War Ⅱ, because her brother was already serving in the Navy, she joined the Women Accepted for Volunteer Emergency Service, WAVES.

After training in the Navy, she was assigned to work at the US Naval Hospital in Mare Island, California. She was responsible for nursing wounded soldiers who lost their limbs in the war, helping them regain their self-care ability and confidence.

She loves military uniforms and even wore them at her wedding. After the war, she settled in Oakland, California, where she bore and raised three children.

◉《中士朱莉娅·拉姆·阿什福德》
*Sergeant Julia Larm Ashford*

茉莉画　画
by Moli

### 中士朱莉娅·拉姆·阿什福德

朱莉娅·拉姆·阿什福德1944年参加陆军女子军团，在太平洋战区服役。战后她跟随太平洋战区的女子军团去往被盟军占领的德国。

她留在陆军直到1948年，然后参加新成立的空军，在空军服务到1953年。

### Sergeant Julia Larm Ashford

Julia Larm Ashford joined the Army Women's Corps in 1944 and served in the Pacific Theater. After the war, she followed the Women's Corps in the Pacific Theater to Germany, which was occupied by the Allies them.

She remained in the Army until 1948, then joined the newly formed Air Force, serving in the Air Force until 1953.

第三部分　战争篇
Part Three　The Wars

◉《军事翻译海伦·M. 李》
*Military Interpreter Helen M. Lee*

龙可为　画
by Claire Fillon

## 军事翻译海伦·M. 李

海伦·M. 李出生在加州威洛斯，于1943年8月参加美国陆军女子军团。

美国陆军女子军团成立后，招募了50名在美国出生的双语华裔女青年，把她们送入明尼苏达州斯内林堡军事情报中心语言学校学习，训练她们为军事翻译。下士海伦·M. 李被分配做帮助美军与中国盟军沟通的工作。后来，她被派到加州洛瑞空军基地 (Lowry Army Air Field) 当训练美军的中文翻译。

## Military Interpreter Helen M. Lee

Helen M. Lee was born in Willows, California, and enlisted in the Women's Army Corps in August 1943.

After the establishment of the US Women's Army Corps, fifty bilingual Chinese-American young women born in the United States were recruited and sent to the Language School of the Military Intelligence Center in Fort Snelling, Minnesota, to be trained as military translators. Corporal Helen M. Lee, was assigned to help the US military communicate with the Chinese allies. Later, she was sent to Lowry Army Air Field in California as a Chinese interpreter for training American troops.

◉《女飞虎队军官陈贞洁》
*Female Flying Tiger Officer Elsie Seetoo*

田芯语　画
by Melody Tian

**女飞虎队军官陈贞洁**

　　陈贞洁出生于加州，童年时跟随父母回到广东新会老家生活。1942年，她在香港玛丽医院接受医疗训练后，徒步1100千米到贵阳，加入了中国红十字会救护总队，随队辗转至昆明、印度等地。

　　1944年，当陈贞洁向美军提交入伍申请时，被认为是中国公民而遭到拒绝。但在美军服役期间，陈贞洁曾在陈纳德将军指挥的美国第14航空队担任军官。

　　1946年，陈贞洁随部队返回美国后，完成大学学业，后随丈夫迁至华盛顿，在海军医疗中心和国立卫生研究院工作多年。2019年，年过百岁的陈贞洁作为"二战"华裔女兵，获美国国会金质奖章。

第三部分　战争篇
Part Three　The Wars

**Female Flying Tiger Officer Elsie Seetoo**

Elsie Seetoo was born in California. She followed her parents back to their hometown in Xinhui, Guangdong when she was a child. In 1942, after receiving medical training at the Queen Mary Hospital in Hong Kong, she walked 1,110 kilometers to Guiyang. She joined the Chinese Red Cross Ambulance Corps, and traveled with the team to Kunming, India and other places.

In 1944, when Elsie Seetoo applied for enlistment to the US military, she was considered a Chinese citizen and was rejected. But while serving in the US military, Elsie Seetoo served as an officer in the US 14$^{th}$ Air Force commanded by General Chennault.

In 1946, after returning to the United States with the army, Elsie Seetoo completed her university studies. She moved to Washington DC with her husband, where she worked for many years at the Naval Medical Center and the National Institutes of Health. In 2019, Elsie Seetoo, who was over 100 years old, won the US Congressional Medal as a Chinese female soldier in World War Ⅱ.

◎《玛格丽特·杰西·张》
*Margaret Jessie Chung*

穆烊昕　画
by Emily Mu

## 玛格丽特·杰西·张

玛格丽特·杰西·张是美国第一位在旧金山唐人街附近开设西医诊所的华人女医生，作为当时知名的社会活动家，她也是最早支持女性加入海军服役的民权人士。

1889年，她出生于加州的圣塔芭芭拉（Santa Barbara），1902年全家移居洛杉矶，她是家中11个孩子中的老大。因母亲患结核并且早逝，她从10岁起，就开始帮助父亲养家糊口，抚养弟妹。1905年，年仅15岁的她，就开始在《洛杉矶先驱报》发表诗歌和论文，被该报誉为有前途的学生。1907年，她就读于南加大预备学校，被评为该校女子体育课的"杰出明星"。1909年，她从南加大毕业后，就读于该校医学院，成为该州第一位进入医学院的华人女孩，也是班上唯一的女生。1916年，她获得医学博士学位。

有了博士学位，她去了芝加哥的汤普森妇女儿童医院做实习医生，接着在另一家州立医院做住院医生、医生助理等。1918年她父亲去世，于是她回到洛杉矶，在一家医院做外科医生。

# 第三部分 战争篇
Part Three　The Wars

## Margaret Jessie Chung

Margaret Jessie Chung was the first Chinese female doctor in the United States to open a Western medicine clinic near San Francisco's Chinatown. As a well-known social activist at the time, she was also the first civil rights advocate to support women's service in the Navy.

In 1889, she was born in Santa Barbara, California, and in 1902, the family moved to Los Angeles. She is the eldest of 11 children in the family. Since her mother suffered from tuberculosis and died young, since she was 10 years old, she had been helping her father with the family and raising her younger siblings. In 1905, when she was only 15 years old, she began publishing poems and essays in the *Los Angeles Herald*, which was hailed as a promising student. In 1907, Margaret Jessie Chung attended the USC Preparatory School and was named the "outstanding star" of the school's women's physical education class. In 1909, after graduating from USC, she enrolled in the school's medical school, becoming the first Chinese girl in the state to enter medical school and the only female student in her class. In 1916, Margaret Jessie Chung received her MD.

With her Ph.D., she went to Thompson Women's and Children's Hospital in Chicago as a trainee, then another state hospital as a resident, physician assistant, etc. When her father died in 1918, she returned to Los Angeles to work as a surgeon in a hospital.

◉《飞虎队员叫她"妈妈"》　　　　　　　　　　　　穆烊昕　画
   "Mother" of the Flying Tigers　　　　　　　　　　by Emily Mu

**飞虎队员叫她"妈妈"**

　　1922 年，玛格丽特·杰西·张搬到旧金山，在唐人街建立了最早的西医诊所。1932 年，有 8 名海军预备役飞行员为中国抗日提供自愿服务，他们到诊所来时，她看到他们一个个都很饿，就给他们做了可口饭菜，还按中国人习惯，给他们脖子上戴玉佛项链。于是他们戏称自己是"张妈妈"的金发养子。终身未婚的张玛珠，在"二战"前后名义上收养了 1500 个"儿子"，其中大部分是美军白人军官和士兵，也有不少国会议员、参议员及社会名流，其中就包括美国前总统罗纳德·里根。

　　图为"二战"期间，张玛珠在感恩节宴请飞虎队队员们。"二战"期间，她在感恩节时，在自己的家中宴请过多达 175 人，并寄出过 4000 份圣诞节礼物。来宾包括美国参议员和国会众议员。

第三部分　战争篇
Part Three　The Wars

## "Mother" of the Flying Tigers

In 1922, Margaret Jessie Chung moved to San Francisco and established the earliest western medicine clinic in Chinatown. In 1932, eight navy reserve pilots provided voluntary services for China's anti-Japanese war. When they came to the clinic, she saw they were all hungry, so she cooked them delicious meals and gave them jade Buddha necklaces according to Chinese custom. They jokingly called themselves "Mama Chung" 's blond adopted sons. The unmarried Zhang Mazhu nominally adopted 1,500 "sons" before and after World War II, most of whom were white US military officers and soldiers, as well as many congressmen, senators, and celebrities, including former US President Ronald Reagan.

The image shows that, Mama Chung entertained the Flying Tigers on Thanksgiving Day during World War II. During World War II, she entertained as many as 175 people at her home on Thanksgiving and sent out 4,000 Christmas gifts. Guests included US senators and members of Congress.

317

◉ 《张妈妈要塞》 穆烊昕 画
*Mama Zhang Fortress* by Emily Mu

第三部分　战争篇

Part Three　The Wars

**命名为"张妈妈要塞"**

　　1937年中国抗日战争全面爆发，张玛珠曾自愿报名担任前线外科医师，但被劝退。鉴于她在白人圈子的影响，中国国民政府请她为飞虎队招募了最初的200名美军飞行员。

　　据说，张玛珠收养了整个飞虎队二中队。1944年6月，二中队单日就击落67架日本战机，从而创下美国纪录。

　　"二战"期间，为感谢张妈妈，至少有三个飞行要塞被她的"养子们"命名为"张妈妈要塞"。

**Named "Mama Zhang Fortress"**

When the Anti-Japanese War broke out in China in 1937, she volunteered to be a front-line surgeon but was persuaded to quit. Given her influence in white circles, the Chinese Nationalist government asked her to recruit the first 200 American pilots for the Flying Tigers.

It is said that Mama Chung adopted the entire No. 2 Squadron of the Flying Tigers. In June 1944, the No. 2 Squadron shot down 67 Japanese fighter jets in a single day, setting an American record.

During World War II, to thank Mama Chung, at least three flying fortresses were named "Mama Chung Fortress" by her "adopted children".

◎《救援女兵李黄翠娟》　　　　　　　　　　　　　吴鸣玥　画
　 *Battlefield Angel, Peggy Lee*　　　　　　　　　　by Thelia Wu

## 救援女兵李黄翠娟

　　李黄翠娟出生于加拿大卑诗省鲁珀特王子港。父亲是太平洋铁路华工。1940年，她来到温哥华，年仅19岁，她自愿当圣约翰女子救护队的救援女兵。

　　2018年，加拿大卑诗省政府为95岁高龄的华裔"二战"女兵李黄翠娟颁发了"良好公民勋章"。

## Battlefield Angel, Peggy Lee

　　Peggy Lee was born in Prince Rupert, British Columbia. Her father was a Chinese worker in the Pacific Railroad. She came to Vancouver in 1940 at 19 and volunteered to be a female rescue soldier with the St. John's Women's Ambulance Corps.

　　In 2018, the British Columbia provincial government awarded the "Good Citizen Medal" to the 95-year-old Chinese World War Ⅱ female soldier Angel, Peggy Lee.

第三部分　战争篇
Part Three　The Wars

◉《皇家信号兵玛丽·劳拉·马》
*Royal Signals, Mary Laura Mah*

吴鸣玥　画
by Thelia Wu

**皇家信号兵玛丽·劳拉·马**

出生于加拿大的华裔玛丽·劳拉·马，19岁入伍，原想当空军，因女性配额限制，她被送往温哥华，成为加拿大皇家信号兵团里的一名电传打字员。她也是军营里唯一的华裔女兵。

**Royal Signals, Mary Laura Mah**

Mary Laura Mah enlisted in the army at the age of 19. She originally wanted to take part in the air force, but due to female quota restrictions, she was sent to Vancouver and became a teletype typist in the Royal Canadian Signal Corps. She was also the only female Chinese soldier in the barracks.

◎《黄国丽》
*Mary Ko Bong*

邹安琪　画
by Angela Zou

## 黄国丽

"二战"期间，30万名加拿大妇女在军工制造行业工作，当时加拿大工厂里近三分之二的工人是女性。无数加拿大女子穿着围裙推销25美分一张的"战争储蓄邮票"，共为军队筹得3亿余美元。其中，出生于卑诗省维多利亚市一个虔诚的华人基督徒家庭的黄国丽，她与四个兄弟在"二战"中都加入了加拿大军队，她在军中担任机械师。

## Mary Ko Bong

During World War Ⅱ, 300,000 Canadian women worked in the military manufacturing industry, and nearly two-thirds of workers in Canadian factories were women. Countless Canadian women wore aprons to sell the 25-cent "War Savings Stamp", raising more than $300 million for the military. Among them, Mary Ko Bong, born and raised in a devout Chinese Christian family in Victoria, British Columbia, joined the Canadian Army with her four brothers during World War Ⅱ, where she served as a mechanic.

（译文/王小龙　责编/许静）

# 第十八章　家族参战

Chapter 18　Families in the War

100 Years of Chinese Immigration in the United States and Canada

### 加拿大马氏兄弟

1941年底，太平洋战争爆发后，日军为了迫使重庆国民政府投降，对香港和仰光实行轰炸，接着又切断了滇缅公路，使大量的援华物资无法运进中国。面对如此严峻的局势，为保证"二战"亚洲战场上对日作战的军备物资，中美两国决定联合开辟新的国际运输线，于是诞生了举世闻名的"驼峰"航线。而美国则成为抗战后期援华的最主要国家。1942年7月，美国陆军航空队一个新的航空运输司令部成立，由威廉·腾纳尔上校指挥，组织空运和提供后勤支持。大多数的人员和设备来自美国陆军航空队，也有英国和印度的英联邦部队、缅甸劳工团队和中国国民航空空运科。飞越驼峰对于盟军飞行人员而言是近乎自杀式的航程，但是在加拿大出生的马家兄弟却毅然加入，并因在"二战"中的功勋，得到崇高的荣誉——亚洲太平洋军功章、美国军功章、"二战"胜利奖章、驼峰胜利奖章。

战争结束后，兄弟俩都定居在加拿大。

第三部分　战争篇
Part Three　The Wars

## Canadian Ma Brothers

At the end of 1941, after the outbreak of the Pacific War in World War II, the Japanese army bombed Hong Kong and Yangon in order to force the National Government of Chongqing to surrender, and then cut off the Yunnan-Burma Road, making it impossible for a large number of aid materials to be transported into China. Faced with such a severe situation, China and the United States decided to open up a new international transportation line joinly in order to ensure the armament materials for the war against Japan on the Asian battlefields of World War II. Thus was born the world-famous "Hump" route. The United States became the most important country that aided China in the later period of the Anti-Japanese War. In July 1942, a new US Army Air Forces Air Transport Command was established, under the command of Colonel William H. Tunner, to organize airlifts and provide logistical support. Most of the personnel and equipment came from the US Army Air Corps, but there are also British and Indian Commonwealth Forces, the Burmese Labour Team, and the Air Transport Section of the Chinese Civil Aviation. Flying over the hump was a near-suicidal voyage for the Allied pilots. Still, the Ma brothers, who were born in Canada, joined resolutely, and received high honors for their exploits in World War II -receiving the Asia Pacific Military Merit, American Military Merit medal, World War II Victory Medal, Hump Victory Medal. After the war, both brothers settled in Canada.

●《哥哥马邦基》
*Older Brother Bangji Ma*

邓依然 画
by Melissa Deng

# 第三部分　战争篇
Part Three　The Wars

**哥哥马邦基**

马邦基 1920 年出生于加拿大。其父亲经营着便利店、面包店和中餐馆。但他 15 岁时，父亲去世。母亲带着父亲的遗骨和他的妹妹回到了中国。18 岁时，他是英属哥伦比亚省拳击比赛业余组的冠军，夺得了"金手套"。那时，日军已经攻进上海。1938 年，他前往美国加州学习驾驶飞机，并取得飞行资格。3 年后，他回到加拿大，在雷蒙顿地区培训加拿大空军进行空中侦察和轰炸的技巧。不久，传来日军占领广东的消息。他毅然决定回到家乡救出自己 12 岁的妹妹。他不会说中国话，因此在穿越日军封锁线时，他机智地扮作聋哑人，在朋友的帮助下终于回到老家。后来，兄妹俩藏身一具棺材里，才通过了日军的岗哨。但当他们在一艘小船上向国统区转移时，曾遭到日军飞机的追杀。

**Older Brother Bangji Ma**

Bangji Ma was born in Canada in 1920. His father ran a convenience store, bakery and Chinese restaurant. But when he was 15, his father died. His mother returned to China with his father's remains and his sister. At 18, he was the amateur boxing champion in British Columbia, winning the "Golden Glove". At that time, the Japanese army had already invaded Shanghai. In 1938, he went to California to learn to fly an airplane and obtained a flying qualification. After three years, he returned to Canada to train the Canadian Air Force in aerial reconnaissance and bombing skills in the Raymonton area. Soon, news came that the Japanese army occupied Guangdong. He resolutely decided to return to his hometown to rescue his 12-year-old sister. He doesn't speak Chinese, so when crossing the Japanese blockade, he cleverly pretended to be a deafmute and finally returned to his hometown with the help of his friends. Later, the brother and sister hid in a coffin before passing the Japanese outpost. But when they were moving to the Kuomintang area on a small boat, they were chased and killed by Japanese aircraft.

◉《420次飞越"驼峰航线"》
*420 Times Flying Over the "Hump Route"*

钟骐励 画
by Qili Zhong

**420次飞越"驼峰航线"**

1945年8月8日,马邦基奉命从重庆将20名旅客送到他们指定的任何地点。登机后,他发现这20名乘客人人穿着日本军服,他以为是日军俘虏。后来才知道他们是日本派来谈判投降事宜的军事代表团,其中还有日本天皇的弟弟。这些人是在广岛被原子弹轰炸后第二天来中国的。

1995年,美军为马邦基颁发了勋章,以嘉奖他在"驼峰航线"上的功勋。在中国抗战的最后3年里,他在"驼峰航线"上飞行了420次。

**420 Times Flying Over the "Hump Route"**

On August 8, 1945, Bangji Ma recived an order to deliver 20 passengers from Chongqing to any place they designated. After boarding the plane, he found that the 20 passengers were all wearing Japanese military uniforms, and he thought they were Japanese prisoners. Later, he learned that they were a military delegation sent by Japan to negotiate about the surrender, the younger brother of the Emperor of Japan in it. These people came to China the day after Hiroshima was bombed by the atomic bomb.

In 1995, the US military awarded Albert a medal for his exploits on the "Hump Route". In the last three years of China's Anti-Japanese War, he flew 420 times on the "Hump Route".

第三部分　战争篇
Part Three　The Wars

◉《弟弟马绍基》　　　钟骐励　画
　Younger Brother Shaoji Ma  by Qili Zhong

◉《弟弟马绍基》　　　马萧萧　画
　Younger Brother Shaoji Ma  by Tyler Ma

**弟弟马绍基**

1922 年，马绍基生于加拿大，比哥哥马邦基小两岁。1937 年，马绍基在加拿大取得飞行执照。1944 年，他回到中国，也成为"驼峰航线"上的一员，他飞行了 370 次，运送了无数抗战人员和军需物资。

**Younger Brother Shaoji Ma**

In 1922, Shaoji Ma was born in Canada. He was two years younger than his brother. In 1937, Shaoji Ma obtained his pilot's license in Canada. In 1944, he returned to China and became a member to the "Hump Route". He flew 370 times and transported countless anti-Japanese soldiers and military supplies.

## 亚利桑那凤凰城关氏兄弟
## The Guan Brothers from Phoenix, Arizona

### 哥哥关卫理

1940年,关卫理加入美国陆军,在俄克拉荷马州和得克萨斯州接受战前训练,1942年被任命为步兵少尉,并派往巴拿马,后经过北非和波斯湾前往中国。

1943年至1944年,他被派往印度训练中国军队。之后,到缅甸北部的作战司令部,并在滇缅战役中于缅甸北部和中部打击日军。

关卫理战功彪炳,得过了亚太区征战勋章、第二次世界大战胜利勋章等5枚勋章。

关卫理在军中服役长达20年,官至上校。

### Older Brother Weili Guan

Weili Guan joined the US Army in 1940 and received prewar training in Oklahoma and Texas before being sent to Panama in 1942 and then to China via North Africa and the Persian Gulf.

From 1943 to 1944, he was sent to India to train Chinese troops. Afterward, he went to the Combat Command in northern Burma and fought against the Japanese during the Burma campaign in northern and central Burma.

Weili Guan's military exploits were outstanding, and he won 5 medals including the Asia-Pacific Region Battle Medal and the World War II Victory Medal.

Weili Guan served in the army for 20 years and was promoted to colonel.

第三部分　战争篇
Part Three　The Wars

◉《弟弟关护理》
*Younger Brother Huli Guan*

刘阅辰　画
by Scarlett Liu

**弟弟关护理**

关护理于1942年服役，加入美国陆军航空兵，是一名特种兵。他是投弹瞄准和飞行控制专家。

1943年1月，关护理进入俄亥俄州著名的赖特－帕特森空军基地，研习飞机仪器－导航－投弹瞄准器和自动飞行控制。同年，他被分配到北非战区。

1944年至1945年12月，他在中国服务于中美空军第14航空队，成为第20大队轰炸司令部的成员，协助中国军民打击日本侵略者。

关护理获得了包括欧洲－中东战区、大西洋－太平洋战区勋章等5枚奖章。

**Younger Brother Huli Guan**

Huli Guan served in 1942 and joined the US Army Air Corps as a special forces soldier. He is an expert in bomb targeting and flight control.

In January 1943, Huli Guan entered the famous Wright-Patterson Air Force Base in Ohio to study aircraft instruments-navigation-bombsights, and automatic flight control. In 1943, he was assigned to the North African Theater.

From 1944 to December 1945, he had served in the 14th Air Force of the Chinese and American Air Forces in China and became a member of the 20th Bomb Command, assisting the Chinese military and civilians in fighting the Japanese invaders.

Huli Guan received five medals including the European-Middle East Theater and the Atlantic-Pacific Theater Medal.

◉《旧金山唐人街三兄弟》　　　　　　　　　　　　　祝云姝　画
　　The Three Brothers From San Francisco's Chinatown　　by Maggie Zhu

## 旧金山唐人街三兄弟

"二战"爆发后，生于美国旧金山唐人街的 Wing Y Lai 家三兄弟一起报名上战场。

大哥刚刚高中毕业。他收到当地征兵办公室的信，得知自己被抽签选中服兵役。

二弟志愿当飞行员，到亚利桑那图森飞行训练基地，因色盲被刷下来，后加入美国空军第 43 情报中队。

三弟被派往距离日本最近的阿拉斯加驻守。

第三部分　战争篇
Part Three　The Wars

## The Three Brothers From San Francisco's Chinatown

After the outbreak of World War II, the three brothers of Wing Y Lai, family who were born in San Francisco's Chinatown, signed up for the battlefield.

When World War II broke out, Wing had just graduated from high school. He received a letter from the local recruiting office that he had been selected for military service.

The second brother volunteered to be a pilot and went to the Tucson flight training base in Arizona. He was brushed off for color blindness and enlisted in the 43$^{rd}$ Intelligence Squadron of the US Air Force.

The third brother was sent to be stationed in Alaska, which is the closest to Japan.

◎《亚利桑那凤凰城一门四杰》　　　　　　　　　　祝云姝　画
　Four of the Best in Phoenix, Arizona　　　　　　by Maggie Zhu

**亚利桑那凤凰城一门四杰**

　　1940年，美国亚利桑那州凤凰城总人口共65400人，华人仅431人。据记载，"二战"期间，凤凰城却有74名华裔青年应征加入美国军队，平均每6个华人中就有一个入伍。他们被分配到海军、陆军、空军和特种部队服役，并勇赴欧洲战场、亚太战区和中国－缅甸－印度战区，与德国、日本法西斯决一死战。

　　其中邓氏四兄弟邓粤昂(Robert Ong)、邓粤寅(Fred Ong)、邓粤钿(Henry Ong)和邓粤铨(Frank Ong)一起入伍。四兄弟中老大、老二参加美军后备队，留守美国本土，没有被派遣海外；老三和老四则被派往欧洲战场。

第三部分　战争篇
Part Three　The Wars

**Four of the Best in Phoenix, Arizona**

In 1940, the total population of Phoenix, Arizona, USA was 65,400, of which only 431 were Chinese. According to records, during World War II, 74 Chinese youths in Phoenix were drafted into the US military, one in six Chinese in average. They were assigned to serve in the navy, army, air force, and special forces, and went to the European theater, the Asia-Pacific theater, and the China-Myanmar-India theater to fight against the German and Japanese fascists bravely.

Among them, the four Deng brothers, Robert Ong, Fred Ong, Henry Ong, and Frank Ong, joined the army. The eldest and the second of the four brothers joined the US military reserve team, stayed in the United States, and were not sent overseas; the third and fourth were sent to the European battlefield.

**老三邓粤钿**

邓粤钿 1942 年当兵，开始被派往密苏里州、佛罗里达州等地学习军事通信技术。随后，他被分配到亚利桑那州图森的戴维斯－蒙森空军基地，担任 B-24 轰炸机上的无线电通信兵。他在新墨西哥州的阿拉莫戈多空军基地作最后的训练后，被派往英国，分配到第 487 轰炸大队的 837 轰炸中队，驻扎于伦敦南部。

邓粤钿参加过著名的诺曼底登陆战役。1944 年 8 月 6 日，邓粤钿执行第 30 次任务，去轰炸德国柏林的发动机工厂。这次任务完成后，他们就可以回美国整编。当时炸弹投中目标后，飞机不幸被防空炮火击中，飞机急坠，机组人员奉命跳伞，但所有美国军人被俘。邓粤钿身上多处受伤。战友爱德华·赖歇尔受伤最严重，因为他是犹太血统，德国人拒绝为他治疗，次日就死了。

邓粤钿被送往德国东部一个俘虏营。两节车厢挤满了战俘，他们几乎没有任何食物和水，受尽了折磨。

1945 年 2 月，为逃避苏军的攻势，德国人决定步行迁移整个战俘营。邓粤钿与超过 10000 名战俘步行 1000 英里，从德国东部走到西部。因战况不利于德军，整个俘虏营又从西部折返东部。他们足足步行了 100 多天，许多战俘死于冻饿与疾病。1945 年 5 月 4 日，邓粤钿被英军救出，重获自由。

战后，美国政府授予邓粤钿多枚奖章，有战争先锋勋章、第二次世界大战胜利奖章等。邓粤钿退役后，服务社会，担任过全美退役军人战俘亚利桑那州总指挥。2005 年入选亚利桑那退伍军人名人堂。为表彰邓粤钿在第二次世界大战期间的贡献，2007 年凤凰城市长菲尔·戈登把 1 月 16 日定为"邓粤钿日"。

第三部分 战争篇
Part Three　The Wars

**The Third Yuedian Deng**

Yuedian Deng joined the army in 1942 and was sent to Missouri, Florida, and other places to study military communication technology. He was then assigned to Davis-Monthan Air Force Base in Tucson, Arizona, as a radio operator on a B-24 bomber. After his final training at Alamogordo Air Force Base in New Mexico, he was sent to England, assigned to the 837$^{th}$ Bomb Squadron of the 487$^{th}$ Bomb Group, stationed in south London.

Yuedian Deng participated in the famous Normandy landing campaign. On August 6, 1944, Yuedian Deng performed his 30$^{th}$ mission to bomb the engine factory in Berlin, Germany. After this mission was completed, they could return to the United States for reorganization. However after the bomb hit the target, the plane was hit by anti-aircraft fire. The plane crashed and the crew was ordered to parachute, but unfortunately all American soldiers were captured. Yuedian Deng suffered multiple injuries. His comrade-in-arms, Edward Reichel, was the worst injured. Bbcause Reichel was of a Utah descent, the Germans refused to treat him. He died the next day.

Yuedian Deng was sent to a prison camp in eastern Germany. The two carriages were crowded with prisoners of war. They could have hardly any food and water, and suffered a lot.

Group photo in front of a large bomber during World War II. Yuedian Deng is the second from the left in the front row.

In February 1945, to escape the Soviet attack, the Germans decided to relocate the entire POW camp on foot. Yuedian Deng walked a thousand miles from eastern Germany to the west with more than 10,000 prisoners of war. Due to the unfavorable situation of the German army, the prison camp was turned back from the west to the east. They walked for more than 100 days, and many prisoners of war died of starvation and disease. On May 4, 1945, Yuedian Deng was rescued by the British army and regained his freedom. After the war, the US government awarded Yuedian Deng many medals, including the War Vanguard Medal and the World War II Victory Medal.

After Yuedian Deng retired, he served as the commander-in-chief for a retired war prisoner in Arizona. In 2005, he was inducted into the Arizona Veterans Hall of Fame. In recognition of Yuedian Deng's contribution during World War II, in 2007, Phoenix Mayor Phil Gordon designated January 16 as Yuedian Deng Day.

◉《老四邓粤铨》
The Fourth Yuequan Deng

王小虎 画
by Bryant Wang

**老四邓粤铨**

1943年10月，邓粤铨加入美国陆军，成为一名野战炮手。1944年邓粤铨被派往菲律宾，到马里亚纳群岛的塞班岛、天宁岛作战。邓粤铨参加了冲绳岛的作战。冲绳岛战役打响的前一天，他所在的炮兵部队已经在离冲绳岛仅5英里的一个小岛上登陆并架炮。大炮威力强大，炮弹射程能打击17英里外的目标，火力覆盖众多日军军事目标。3月26日，冲绳岛总攻战役开始，炮兵部队为美军登陆扫清了障碍。之后，他随部队登岛，并全程参与了攻占冲绳岛的战斗。邓粤铨在"二战"中获得了4枚奖章。

**The Fourth Yuequan Deng**

In October 1943, Yuequan Deng joined the US Army as a field gunner. In 1944, Yuequan Deng was sent to the Philippines, where he fought on Saipan and Tinian in the Mariana Islands. Yuequan Deng participated in the battle on Okinawa. Before the Battle of Okinawa, his artillery unit had landed and mounted artillery on a small island just five miles from Okinawa. The cannon was powerful, and the shells could hit targets 17 miles away. The firepower covered many Japanese military targets. On March 26, the Battle of Okinawa Island began. The artillery units cleared obstacles for the landing of the US military. After that, he landed on the island with the troops and participated in the battle to capture Okinawa. Yuequan Deng won four medals in World War II.

第三部分 战争篇
Part Three　The Wars

◉《密尔沃基母子四人》　　　　　　　　　　　　　　　张云想　画
　*Mother Milwaukee and Her Three Sons*　　　　　　　by Yunxiang Zhang

## 密尔沃基母子四人

"二战"爆发时，威斯康星的密尔沃基市仅有300名华人。但中国商人梅彩遒一家就有5个兄弟参战；另一个家庭，母亲珍妮（Jenny Chan）作为护士参加中国抗战，她有4个孩子，其中3个孩子分别参加了位于中国昆明和湖南芷江的飞虎队，还有陈纳德将军的美国第14航空队。

## Mother Milwaukee and Her Three Sons

When World War II broke out, there were only 300 Chinese in Milwaukee, Wisconsin. Yet the Chinese businessman Mei Caiqiu's family had five brothers who participated in the war. Another family, mother Jenny Chan participated in the Chinese war as a nurse. She has four children, three of whom joined in the Flight Tigers at Kunming, China and Zhijiang, Hunan, China, and General Chennault's US 14th Air Force.

●《黄国丽》
*Guoli Huang*

邹安琪　画
by Angela Zou

## 加拿大黄氏四姐弟

在加拿大卑诗省的维多利亚市，有一个黄姓华人基督教家庭，姐弟四人都入伍参战。姐姐是家中唯一的女孩，却也是第一个偷偷跑去参军的，她的举动影响了三个弟弟，他们也相继入伍。

## The Four Siblings of the Huangs' in Canada

In Victoria, British Columbia, Canada, there was a Chinese Christian family surnamed Huang. All four sisters and brothers enlisted in the army. The elder sister was the only girl in the family. She was also the first to join the army. She joined the army without letting her family konwing. Her actions affected the three brothers, who also joined the army later.

### 姐姐黄国丽

黄国丽学过声乐和舞蹈，也曾为军人们表演。

### Elder sister Guoli Huang

Guoli Huang studied vocals and dance, and used to perform for the military.

第三部分 战争篇
Part Three　The Wars

◉《弟弟黄国雄》
*Younger Brother Guoxiong Huang*

邓佳宜　画
by Kelly Deng

**弟弟黄国雄**

黄国雄于 1917 年出生。由于华裔不能就读公立学校，他只能在教会以及中华会馆学习中英文，至 11 岁时才获准到公立学校读书。黄国雄在温哥华工业中学学习木工等技术。1939 年，他尝试参军但被拒绝，直到 1941 年才被允许加入，他成为首位加入空军部队的加拿大华人。

在服役 4 年期间，他被训练成为一名空军工程师，后在卡尔加里受训后，成为一名飞机检验师。

**Younger Brother Guoxiong Huang**

Guoxiong Huang was born in 1917. Since no Chinese were allowed to attend public schools, he could only study Chinese and English at the church or the Chinese Association. He was not allowed to study in public schools until he was 11 years old. Guoxiong Huang studied woodcraft and other skills at Vancouver Tech. In 1939, he tried to join the army but was rejected. He was not allowed to join the army until 1941, when he became the first Chinese-Canadian to join the Air Force.

During his 4 years of service, he was trained as an Air Force engineer. After training in Calgary, he became an aircraft inspector.

◉ 《加入特种部队》　　　　　　　　　　　　　　David 田　画
　 *Join Special Forces*　　　　　　　　　　　　　by David Tian

**加入特种部队**

黄国雄和另外 12 名华人士兵被抽调组成了一支特种部队,任务是到东南亚战场展开敌后游击战。这是一个风险极高的任务,但他们毫无惧色地接受了挑战。战争结束的时候,黄国雄带着他在澳大利亚爱上的一名中国女孩,准备回到加拿大的故乡,退役、结婚。然而,黄国雄从加拿大政府却获得了一个尴尬的答复——他的中国妻子被拒绝入境。按照仍在生效的《排华法案》,华人无权带自己的妻小进入加拿大。

1945 年他退役回到温哥华,成为一名工程师,也曾在温哥华市华埠开设杂货店。

第三部分　战争篇
Part Three　The Wars

**Join Special Forces**

Guoxiong Huang and 12 other Chinese soldiers were recruited to form a special force. Their task was to launch guerrilla warfare behind enemy lines in the Southeast Asian battlefield. It was a risky task, but they accepted it without fear. At the end of the war, Guoxiong Huang brought a Chinese girl with whom he fell in love in Australia and return to his hometown in Canada. He wanted to retire and get married. However, he received an embarrassing answer from the Canadian government, for his Chinese wife was refused to entry. According to the *Chinese Exclusion Act*, still in effect at that time, Chinese people did not have the right to bring their wives and children into Canada.

In 1945, he retired from the military and returned and Vancouver and work as an engineer. He also ran a grocery store in Vancouver's Chinatown.

343

◎《百岁过世》
*Passed Away After His 100th*

邓佳宜 画
by Kelly Deng

## 百岁过世

2017年，列治文华裔协会向包括黄国雄在内的5名"二战"华裔老兵授予"华裔荣耀"奖项，以纪念华裔老兵在为全体华裔争取平等权利当中做出的巨大贡献。2019年3月10日，黄国雄在加拿大的大温列治文医院去世，享年101岁。

## Passed Away After His 100th

In 2017, the Richmond Chinese Association awarded the "Chinese Glory" award to five Chinese veterans of World War Ⅱ, including Guoxiong Huang, to commemorate his great contributions in fighting for equal rights for all Chinese. On March 10, 2019, Guoxiong Huang Died at Richmond Hospital in Greater Vancouver, Canada, at the age of 101.

（译文/田芯语 责编/陈小洁）

# 第十九章 加华军人

## Chapter 19　Canadian Chinese Soldiers

◎《136 特种部队》 李炳毅 画
*136 Special Forces* by Bingyi Li

## 136 特种部队

1944 年，日本军队在全亚洲设防，占领了新加坡、中国香港等。英国情报部门决定在远东战场设立一个敌后特别行动部队，需要有能够深入敌后的战士，能隐藏并破坏日军的设施，于是，一支高度机密的"136 特种部队"成立了。

该部队由英国特别行动局指挥。但是派遣白人面孔的士兵相貌容易被认出，所以盟国从温哥华唐人街招募华人。到"二战"结束时，136 特种部队有 150 名华裔，他们的足迹遍布马来西亚、缅甸等地，主要从事谍报、游击战、颠覆、协调当地抵抗运动、解救战俘、最终胁迫日军投降等活动。

第三部分 战争篇
Part Three　The Wars

**136 Special Forces**

In 1944, the Japanese Army set up defense all over Asia and occupied Singapore and Hong Kong, China, and other places. In order to recruit soldiers who could penetrate deep behind enemy lines and sabotage Japanese Army supply lines and equipment secretly, the British intelligence department decided to sct up a branch of the Special Operations Executive (SOE) based in the Far East battlefield. It was named "Force 136".

Force 136 was under the command of the British Special Operations Bureau. Because white man were easily recognized among the Asian people, they decided to recuit some Chinese from the Vancourer China town. At the end of the war, there were 150 Chinese in the the Force 136. They could be seen over Malaya, Burma, and other places, and they were engaged in activities such as espionage, guerrilla warfare, subversion, coordination of local resistance movements, rescue of prisoners of war, and eventual intimidated the of Japanese forces to surrender.

◉《埋没行动》　　　　　　　　　　　　　　　　　David 田　画
　 Death Action　　　　　　　　　　　　　　　　　by David Tian

## 埋没行动

　　1944年6月，12名华人自愿加入一个敢死队，他们被指派的军事行动定名为"埋没行动"。他们被告知自己不同于普通的士兵，需要宣誓严守秘密，如果被日军俘虏，他们将不会被承认，也不会受到日内瓦战俘公约的保护。他们在入伍时就受到相关培训，每个人都带着氰化物的毒药片，准备在被俘虏时抢先结束自己的生命。

　　然而，令人心酸的是，入伍前这些敢死队员并不是加拿大公民，他们一直被禁止进入公共部门打工，禁止参军。1907年，温哥华曾爆发打砸抢唐人街的恶性事件，一万多名当地白人发起反亚裔移民的示威游行。

第三部分　战争篇
Part Three　The Wars

**Death Action**

In June 1944, 12 Chinese volunteered to join a suicide squad and were assigned to perform a military operation named "Operation Oblivion". They were told that they are different from ordinary soldiers and need to take an oath to keep secrets. If they were captured by the Japanese Army, they would not be recognized as a Canadian soldier, nor would they be protected by the Geneva Convention on the Treatment of Prisoners of War. When they enlisted in the army, they received some relevant training. Everyone took some cyanide poison pills with them. They would swallow them and end their lives first when they were captured.

However, the poignant thing was that they were not Canadian citizens before enlisting. They had been barred from entering the public sector to work joining the military. In 1907, more than 10,000 local white people launched an anti-Asian protest. There was an incident of beating, smashing and looting in Vancouver's Chinatown.

◎《汉克黄》　　　　　　　　　　　　　　　　　　　　　钟骐励　画
　*Hank Wong*　　　　　　　　　　　　　　　　　　　　by Qili Zhong

第三部分　战争篇
Part Three　The Wars

## 汉克黄

汉克黄于1919年出生于安大略省伦敦市，他的父母从中国广东移民到加拿大，开了家中餐馆。母亲死于1918年的西班牙流感。父亲照顾不了三个孩子，把他送到孤儿院，直到长大他才回到家。

1940年，汉克黄报名参加海军，1944年他被招募参加"遗忘行动"，因为他的枪械技能，为他赢得了"扳机"的绰号，他成了一名枪械教官。

## Hank Wong

Hank Wong was born in London, Ontario in 1919. His parents immigrated from Guangdong to Canada and opened a Chinese restaurant. His mother died from the Spanish flu in 1918. The father couldn't take care of the three children, so he sent Hank to an orphanage IIank didn't rcturn homc until hc grcw up.

Hank enrolled in the Navy in 1940 and was recruited in Operation Oblivion in 1944. Because of his firearms skills, Hank earned himself the nickname "The Trigger" and became a firearms instructor.

◉《流浪回到加拿大》
*Wandering Back to Canada*

胡锦海　画
by Elmer Hu

## 流浪回到加拿大

　　战后汉克黄坐流浪轮船回到加拿大,在通用钢铁公司工作,担任实验室技术员。

## Wandering Back to Canada

　　After the war, Hank Huang returned to Canada on a wandering steamship and worked for General Steel as a laboratory technician.

第三部分　战争篇
Part Three　The Wars

◉《无线电操作员李庆芳》　　　　　　　　　　　　邓佳宜　画
*Rodio Operator Ronald Lee*　　　　　　　　　　　by Kelly Deng

**无线电操作员李庆芳**

李庆芳出生于1919年，在温哥华唐人街长大。

1941年，李庆芳被选中加入"136特种部队"，成为一名无线电操作员。他的工具包里有鸦片药丸（用于交易）和氰化物药丸（一旦被抓便吞服自杀）。所幸他活着回到了加拿大。

**Radio Operator Ronald Lee**

Ronald Lee was born in 1919 and grew up in Chinatown, Vancouver.

In 1941, Ronald Lee was recruited to join Force 136, a special force of the British intelligence service, and became a radio operator. In his kit, he had some opium pills and cyanide pills. Opium pills were for trading, if caught, he would swallow the cyanide pills and commit suicide. Fortunately, he returned to Canada alive.

◎《机电工程师黄炳章》
*Mechanical and Electrical Engineer Bingzhang Huang*

吴鸣玥　画
by Thelia Wu

**机电工程师黄炳章**

　　他于1919年出生在加拿大，1942年加入加拿大军队，22岁时，在加拿大派往欧洲的首批部队担任机电工程师，他随部队到过挪威、法国、波兰、德国等国家。

　　1944年6月，他参加了加军在诺曼底朱诺海滩登陆行动。那时在欧洲作战的加拿大军队280小组中，只有他一个华裔。当时他身边的20多个战友被敌军打死，他幸存下来。

　　1981年，黄炳章的女儿与一位加拿大的德裔青年结婚了。两家聊天时，意外得知，他们都曾经在欧洲战场，而且亲家还被加拿大部队俘虏，直到"二战"结束，亲家才返回德国，后来移民到加拿大。曾经的敌人变成了好朋友。战争导致的人间悲喜令人沉思。

　　1995年荷兰被加拿大解放50周年纪念庆典，黄炳章受邀出席大典，是唯一一位获得荷兰颁发纪念奖章的华裔军人。

第三部分 战争篇
Part Three  The Wars

**Mechanical and Electrical Engineer Bingzhang Huang**

He was born in Canada in 1919 and joined the Canadian army in 1942. At the age of 22, he served as an electromechanical engineer in the first Canadian troops to Europe. He accompanied the troops to Norway, France, Poland, Germany and other countries. In June 1944, he participated in the Canadian Army's landing operation on Juneau Beach, Normandy. At that time, he was the only Chinese in the 280th Group of the Canadian Army fighting in Europe. More than 20 comrades around him were killed by the enemy, but he survived.

In 1981, Bingzhang Huang's daughter married a young German Canadian. They accidentally learned that Bingzhang Huang and the in-law both went to the European battlefield. The in-law was captured by the Canadian army. It was not until the end of World War Ⅱ that the in-law returned to Germany and later immigrated to Canada. The former enemies become good friends. The joys and sorrows caused by the war are thought-provoking.

In 1995, at the celebration of the 50th anniversary of the liberation of the Netherlands by Canada, Huang Bingzhang was invited to attend the ceremony. He was the only Chinese soldier who received the commemorative medal from the Netherlands.

◉《英联邦海军大副罗景鎏》
Chief Mate of the Commonwealth
Navy William Lore

David 田　画
by David Tian

### 英联邦海军大副罗景鎏

他于1909年出生在不列颠哥伦比亚省的维多利亚，毕业于蒙特利尔的麦吉尔大学。

1939年，他成为第一位进入加拿大公务员队伍的加拿大华裔，担任交通部无线接线员。"二战"爆发后，他成为加拿大皇家海军的第一位华裔，最初被任命为临时中尉，曾为英联邦海军大副。

### Chief Mate of the Commonwealth Navy William Lore

William Lore was born in Victoria, British Columbia, Canada in 1909. He graduated from McGill University in Montreal.

In 1939, Lore became the first Chinese Canadian to enter the civil service when he was employed as a wireless operator for the Department of Transport. With the outbreak of World War II, Lore was the first Chinese Canadian to officially serve in the Royal Canadian Navy and the first officer of Chinese descent to serve in any of the Royal Navies of the British Commonwealth. He was initially appointed as an acting sub-lieutenant.

第三部分　战争篇
Part Three　The Wars

◉《首位登岸中国香港的中尉》
*First Lieutenant to Land in Hong Kong*

David 田　画
by David Tian

## 首位登岸中国香港的中尉

1945 年 8 月，日本投降，罗景鎏率一支海军陆战队，成为首位登岸中国香港的海军军官。

1946 年，他晋升为加拿大皇家海军中尉指挥官。

战后，他在牛津大学获得法律学位。103 岁离世。

## First Lieutenant to Land in Hong Kong

In August 1945, Japan surrendered. William Lore led a party of Royal Marines ashore. He was the first Allied officer to enter Hong Kong since its capture. In 1946, he was promoted to Lieutenant Commander RCN. After the war, he obtained a law degree at Oxford University. William Lore died at the age of 103.

◎《周镜球》　　　David 田　画
George Chow　　　by David Tian

◎《周镜球》　　　邓依然　画
George Chow　　　by Melissa Deng

**高射炮手周镜球**

　　他出生于维多利亚市，随后搬迁到温哥华的一个岛上。1940 年，在将满 19 岁时，他在维多利亚征兵站报名加入了高射炮营，被派往欧洲战场，在诺曼底登陆，穿越法国、比利时、德国和荷兰。在英国，他和同班战友击落了一架德军飞机，这也是加拿大军队击落的第一架飞机。

**Anti-Aircraft Gunner George Chow**

　　George Chow was born in Victoria and later moved to Vancouver. In 1940, he joined the anti-aircraft artillery battalion at the age of 19 and was sent to the battlefields of Europe. He landed in Normandy and crossed France, Belgium, Germany, and the Netherlands. In Britain, he and his comrades shot down a German aircraft in England. It was the first-ever shot down aircraft by the Canadian army.

## 第三部分　战争篇
## Part Three　The Wars

◉《幸运的战地爱情》　　　　　　　　　　　　　　　邓依然　画
　*Lucky Battle Love*　　　　　　　　　　　　　　　by Melissa Deng

## 幸运的战地爱情

周镜球在英国参加一个村庄舞会时，与玛贝尔·露丝一见钟情，两人相爱结婚，战争还没结束，就生下一对双胞胎。

婚后周镜球继续转战各地。战后玛贝尔·露丝随周镜球回到加拿大。

"二战"结束后，周镜球加入了加拿大皇家炮兵团下属的温哥华第 15 野战团。他担任炮兵教官，后来晋升高级准尉。

## Lucky Battlefield Love

While attending a village dance party in Britain, George Chow fell in love with Mabel Rose at first sight. They got married and had twins before the war ended. After marriage, George Chow continued to travel to various places. After the war, Mabel Rose came to Canada with him.

Following World War Ⅱ, Chow joined the 15th Field Regiment, RCA, in Vancouver. He was a gunnery instructor, eventually promoted to the rank of master warrant officer.

◎《加拿大国家骑士》
*Canadian National Knight*

邓佳宜　画
by Kelly Deng

**加拿大国家骑士**

　　1963年，周镜球退伍。

　　2012年，他获得女王钻石纪念奖章。

　　2015年，法国政府授予他荣誉国家骑士头衔。

　　2020年，99岁的周镜球刚过完生日，在温哥华去世。

**Canadian National Knight**

　　George Chow was honorably discharged in 1963. He received the Queen's Diamond Jubilee Medal in 2012. He was awarded the rank of Knight of the National Order of the Legion of Honour by the French government in 2015. In 2020 George died in Vancouver, the day after his 99 birthday.

第三部分　战争篇
Part Three　The Wars

## 爆破专家高登权

他的父辈是帮助加拿大修建铁路的华工。"二战"期间，他希望能加入加拿大军队，但开始并未被允许。他先是志愿在加拿大军队培训，后被转移到英国陆军，为东南亚司令部提供特殊服务。直到1944年，被告知志愿选择在东南亚服务，因为他懂当地语言，容易和东南亚居民混在一起，其实就是盟军派出的间谍。因为他急切想要参军，希望自己的努力能改变加拿大人对华人的偏见，从而有好的看法，他便自愿接受了这项危险任务。

他在136特种部队接受了强化训练，成为爆破专家。然后被派往马来西亚的丛林中。

然而"二战"结束后，加拿大政府仍然没有给予华裔投票的权利，于是曾参加过136特种部队的华裔士兵联合起来争取，最终，1947年加拿大的《排华法案》被废除，他也成为加拿大公民，拥有平等权利。

## Demolition Expert Cordon Quan

Cordon Quan's parents were Chinese laborers who helped build railways in Canada. During World War Ⅱ, he tried to join the Canadian Army, but was not allowed. He volunteered to be trained in the Canadian Army before transferred to the British Army to provide special service to the Southeast Asia Command. Until 1944, he was chosen to serve in Southeast Asia as he knew the local language and could easily go with Southeast Asian residents. In fact, he was a spy sent by the Allied forces. Because he was eager to join the army and hoped that his efforts would change Canadians' prejudice against the Chinese, he voluntarily accepted this dangerous task.

He received intensive training in the 136 Special Section to become a demolition specialist and was then sent to the jungles of Malaysia.

However, after World War Ⅱ, the Canadian government still did not grant Chinese Canadians the right to vote. The Chinese Canadians who had participated in the 136 Special Forces united to fight for the right. In 1947, Canada's "Chinese Exclusion Act" was eventually repealed, and Cordon Quan became a Canadian citizen with equal rights to the other citizens.

◉《郑兆根——获得大英帝国勋章》 马倩芸 画
*William Bill Gun Chong—Awarded the Order of the British Empire* by Annissa Ma

第三部分　战争篇
Part Three　The Wars

**郑兆根——获得大英帝国勋章**

他于1911年出生在卑诗省温哥华市。他几乎没有接受过正规教育，参战之前，他是一名厨师和管家。

1941年日本入侵中国时，他正在中国香港。他自愿为英国军事情报局的英军服务团MI-9服务，代号Agent50。

1942—1945年，他扮成乞丐，经常每天步行30英里，他的手杖里藏着药品和文件。他的主要任务是将医疗用品走私到日军占领区；他也把盟军飞行员偷渡回去；他曾被日军抓获三次，但每次都得以逃生。

他是唯一获得大英帝国勋章的华裔加拿大人，获得了英国授予非英国公民的最高荣誉。

**William Bill Gun Chong—Awarded the Order of the British Empire**

He was born in Vancouver, British Columbia in 1911. He had little formal education and was employed as a cook and houseboy.

Chong was visiting Hong Kong when Japan invaded it in 1941. He volunteered for the British Army Aid Group, a paramilitary unit of MI9, known as Agent 50.

Between 1942 and 1945, he dressed as a beggar and traveled on foot, often walking 30 miles per day, with medicines and documents hidden in his walking cane. Chong's main tasks were to smuggle medical supplies into Japanese-occupied areas. He also smuggled Allied aviators out. He had been captured by the Japanese three times, but every time he escaped.

He was the only Chinese Canadian to be awarded the British Empire Medal, the highest honor that awarded to a non-British citizen by the Birtish.

◉《咖啡馆老板》
*Cafe Owner*

吴鸣玥 画
by Thelia Wu

**咖啡馆老板**

"二战"结束后,郑兆根回到加拿大,在温哥华经营一家咖啡馆,2006 年离世。值此 2014 年亚裔传统月之际,加拿大移民局网站介绍了他参加"二战"的故事。

**Cafe Owner**

After the war, Chong returned to Canada and operated a cafe in Vancouver. He died in 2006. On the occasion of Asian Heritage Month in 2014, the Canada Citizenship and Immigration Services featured Chong's story of his involvement in World War Ⅱ on the website.

(译文 / 殷思齐 责编 / 王瑾)

# 第四部分　融入篇
# PART FOUR
# INTEGRATION

# 第二十章 美加百年杰出华人

## Chapter 20  Centurial Outstanding Chinese in the United States and Canada

自1785年3名中国水手随"帕拉斯号"抵达美国,到1947年的160的年间,三代华人为美国的建设和发展做出了巨大贡献,也涌现出许多杰出华人。他们中第一代华人有百余人参加过南北战争、北极探险以及在没有现代汽车和电动工具的时代成为修建铁路的主力军,为美国建国后的第一个百年崛起做出了不可磨灭的贡献;第二代华人参加了第一次世界大战、发明了水上飞机、担任波音飞机公司第一任航空工程师、改进研发出B&W-C型水上飞机;第三代华人,有20%参加了第二次世界大战,并成为美国各族裔中参战人数比例最多、捐款比例最大的族群。

由于篇幅限制,本章手绘内容仅呈现少部分三代华人的代表。

Since three Chinese sailors arrived in the United States on the merchant vessel "Pallas" in 1785, three generations of Chinese Americans had made significant contributions to the construction and development of the United States, and many outstanding Chinese Americans have emerged during the 160 years that was from 1785-1947. Among them, over a hundred first-generation Chinese people participated in the Civil War, Arctic exploration, and became the main force in building railways in an ear without modern cars and electric tools, making indelible contributions to the rise of America in its first century after independence; the second generation of Chinese Americans participated in World War I, invented seaplanes, served as Boeing's first aviation engineer and improved and developed the B&W-C seaplane; the third generation of Chinese Americans, 20% of whom participated in World War II and became the ethnic group with the highest proportion of participants and donations among the society in the United States.

As the length limit, this chapter only presents a small portion of the representatives of the three generations of Chinese Americans in hand-drawn content.

第四部分　融入篇
Part Four　Integration

◎《梅彩逎》
*Moy Toy Ni*

贾佳茵　画
by Kaela Jia

**梅彩逎——从华工到百万富翁**

梅彩逎出生于广东台山县瑞芬锦屏村，1880 年他 18 岁时，买了一个纸儿子（"Son of Paper"）身份来到美国，通过辛勤努力，他在美国建造了全美最大的中餐馆，创立了密尔沃基最成功的贸易公司，并成为一名百万富翁。

梅彩逎被称为 20 世纪美国最成功的中国商人。

**Moy Toy Ni—From Chinese Worker to Millionaire**

Moy Toy Ni was born in Jinping Village, Ruifen, Taishan County, Guangdong. In 1880 at 18, he purchased some documents and came to the United States as a "Paper Son". Through hard work, he built the largest Chinese restaurant in the United States, founded Milwaukee's most successful trading company, and became a millionaire.

Moy Toy Ni was known as the most successful Chinese businessman in the United States in the 20th century.

◉《最豪华的中国餐厅》　　　　　　　　　　　　　　　　　黄嘉怡　画
　　*The Most Luxurious Chinese Restaurant*　　　　　　　　　by Olia Huang

第四部分 融入篇
Part Four  Integration

**最豪华的中国餐厅**

图为梅彩逎 1913 年建造的密尔沃基市托伊大厦。它被称为那个年代美国最大和最豪华的中国餐厅。1920—1930 年,托伊大厦是密尔沃基大众娱乐的场所,其有六层楼,其中一楼有 460 个座位、剧院和影院;二楼有乐队和宴会厅;三楼有舞台和台球厅;四楼是棋牌活动室;五楼和六楼是办公区和员工宿舍区。因与当时政府有冲突被拆毁,该建筑于 1937 年改为停车场。

**The Most Luxurious Chinese Restaurant**

The image shows the Toy Building in Milwaukee, built by Moy Toy Ni in 1913. It was considered the largest and most luxurious Chinese restaurant in the United States of that era. From 1920 to 1930, the Toy Building was the place for entertainment in Milwaukee. It had six floors. There were theaters with 460 seats on the first floor; a band and ballroom on the second floor; A stage and billiards hall on the third floor. The fourth floor was the chess and card activity room; the fifth and sixth floors were the office area and the staff dormitory area. The building was demolished in 1937 and converted into a parking lot due to the conflicts with the then government.

◎《落叶归根》　　　　　　　　　　　　　　　　　　　贾佳茵　画
　Going Home　　　　　　　　　　　　　　　　　　　by Kaela Jia

## 落叶归根

1946年，梅彩逎86岁时，决定落叶归根。图为托伊大厦员工们为他举办的欢送晚宴。此后他一直待在广州，直到1955年去世，享年95岁。

## Going Home

In 1946, at the age of 86, Moy Toy Ni decided to return to his motherland, China. The Toy Building staff held a farewell dinner for him. After that, he stayed in Guangzhou until he died at 95 in 1955.

第四部分　融入篇
Part Four　Integration

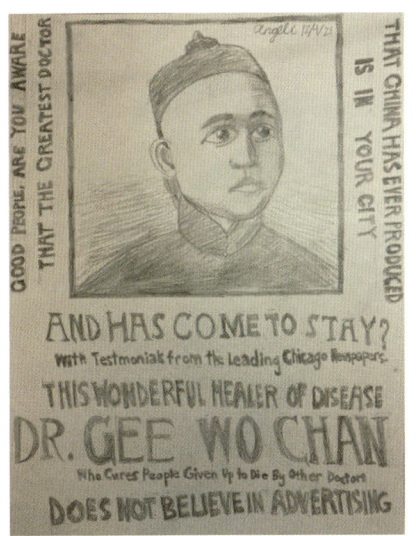

◉《中医陈》
*CMP Chan*

宿佳博　画
by Angeli Su

## 中医陈

　　美国威斯康星州密尔沃基市是很多有影响力的华裔美籍人士成功创业的所在地，其中包括医生。据《密尔沃基华人史记》一书介绍，陈医生于1894年搬到密尔沃基，此前他曾通过华美展览公司融资筹划了1893年芝加哥世博会上的中国展厅。该博览会吸引了多达2700万名游客（超过美国当时人口的一半）前来参观中国展厅。此次展出使美国人首次有机会观赏到中国戏剧、宗教、建筑，以及其他包括舞蹈在内的中国文化。展览结束后陈医生留在了密尔沃基，他在市中心经营了一所诊所，行医多年。

## CMP Chan

　　Milwaukee, Wisconsin, USA, is home to many successful businesses by some influential Chinese-Americans, including Dr. Gee Wo Chan. According to the book *The History of the Chinese in Milwaukee*, Dr. Chan moved to Milwaukee in 1894. Before that, he collected funds and planned for the China showroom at the 1893 Chicago World's Fair. The expo attracted as many as 27 million visitors (more than half of the US population at the time) to visit the Chinese showroom. The exhibition provides Americans with the first opportunity to watch the opera religious architecture dance, and other culture from China. Dr. Chan stayed in Milwaukee after the exhibition, where he ran a clinic in the city center and practiced medicine for many years.

◉《清政府留美幼童》　　　　　　　　　　　　　　　　　　张蕴涵　画
*Children Sent by the Qing Government to the US*　　　by Yunhan Zhang

**清政府留美幼童**

1868年初，近代中国留美第一人容闳向清政府提出他的留学教育计划：选派少年出国留学，先以120名做实验，每年派30人，4年完成；限12—15岁的少年，学习期限15年；在美国设立留学生事务所，设正、副监督官，管理留学生的学习和生活；从海关收入中拨出一定的经费，作为留学生的费用。1870年清政府批准该计划。1872年8月，首批30名幼童留学生赴美，到1880年，共有50多名幼童进入美国著名大学学习，在学成回国的学生中，有"中国铁路之父"詹天佑、物理学家周培源、建筑学家梁思成、气象学家竺可桢等；而留在美国的容揆获职中国驻美公使参赞；谭耀勋获职中国总领馆；李恩富则成为首位在美国出版图书的亚裔作者，他一直用演讲和书写的方式为华人争取平等权益。

图为1872年9月，首批来美的幼童留学生合影。

第四部分　融入篇
Part Four　Integration

**Children Sent by the Qing Government to the US**

At the beginning of 1868, Yung Wing (Rong Hong), the first person in modern China to study in the United States, proposed to the Qing government an education plan: sending some young people to study abroad. The first trial included 120 people, 30 people each year within 4 years; They were boys only and aged 12—15; They should for a study 15 years; An international student office should be set up in the US, with a supervisor and deputy supervisor to supervice the study and life of international students; Funding from the customs revenue was used to sponsor the international students. The Qing government approved the plan in 1870. In August 1872, the first 30 young Chinese students went to the US. By 1880, more than 50 young children had entered some well-know universities in the US. Among the students who returned home after graduation was the father of the railway, Zhan Tianyou, the physicist Peiyuan Zhou, the architect Sicheng Liang, the meteorologist Kezhen Zhu, etc. Kui Rong, who stayed in the US, was appointed as the Chinese Minister-Counselor in the United State. Yaoxun Tan was appointed as the Chinese Consulate General. Li Enfu became the first Asian author to publish a book in the US.

The picture above shows the first group of young Chinese students who came to study in the US in September 1872.

◎《北极探险》  邓依然 画
*Arctic Expedition*  by Melissa Deng

## 林通盛——北极探险

1879年，纽约报业大亨本内特（James Gordon Bennett Jr.）和美国海军决定赞助一次美国北极探险（the US Arctic Expedition）。

林通盛是船长亲自从旧金山唐人街招来的炊事兵。那年林通盛不到20岁。

图为探险队员在北极逃生的场面。

## Tongsheng Lin—Arctic Expedition

In 1879, New York newspaper tycoon James Gordon Bennett Jr. and the US Navy decided to sponsor the US Arctic Expedition.

Tongsheng Lin was a cook recruited from Chinatown in San Francisco by the captain. Lin Tongsheng was no more than 20 years old that year.

The image shows the expedition team escaping in the Arctic.

## 第四部分　融入篇
## Part Four　Integration

◎《幸存回家》　　　　　　　　　　　　　　　　　李炳毅　画
　Surviving and Going Home　　　　　　　　　　by Bingyi Li

## 幸存回家

1881年冬,"珍妮特号"幸存者中的六人合影,后排左一是林通盛。

## Surviving and Going Home

In the winter of 1881, six Janet survivors took a group photo. The first from the left in the back row was Tongsheng Lin.

100 Years of Chinese Immigration in the United States and Canada

◉《获得勇敢奖》　　　　　　　　　　　　　　　　李炳毅　画
　　*Get Bravery Award*　　　　　　　　　　　　　　by Bingyi Li

第四部分 融入篇
Part Four　Integration

**获得勇敢奖**

1890年，美国国会通过法案，向所有"珍妮特号"上的探险队员颁发国会金质或银质奖章。林通盛荣获美国国会颁发的银质奖章一枚。

1892年12月，林通盛收到了这枚国会颁发的银质奖章，这是美国历史上华人第一次荣获勇敢奖。

**Get Bravery Award**

In 1890, the US Congress passed a bill to award the Congressional Gold or Silver Medal to all members of the Janet expedition. Lin Tongsheng was awarded a Silver Medal.

In December 1892, Tongsheng Lin received the silver medal from the Congress. It was the first time in American history that a Chinese had won a Brave Award.

◉ 《梁亚娣》  邹安琪 画
*Tye Leung Schulze*  by Angela Zou

## 梁亚娣

她出生在美国。1912年5月19日，她成为首位行使总统选举权的女性，比美国白人女性享有总统选举投票权提前了8年。当时美媒称，梁亚娣投票选总统，是女性完全解放的现代运动！

## Tye Leung Schulze

Tye Leung Schulze was born in America. On May 19, 1912, she became the first woman to exercise the right to vote for president, eight years before white American women had the right to vote. At that time, the US media said that Tye Leung Schulze's vote for president indicated a modern movement for the complete liberation of women!

第四部分　融入篇
Part Four　Integration

◎《移民站翻译》　　　　　　　　　　　　　　　　邹安琪　画
　　*Immigration Station Interpreter*　　　　　　　　by Angela Zou

**移民站翻译**

　　梁亚娣是首位联邦政府雇用的在天使岛移民站当翻译的中国女性。

**Immigration Station Interpreter**

Tye Leung Schulze was the first Chinese woman employed by the federal government as an interpreter at the Angel Island immigration station.

◉《骑马游行的李美步》  邹安琪 画
  *Mabel Ping-Hua Lee in Marching*  by Angela Zou

### 骑马游行的李美步

她 3 岁时随家人来到纽约，她的父亲是纽约唐人街的一位牧师。

1912 年她 15 岁时，骑马在纽约大街上参加争取妇女选举权的大游行。

### Mabel Ping-Hua Lee in Marching

She came to New York with her family when she was 3. Her father was a pastor in New York's Chinatown.

In 1912, when she was 15 years old, she rode a horse through the streets of New York in a march for women's suffrage.

第四部分 融入篇
Part Four　Integration

◎《首位华人女博士》
*The First Chinese-American Female Ph.D.*

喻玲珑　画
by Annie Yu

**首位华人女博士**

李美步在 1917 年成为首位申请到庚子赔款奖学金的女性。

1920 年，美国宪法第十九修正案通过，全美女性被赋予合法选举权。但她作为非美国公民却没有选举权。她是哥伦比亚大学首位华人女博士。

图为 18 岁时的李美步。

**The First Chinese-American Female Ph.D.**

In 1917, Mabel Ping-Hua Lee became the first woman awarded the Boxer Indemnities Scholarship.

In 1920, the Nineteenth Amendment to the US Constitution was passed, giving women the legal right to vote. But as a non-US citizen, she did not have the right to vote. She is the first Chinese female Ph.D. at Columbia University.

The image shows Mabel Ping-Hua Lee at the age of 18.

◉《冯如——创办首家华人飞机制造厂》　　　　　　　　　　胡锦海　画
Ru Feng—Founder of the First Chinese Aircraft Factory in the US　　by Elmer Hu

## 冯如——创办首家华人飞机制造厂

1884年，冯如出生于广东恩平县，12岁时，舅舅将他带到旧金山生活、读书。18岁时，他转往纽约读机器制造专业，期间发明了抽水机和打桩机。

1902年，莱特兄弟发明了飞机，在国际上引发强烈反响。冯如游说华侨，给他凑集1000余美元。1907年秋，他办起第一家华人飞机制造公司。1908年，飞机制造出来了，他在奥克兰市的麦园进行试飞，结果失败。1909年，他在哥林达市再次试飞并获成功。他的飞机首飞2600多英尺，比莱特兄弟的首飞纪录远1700多英尺。

第四部分　融入篇
Part Four　Integration

**Ru Feng—Founder of the First Chinese Aircraft Factory in the US**

Ru Feng was born in Enping County, Guangdong, in 1884. When he was 12 years old, his uncle brought him to San Francisco to live and study. At 18, he moved to New York to study machine building, where he invented the pump and pile driver.

In 1902, the Wright brothers invented the airplane, causing a strong international response. Ru Feng lobbied the overseas Chinese people and collected more than a thousand dollars from them. In the autumn of 1907, he established the first Chinese aircraft manufacturing company. In 1908, the plane was made, but he failed in a test flight at Wheat Field in Oakland. In 1909, he made another successful test flight in Corinda. His plane flew more than 2,600 feet on the first attempt, over 1,700 feet farther than the Wright brothers' first flight record.

◎《华人飞行家》　　　　　　　　　　　　　　　　　　　　胡锦海　画
　 *Chinese Aviator*　　　　　　　　　　　　　　　　　　　by Elmer Hu

## 华人飞行家

　　三年后，冯如驾驶着新设计出的一种性能更好的飞机，参加旧金山举办的国际飞行比赛。他是举世公认的飞机设计师、制造家和飞行家。

## Chinese Aviator

　　Three years later, Ru Feng flew a newly designed aircraft with better performance. He participated in the international flying competition in San Francisco. He was known as a world-recognized aircraft designer, manufacturer and pilot.

第四部分　融入篇
Part Four　Integration

◉ 《英年早逝》　　　　　　　　　　　　　　　　　喻玲珑　画
　　*Die Young*　　　　　　　　　　　　　　　　　by Annie Yu

## 英年早逝

响应孙中山先生"航空救国"号召，冯如回中国筹建南京机场。

1912年8月，冯如在广州郊区做飞行表演时，为躲避跑道上的两个儿童，飞机失去平衡而坠落，29岁的冯如不幸身亡。

## Die Young

In response to sun Yat-sen's call to "Save the Nation by Air", Ru Feng returned to China to prepare for the construction of Nanjing Airport.

In August 1912, when Ru Feng was performing an air show in the suburbs of Guangzhou, the plane lost its balance and crashed down when trying to avoid two children on the runway. Ru Feng died at the age of 29, unfortunately.

◎《谭根——水上飞机发明人》 邓佳宜 画
Gen Tan—The Inventor of The Seaplane by Kelly Deng

第四部分　融入篇
Part Four　Integration

## 谭根——水上飞机发明人

谭根 1890 年生于旧金山。父辈是铁路华工。

他 5 岁时，莱特兄弟的飞机轰动全球。一心向往飞行的谭根进入加州奥克兰理工高中学习机械，得知广东同乡冯如在奥克兰研制飞机，他虚心向冯如请教。

冯如的飞机试飞成功时，谭根 20 岁。

1910 年，谭根担任美国飞行员助理，成为首位在美国获得国际飞行驾驶执照的华裔美国人。

在华侨的资助下，他开始尝试自己设计和建造水上飞机。

## Gen Tan—The Inventor of The Seaplane

Gen Tan was born in San Francisco in 1890. His parents were Chinese railway workers.

When he was five years old, the Wright Brothers' airplane caused a sensation in the world. Gen Tan, who yearned for flying, entered the Oakland Institute of Technology High School in California and studied machinery there. When he learned that Ru Feng, a fellow from Guangdong, was developing aircraft in Oakland. He humbly asked Ru Feng for advice.

Gen Tan was 20 years old when Feng Ru's test flight succeeded.

In 1910, Tan Fei served as a pilot assistant, becoming the first Chinese American to obtain an international pilot's license in the United States.

With the support of overseas Chinese, he began to design and build seaplanes by himself.

# 100年北美华人移民史
100 Years of Chinese Immigration in the United States and Canada

◉《万国大赛冠军》　　　　　　　　　　　　　　　　　　喻玲珑　画
　　*Championship of Nations*　　　　　　　　　　　　　　by Annie Yu

第四部分 融入篇
Part Four Integration

**万国大赛冠军**

1910年7月,谭根成功制成一种新结构的水上飞机。他把发动机安装在机头上,夺得旧金山万国飞机制造大会比赛冠军。

图为谭根在1910年加利福尼亚洛杉矶国际航空大会表演中获奖,他手握奖杯和中美两国国旗。

**Championship of Nations**

In July 1910, Gen Tan successfully made a new-structure seaplane. He installed the engine on the nose. With it he won the championship at the international airplane convention in San Francisco.

The image shows Gen Tan winning the award at the 1910 International Aviation Congress in Los Angeles, California. He was holding the trophy and the flags of China and the United States.

◉《万名观众欢呼》　　　　　　　　　　　　　　　　　　　喻玲珑　画
　*Thousands of Spectators Cheer*　　　　　　　　　　　　　by Annie Yu

第四部分　融入篇
Part Four　Integration

**万名观众欢呼**

谭根于 1912 年 4 月参加圣地亚哥举行的飞行表演，获得柯蒂斯公司颁发的银质奖杯。

1913 年，谭根受邀在夏威夷檀香山为"中华飞船公司"设计飞机，试飞成功，同时开始培训飞行员。这年 7 月，他在檀香山驾机展翅飞翔，近万名观众在地面欢呼。1925 年，他在上海发生的一次人力车事故中身亡。

图为美国著名飞机制造师、飞行家柯蒂斯与谭根的合影。

**Thousands of Spectators Cheer**

Tan Gen participated in the air show in San Diego in April 1912 and received a silver trophy distributed by Curtiss.

In 1913, Gen Tan was invited to design an aircraft for the "China Spaceship Company" in Honolulu, Hawaii. The test flight was successful, and almost the same time he began to train pilots. In July this year, Tan flew in Honolulu, and nearly 10,000 spectators cheered on the ground. In 1925, he died in a rickshaw accident in Shanghai.

This is a image of Gen Tan with the famous American aircraft manufacturer and aviator Curtis.

# 100年北美华人移民史
100 Years of Chinese Immigration in the United States and Canada

◎《伍冰枝》　　　　　　　　　　　　　　　　喻玲珑　画
*Adrienne Clarkson*　　　　　　　　　　　　　*by Annie Yu*

第四部分　融入篇
Part Four　Integration

**伍冰枝——首位华裔总督**

　　伍冰枝1939年生于香港，祖籍广东台山。父亲是在澳大利亚出生的第一代华人。1942年，年仅3岁的伍冰枝跟随父母，以难民身份撤离香港，来到加拿大首都渥太华。

　　图为1999年，60岁的伍冰枝就任加拿大第26任总督，成为加拿大历史上的首位华裔总督。

**Adrienne Clarkson—The First Chinese Governor-General of Canada**

　　Bingzhi Wu, known as Adrienne Clarkson, was born in Hong Kong in 1939. Her ancestral home was Taishan, Guangdong. Her father was a first-generation Chinese born in Australia. In 1942, Adrienne Clarkson who was only three years old, followed his parents and evacuated Hong Kong as a refugee to Ottawa, the capital of Canada.

　　The image shows that in 1999, 60-year-old Adrienne Clarkson became the 26th Governor-General of Canada. She was the first Chinese Governor-General in Canadian history.

◉ 《战争难民》
War Refugees

吴鸣玥　画
by Thelia Wu

**战争难民**

图为伍冰枝（前排中）与邻家孩子一起在渥太华家中后院玩耍。右一是其哥哥伍卫权。

**War Refugees**

Adrienne Clarkson (middle in the front row) was playing with the neighbor children in the backyard of her home in Ottawa. The first from the right was her elder brother Weiquan Wu.

第四部分 融入篇
Part Four　Integration

◎《参政》　　　　　　　　　　　　　　　　　　　钟琪励　画
　Political Participation　　　　　　　　　　　　　by Qili Zhong

**参政**

　　伍冰枝哥哥的妻子利德蕙博士，成为加拿大历史上第一位亚裔参议员。图为利德蕙与丈夫伍卫权医生共同出席会议。

**Political Participation**

　　Adrienne Clarkson's brother married Vivienne Lee, who became a Asia Senator in the Canadian history.

　　The image is Vivienne Lee and her husband, presenting at a meeting.

◉《华裔国会议员邓天华》 李炳毅 画
*Chinese-American Congressman Douglas Jung* by Bingyi Li

第四部分 融入篇
Part Four  Integration

## 华裔国会议员邓天华

邓天华1924年在卑诗省维多利亚市出生，父辈是早年的太平洋铁路华工。他的英文名字道格拉斯来自维多利亚州道格拉斯街。他生长在加拿大极度反华的年代，那时华人不能从事医药和法律行业，甚至不允许在某些地段买房子。

1946年2月，作为"二战"中的特种部队士兵，邓天华从澳大利亚回到加拿大，他受到英雄式的欢迎。加拿大主流社会渐渐发现，华人也是勇敢而且捍卫自由的群体。退役后，他前往大学深造，攻读法律学位，1953年，他获得文学学士和法律学士学位，1954年拿到律师执业牌照，成为首位出庭的加拿大华人律师。1957年郑天华当选加拿大首位华裔国会议员。

## Chinese-American Congressman Douglas Jung

Douglas Jung, the son of an early Chinese Pacific Railroad worker, was born in Victoria, British Columbia 1924. His English name, Douglas, comes from Douglas Street, Victoria. He grew up in an era when Canada was extremely hostile toChinese. At that time, Chinese people were not allowed to work in the medical and legal professions. They were not even allowed to buy a house in some areas.

In February 1946, as a special forces soldier in World War II, Douglas Jung returned to Canada from Australia. He was greeted as a hero. The mainstream society in Canada gradually found that the Chinese are also a group of people who was brave and could defend freedom. Retiring from the military, he went to study law in the University of British Columbia. In 1953, he obtained a Bachelor of Arts and a Bachelor of Laws. In 1954, he obtained a lawyer's license and became the first Canadian Chinese lawyer to appear in court. In 1957, Douglas Jung was elected Canada's first Chinese-born member of parliament.

100 Years of Chinese Immigration in the United States and Canada

◎《邓天华大楼》　　　　　　　　　　　　　　　　　　　　邓佳宜　画
　 *Deng Tianhua Building*　　　　　　　　　　　　　　　　　by Kelly Deng

第四部分 融入篇
Part Four　Integration

## 邓天华大楼

邓天华曾担任加拿大驻联合国代表。他在1990年获加拿大勋章，1997年获卑诗省勋章及加拿大军人勋章。

邓天华于2002年与世长辞，2007年联邦政府宣布位于温哥华的一栋联邦政府大楼命名为"邓天华大楼"。

## Deng Tianhua Building

Douglas Jung served as Canada's representative to the United Nations. He was awarded the Order of Canada in 1990, the Order of British Columbia and the Order of the Canadian Military in 1997.

Douglas Jung passed away in 2002. In 2007, the federal government announced that a federal building in Vancouver was named after Douglas Jung.

100 Years of Chinese Immigration in the United States and Canada

◎《丁龙》　　　　　　　　　　　　　　　　　　　　　　吴雨芮　画
　Dean Lung　　　　　　　　　　　　　　　　　　　　　by Sherry Wu

第四部分　融入篇
Part Four　Integration

## 丁龙——汉语文化讲座创始人

丁龙于1858年出生在广东，18岁时入境美国。他先到旧金山，在奥克兰市市长贺拉斯·沃尔普·卡朋蒂埃家里当佣工，后跟随雇主到纽约，成为卡朋蒂埃的家庭主管。1901年丁龙写信给哥伦比亚大学校长塞斯·洛，将积蓄12000美元捐给哥伦比亚大学从事汉学研究。雇主卡朋蒂埃为了纪念丁龙，总共捐了226000美元成立汉学讲座。

1902年3月，丁龙基金会举办一系列汉学演讲，首先邀请到剑桥大学汉学教授、威妥玛拼音的共同发明人翟理斯到哥伦比亚大学作了两场演讲，题目分别是"中国语文"与"中文图书"。

1905年，丁龙回到故乡娶妻生子。

## Dean Lung—Founder of Chinese Culture Lecture

Dean Lung was born in Guangdong in 1858, and entered the United States at 18. He first went to San Francisco, where he worked as a servant in the house of Oakland Mayor Horace Volpe Carpentier. Later, he followed his master to New York, where he became Carpentier's family supervisor. In 1901, Dean Lung wrote to Seth Lowe, the President of Columbia University, donating $12,000 form his savings to Columbia for Sinology research. His employer, Carpentier, donated a total of $226,000 to set up Sinology Lectures in honor of Ding Long.

In March 1902, the first series of talks on sinology organized by the Dean Lung Foundation, invited Herbert Allen Giles to give two lecture at Columbia. Giles was a professor of sinology at Cambridge University and the co-inventor of Wade-Giles, a romanization system for Mandarin Chinese. He talked on the topics of "Chinese Language" and "Chinese Books".

In 1905, he returned to his hometown to marry and have children.

◉《王清福》
Wong Chin Foo

吴雨芮 画
by Sherry Wu

**华文报纸创始人王清福**

王清福是美国华裔报人，民权领袖。1847年出生于中国山东即墨，少年时代跟随美国传教士夫妇来到美国东岸，先后在华盛顿的哥伦比亚学院、宾夕法尼亚的路易斯伯格学院就读。1883年，王清福在纽约创办了美国的第一份华文报纸《华洋新报》。

1884年，王清福在纽约组织了华人聚会，建议组建华人参政联盟。

1892年9月1日，美国东部的华人在纽约市举行大会，讨论如何应对排华的吉利法案。"美国华人平等权利联盟"在大会上宣告组成，王清福被推举为联盟的秘书长。

1893年1月，王清福作为"美国华人平等权利联盟"的代表前往美国国会出席听证会，就《排华法案》做证。

1897年秋，王清福再次发动了向美国国会请愿废除《排华法案》并争取华人投票权的运动。此时，王清福已担任"美国华人平等权利联盟"主席。

1898年，王清福借赴中国香港为美国的奥马哈世博会组织中国展团之机，回到家乡，因心脏病发作离世。

图为1879年维权先驱王清福通过《美华时报》下战书，要用算盘和筷子与丹尼斯公开辩论。

第四部分　融入篇

Part Four　Integration

**Founder of Chinese Newspaper, Wong Chin Foo**

Wong Chin Foo was a Chinese American journalist and civil rights leader. Born in Jimo, Shandong, China in 1847, he followed an American missionary couple to the United States east coast when he was a boy. He studied at Columbian College in Washington and later at University at Lewisburg in Pennsylvania. In 1883, Wong Chin Foo founded the first Chinese-language newspaper of the United States, *The Chinese American Huayang Xinbao*, in New York City.

In 1884, Wong Chin Foo organized a Chinese gathering in New York and suggested the formation of a Chinese political alliance.

On September 1, 1892, the Chinese in the eastern United States held a convention in New York City to discuss how to deal with the Chinese Exclusion Act. The "American Chinese Equal Rights Alliance" was announced then, and Wong Chin Foo was elected as the alliance's secretary-general.

In January 1893, Wong Chin Foo, as a representative of the "American Chinese Equal Rights Alliance," went to the US Congress to attend a hearing to testify on the "Chinese Exclusion Act".

In the autumn of 1897, Wong Chin Foo once again launched a campaign to petition the US Congress to repeal the *Chinese Exclusion Act* and to fight for the voting right of the Chinese. By then, Wong Chin Foo had already become the chairman of the American Chinese Equal Rights Alliance.

In 1898, Wong Chin Foo went to Hong Kong to help organize a Chinese pavilion in the Omaha World Expo in the United States. He returned to his hometown and died of a heart attack.

The image shows that in 1879, Wong Chin Foo, a pioneer of civil rights, submitted a battle letter through the US and *China Times*. He used an abacus and chopsticks to debate with anti-Chinese activist Denis Kearney openly.

◎《李恩富——呼吁中国人必须留下》
Lee Yen Fu—Call on the Chinese to Stay

刘阅辰　画
by Scarlett Liu

### 李恩富——呼吁中国人必须留下

李恩富出生于广东。1872年，12岁的他成为第二批清政府的留美幼童，毕业于耶鲁大学。在他大学二年级时，他在演讲、辩论等多种语言文字比赛中，展示出超人的语言天赋。他曾出版《我的中国童年》，是首位在美国出版图书的华裔。

他曾为许多美国报纸工作。他四处发表演说，准确剖析中国华工问题，强烈谴责反华运动。李恩富最有名的论文题目是"中国人必须留下"，质疑当时的政府没有秉承美国先父自由平等的开国理念！

1890年，为了把反对排华的声音传递到美国西部，他踏上西部演讲之旅，他想唤醒华人为自己的平等权利而努力，想帮助华工成立中国劳工工会，但在一群没有受过西式教育的华人面前他失败了。

1917年，他因改写美国国歌《星条旗》而受到关注。

1938年，李恩富在中国香港辞世。

图为正值美国《排华法案》出台第五年，李恩富与当地望族——新英格兰的伊丽莎白小姐结婚，并育有两个女儿。

第四部分　融入篇
Part Four　Integration

**Lee Yen Fu—Call on the Chinese to Stay**

Lee Yen Fu was born in Guangdong. In 1872, when he was 12 years old, he became the second group of young children sent by the Qing government to study in the United States. He graduated from Yale University. In his sophomore year, he showed extraordinary language talent in speech, debate and other multi-language competitions. He published the book *When I Was a Boy in China* and became the first Chinese American to publish a book in the United States.

Lee Yen Fu worked for many American newspapers. He delivered speeches everywhere, accurately analyzing the issue of Chinese laborers in US, and strongly condemning the anti-China movement. Lee Yen Fu's most famous thesis was *The Chinese Must Stay*, questioning the government not adhering to the founding concept of freedom and equality by the American father!

In 1890, to spread the voice against the anti-Chinese movement to Western America, he embarked on a speaking tour in the West. He wanted to awaken the Chinese to work hard for their equal rights. He hoped to help Chinese workers to establish a Chinese labor union. However, he failed to convince the Chinese people, who had never received a Western education.

In 1917, he gained the attention from the peole for rewriting the American national anthem, "The Star-Spangled Banner."

Lee Yen Fu died in Hong Kong in 1938.

The picture shows that in the fifth year of the introduction of the *Chinese Exclusion Act* in the United States, Lee Yen Fu married a girl from a locally prominent family, Miss Elizabeth of New England, and had two daughters.

◎《学英文》 祝云姝 画
*Learning English* by Maggie Zhu

第四部分　融入篇
Part Four　Integration

## 学英文

1860年，只有16岁的陈宜禧从台山来到西雅图当筑路工。后来到一个铁路工程师家帮佣。热心的工程师夫人教他英语，工程师送他到铁路夜校学知识。

## Learning English

In 1860, Chin Gee Hee, who was only 16 years old, came to Seattle from Taishan to work as a road construction worker. Later, he worked as a domestic helper for a railway engineer. The engineer's wife kindly taught him English, and the engineer sent him to the railway night school to study.

◉ 《温尼玛卡铁路》　　　　　　　　　　　　　　　贾佳茵　画
　　*Winnemucca Tunnel*　　　　　　　　　　　　　by Kaela Jia

### 陈宜禧——新宁铁路发起人

　　陈宜禧来到温尼玛卡隧道，他升为助理工程师。一次华工营地遭袭，他立即将华工损伤情况提交国会，并得到赔偿。

　　排华期间，陈宜禧经常同政府交涉，要求保护华人、严惩肇事者，还自费聘请律师来帮助华工主张自己的权益。1889 年西雅图大火，陈宜禧发起了募捐以救济同胞，逐渐成为当地著名的侨领。1896 年，当地侨民要求清政府在西雅图设立领事馆，并推举陈宜禧为领事候选人。

　　1904 年，陈宜禧回到台山，提出建设新宁铁路的计划，并成为总办，他再次回美国动员筹到 150 万美元。经过 15 年努力，1920 年新宁铁路开通。

　　图为陈宜禧和华工一起修建的温尼玛卡铁路。

第四部分　融入篇
Part Four　Integration

**Chin Gee Hee—Founder of Xinning Railway**

Chin Gee Hee came to Winnemucca Tunnel and was promoted to assistant engineer. When a Chinese worker camp was attacked, he immediately reported the Chinese workers' injury to Congress. The workers received compensation.

During the time when the Chinese were often expelled, Chin Gee Hee often negotiated with the government. He demanded that they provide more protection for the Chinese and severely punish the perpetrators. He hired a lawyer at his own expense to help the Chinese workers claim their rights. During the seattle fire in 1889, Chin Gee Hee launched a fundraising campaign to help his compatriots. He gradually became a famous leader in the local of overseas Chinese. In 1896, local expats asked the Qing government to set up a consulate in Seattle. They nominated Chin Gee Hee as a consular candidate.

In 1904, Chin Gee Hee returned to Taishan and proposed a plan to build the Xinning Railway. He became the General Manager. He then returned to the United States to mobilize the people and family raised a $1.5 million fund. After 15 years of hard work, the Xinning Railway opened in 1920.

This image shows Chinese workers building the unparalleled Winnemucca Railroad.

（译文 / 张天阳　责编 / 卓越）

# 第二十一章　华人之友

## Chapter 21　Chinese Friends

100 Years of Chinese Immigration in the United States and Canada

　　自1785年3名华人船员随"帕拉斯号"商船抵达马里兰州至1945年，这160多年间，华人在美洲大陆这片土地上既经历了磨难，也创造了辉煌，更得到过许多族裔对他们的帮助。中国俗话说，"滴水之恩，当涌泉相报"，意为在困难时，即使受人一点小小的恩惠，以后也应当加倍报答。我们的手绘本，仅选取汉娜、傅烈秘、赛珍珠、加里森、霍尔等美国友人，他们在第一代华人移民危难之际，慷慨而真诚地伸出温暖的援手，今天华裔后代绘画他们，就是为了向他们致谢致敬！

　　Three Chinese sailors on the merchant vessel "Pallas" landed in Maryland in 1785. During the 160 years until 1945, the Chinese have experienced hardship, created wonders, and received help from many other ethnicities. As the Chinese proverb says, "The kindness of a drop of water must be rewarded by a gushing spring," meaning we would return the kindness with a lot more. Our hand drawings featured Maria, Bee, Buck, Garrison, and Hoar among others, who had provided generous and sincere help to the first generation of Chinese immigrants when they had faced adversity. The descendants of Chinese immigrants draw them out of gratitude and respect.

第四部分　融入篇
Part Four　Integration

◉《汉娜·玛丽亚》
*Hannah Maria*

贾佳茵　画
by Kaela Jia

## 汉娜·玛丽亚

　　1869年1月，中央太平洋铁路工地爆发天花瘟疫期间，施工负责人斯托尔布瑞吉夫人汉娜冒着风险，到工地为华工送水。而且在他们夫妇住的火车车厢里，也尽可能护理一些患者。

## Hannah Maria

　　Hannah Maria was James Harvey Strobridge's wife, whose husband was in charge of the Central Pacific railway construction site. During the smallpox outbreak in January 1869, she delivered water to the Chinese railroad workers despite the risk of the disease. The couple also took care of some patients in the train compartment they stayed in within their capacity.

◉《帮助生病的华工》 贾佳茵 画
　　Helping Sick Chinese Workers by Kaela Jia

**帮助生病的华工**

　　在护理患者的过程中，汉娜·玛丽亚也感染了天花。康复后，每逢出门，她总要戴着面纱。

**Helping Sick Chinese Workers**

　　Hannah Maria was infected with smallpox from patients she tended to. After her recovery, she wore a veil whenever going outside.

第四部分 融入篇
Part Four　Integration

◉《傅烈秘》
*Frederick A. Bee*

祝云姝　画
by Maggie Zhu

## 傅烈秘——清政府雇用领事

傅烈秘的祖辈是英格兰和苏格兰移民。由于傅烈秘律师为华人挺身而出，屡次在国会做证伸张正义，《排华法案》出台前期，清政府于旧金山设立总领事馆之初，正式雇用他为领事。傅烈秘为华人服务了14年，1892年在执行公务时突然离世。在教堂举行追思仪式后，有125辆马车陪送他到墓地，其中，百余辆车上下来的都是华人。他是历史上中国驻旧金山总领事馆唯一的美国籍中国领事。此后，中国再没雇用过白人领事。世间已无傅烈秘。

## Frederick A. Bee—Qing Government Hired Consul

Frederick A. Bee was a descendant of England and Scotland. Out of righteousness, he often testified at Congress for the right of Chinese immigrants. Due to these activities. In the early years when the *Chinese Exclusion Act* was released, the Qing dynasty appointed him officially as a consul when the Chinese general consulate opened in San Francisco. Bee worked there for 14 years until he died suddenly when still on duty in 1892. After the memorial ceremony at the church, 125 carriages followed his coffin to the cemetery, among which more than 100 carriages carried with the Chinese attendees. He was the only American that has ever worked at a Chinese consulate as a consul. Since then, no white man has been hired as the consul. There will never be another Bee in the world.

◉《赛珍珠》
*Pearl S. Buck*

吴雨芮　画
by Sherry Wu

**赛珍珠——沟通东西方的文化桥梁**

　　1892年，赛珍珠出生4个月后，即被父母带到中国镇江，其父母在中国传教18年。赛珍珠总共在中国生活40年。作为以中文为母语的美国女作家，她曾写下了描写中国农民生活的长篇小说《大地》，1932年其凭借小说获得普利策小说奖，并在1938年以此获得美国历史上第三个诺贝尔文学奖。

　　1934年，赛珍珠告别了中国，回美国定居。1942年3月，应美国之音、英国BBC电台之邀，她用汉语广播向中国介绍美国人民如何理解支持中国人民的抗日战争。1943年7月，赛珍珠邀请中美作家、学者到她在宾夕法尼亚州的寓所聚会，讨论中美关系。会后，就支持中国抗日等问题，向美国政府发起声势浩大的宣传。

　　赛珍珠还动员1000名美国妇女捐款数十万美元，支持中国抗战。1942年8月15日，宋美龄为此写信感谢赛珍珠。她还动员美国名流和民众，为中国人民写声援信，声援信达上万封，其中有9个州的州长；她也曾热情帮助过老舍、胡适、林语堂等许多中国文化名人，曾安排并主持王莹在白宫的抗日宣传演出，请总统等美国政要观看。

　　1973年3月6日，赛珍珠去世。美国总统尼克松称赞她是一座沟通东西方文明的桥梁。

# 第四部分 融入篇
## Part Four Integration

**Pearl S. Buck—A Cultural Bridge Between East and West**

In 1892 Buck's parents took four months old Buck with them to Zhenjiang, China and started their 18-year missionary. Buck lived in China for 40 years and became an American woman writer, Chinese as her mother tongue. She wrote the novel *The Good Earth*, which described the lives of Chinese farmers. The book won her the Pulitzer prize in 1932 and the Nobel prize in literature in 1938, which was the third Nobel prize in literature for the US

Buck left China and settled in the US in 1934. At the invitation of BBC and Voice of America in March 1942, she spoke in Chinese and told Chinese people how the Americans understood the anti-Japanese War and how they supported the Chinese people. In July 1943, Buck invited some writers and scholars-both Chinese and American-to gather at her apartment in Pennsylvania to discuss the China-US relations. After the gathering, the group started to promote the idea of supporting China's war against Japan's invasion the American government.

Buck also mobilized one thousand American women to donate hundreds of thousands of US dollars to support China's war against Japan. On August 15, 1942, Meiling Song wrote a letter expressing gratitude towards Buck specifically. In addition, Buck inspired the American celebrities and the general public. They wrote nearly ten thousand letters to support Chinese people, including letters from the govenors of nine states. She also helped many Chinese intellectuals enthusiastically, including Lao She, Shi Hu and Yutang Lin. Additionally, she arranged and hosted Ying Wang's performance, which tried to promote the war again Japan, in front of the president and other politicians at the White House.

Buck passed away on March 6, 1973. President Nixon praised her as a bridge between the eastern and western civilizations.

◉《小威廉·劳埃德·加里森》
William Lioyd Garrison JR.

吴雨芮　画
by Sherry Wu

**小威廉·劳埃德·加里森——国会演讲反对排华**

他于1838年出生在波士顿，是单一税制、自由贸易、妇女选举权和废除《排华法案》的杰出倡导者。小威廉·劳埃德·加里森的父亲是美国著名的废奴主义者，并于1831年在波士顿创立了反奴隶制报纸《解放者》。

1882年，美国国会违背"人人平等"的原则，通过了禁止华人入境的《排华法案》。这是美国第一个基于族裔限制移民的法案。1902年国会准备无限期延长《排华法案》。

1900年美国只有9万华人，华人社区处于排华浪潮的困难时期。

1902年，时年64岁的加里森发表演讲，尖锐地指出，排华的实质是政客需要拉拢西海岸的工会获得其选票。同时，针对排华势力对华人的6大罪名，加里森这样回复：（1）华人不融入美国吗？你们根本就没打算与华人套近乎，迫害只能让华人更加团结。（2）华人攒钱寄回家？爱家庭是高尚品格，你们不也都寄钱回家吗？（3）华人抢美国人饭碗？当年修铁路时，美国急需劳动力，华人才来的。（4）华人节俭？林肯说过，节俭是新英格兰地区的美德。（5）华人脏乱差，抱团？这是偏见不允许他们改善生活条件，人家习惯相同、语言相同，又受迫害，当然要抱团取暖。（6）唐人街有妓女？如果把两万白人放在一起，排除女眷，相比之下，唐人街简直就是模范城了。

第四部分　融入篇
Part Four　Integration

## William Lloyd Garrison JR.—Congressional Speaker Against Chinese Exclusion

Garrison Jr. was born in Boston in 1838. He was an outstanding advocate for single tax system, free trade, woman's voting rights, and the abolition of the *Chinese Exclusion Act*. Garrison Jr.'s father was an eminent abolitionist who founded the anti-slavery newspaper "The Liberator" in Boston in 1831.

In 1882, despite the violation of the principle that all men are equal, the US Congress enacted the *Chinese Exclusion Act* to prohibit Chinese immigration. It was the first law in US history that restricted immigration based on ethnicity. In 1902 Congress was getting ready to extend the Act indefinitely.

With merely 90,000 Chinese in the US in 1900, the Chinese community was caught in a difficult time became of the exclusion.

In 1902, 64 year old Garrison pointed out poignantly in his speech that the essence of the exclusion of Chinese people was the need to gain votes from the unions along the west coast. He also rebutted the six accusations of the Chinese by saying the following: 1) "The Chinese were not integrated in America" You did not even have the intention to interact with them. Persecution to the Chinese would only lead to a more united group. 2) "The Chinese remit money home" Love of one's own family was a noble character. Didn't you all remit money home too? 3) "The Chinese have seized the Americans' jobs" The Chinese came to the US when labor for railway construction was urgently needed. 4) "The Chinese were mean" Lincoln once said that frugality was a virtue in New England. 5) "The Chinese were unclean, messy, and not communicate with other group" That was because prejudice got in the way of improving their living conditions. With similar habits, language and persecution, of course they would stick together. 6) "There were prostitutes live in the China town" If you put together 20,000 male white and compare it to the Chinatown, it would be a model town.

◉《乔治·弗里斯比·霍尔》
George Frisbie Hoar

吴雨芮 画
by Sherry Wu

## 乔治·弗里斯比·霍尔——唯一投反对票的议员

1826年，霍尔出生于马萨诸塞州康科德，1846年毕业于哈佛大学法律专业。共和党成立不久他就加入了，并于1877—1904年，代表马萨诸塞州，先是担任四届众议院议员，后任职美国参议院，直到他在第五个任期内的1904年去世。

他长期以来被认为是反对政治腐败的斗士，他既为非裔美国人和美洲原住民的权利而竞选，也坚定地抗击《排华法案》直至暮年。

1902年国会讨论无限期延长《排华法案》时，积极主张排华的俄勒冈共和党参议员约翰·H. 米歇尔（John H. Michell, 1835—1905）发起议案，不仅要加强排华力度，还要把排华法适用的地域从美国本土扩大到所有美国控制的领地，包括菲律宾、夏威夷，甚至要把在这些领地出生的华人也赶走。

霍尔参议员明知不可能改变结果，但他坚决抗议。他说每个人都有其权利，该权利应该取决于其个体价值，而不应取决于肤色或种族，并且所有种族、所有肤色、所有国籍的人都和其他族裔平起平坐。"就算我孤军奋战，也必须将我的抗议记录在案。"《排华法案》延期议案最终以76比1通过。

霍尔是唯一投反对票的议员。

第四部分　融入篇
Part Four　Integration

◉《乔治·弗里斯比·霍尔》
*George Frisbie Hoar*

林之雅　画
by Candice Lin

**George Frisbie Hoar—The Only Congressman Who Voted Against**

Hoar was born in Concord, Massachusetts, 1826 and graduated from Harvard Law School in 1846. Shortly after the Republic party was formed, he joined it and represented Massachusetts as a congressman for four terms. Then, he had been a senator until he passed away in 1904 while he was in his fifth term.

When the Congress discussed extending the *Chinese Exclusion Act* indefinitely in 1902, John H. Michell (1835—1905), an Oregon senator, was and a strong proponent of Chinese exclusion. He initiated the motions, not just to intensify anti-Chinese actions, but also extend the application of the Act from US mainland to all other aress goverred by the US, which this included Philippine and Hawaii. He ever proposed ther all the Chinese born there should be driven out.

Senator Hoar was vehemently against the motions even though he knew he could not change the final outcome. He stated that everyone had the human rights, with value decided by the person themself rather than skin color or ethnicity. People who felt equal to all others could have any ethnicity, color, or nationality. "Even if I had to fight alone, my vote must be recorded." The motion to extend the *Chinese Exclusion Act* was eventually passed with 76 yeas and one nay.

Hoar was the only senator who cast a nay vote.

◉《拉里·迪利奥》  吴雨芮 画
*Larry DeLeeuw*  by Sherry Wu

第四部分　融入篇
Part Four　Integration

### 拉里·迪利奥——保护华人墓地

内华达州的拉夫洛克镇曾是铁路沿线重要的驿站和华人的聚居区。小镇的外围有座山叫寞山，那里有一处华人墓地。每个墓都没有标记，没有姓名，没有生卒年月日，只有墓地附近竖立的铁轨枕木见证了他们和铁路的故事。

拉里·迪利奥从加州搬到拉夫洛克镇后，认识了镇上唯一的华人后裔弗兰克·张，他们成为朋友后，迪利奥开始对华人历史产生兴趣。

迪利奥主动在小镇附近的华工墓地搭建了金属围栏，还按祭祀习俗，砌了一个烧纸用的砖池。多年来，他一直努力保护这片华人墓地。他对从中国来的自由摄影师李炬说："哪天你们来这里，哪天就是清明节。"

### Larry DeLeeuw—Protector of Chinese Cemeteries

Lovelock Nevada was once a prominent rest station along the railway and the gathering place for Chinese. In Lone Mountain outside the town, there is a cemetery of Chinese people. None of the tombs have any marks, names, or dates. Only the nearby railroad sleepers bear witness to the stories between the Chinese and the railway.

After moving to Lovelock from California, Larry DeLeeuw got to know Frank Chang, the only Chinese descendant in the town. After they became friends, DeLeeuw became interested in Chinese history.

DeLeeuw built a metal fence around the cemetery. He also built and a brick fireplace for joss paper burning, one of the Chinese sacrificial customs. For years, DeLeeuw kept maintaining the cemetery. He told JuLi, a photographer from China, that "Whichever day you come, that day would always be the Tomb-sweeping Day".

◎《瑞诺青年乐队》
*Reno the Youth*

张云想　画
by Yunxiang Zhang

## 瑞诺青年乐队

2018年8月，内华达州瑞诺市的6名白人青年，感动于铁路华工的贡献，来到唐纳山顶隧道，举办了一场小型追思音乐会。正在拍摄纪录片《黑色道钉》的导演周敏，正好拍下了这一幕。

## Reno the Youth

In August 2018, six young white men held a small-scale memorial concert at the tunnel in Mount Donna as a tribute to the Chinese railway workers. Min Zhou, the director of the documentary *The Black Spikes*, happened to see them. He took a photo for the scenevry.

（译文／贾佳茵　责编／杨艳华）

# 附 录
## Appendix

### 70名画童

| | | | |
|---|---|---|---|
| 曹奕佳 | Christina Cao | 郑　好 | Eric Zheng |
| 陈子杰 | Alex Chen | 郑可涵 | Oscar Zheng |
| 陈子鉴 | Kent Chen | 周子婷 | Helen Zhou |
| 陈乃仪 | Nia Chen | 杜馨予 | Claire Du |
| 陈睿斌 | Ruibin Chen | 高大牛 | Daniel Gao |
| 高晨曦 | Chenxi Gao | 黄嘉怡 | Olia Huang |
| 韩赫颐 | Helen Han | 贾诗涵 | Cara Jia |
| 黄子恬 | Alita Huang | 李涵融 | Elaine Li |
| 贾佳茵 | Kaela Jia | 林之雅 | Candice Lin |
| 马铭浩 | Mario Ma | 刘娜娜 | Kalina Liu |
| 毛　笛 | Di Mao | 马嘉奇 | Jake Ma |
| 宿佳博 | Angeli Su | 马萧萧 | Tyler Ma |
| 宋毕昕 | Anthony Song | 穆烊昕 | Emily Mu |
| 王琪顸 | Alice Wang | 潘洁棱 | Jieling Pan |
| 王彦博 | Yanbo Wang | 钱书涵 | Justin Qian |
| 吴雨芮 | Sherry Wu | 邵奕霏 | Sophia Shao |
| 肖禹睿 | James Xiao | 王小虎 | Bryant Wang |
| 杨书睿 | Suri Yang | 王小龙 | Joy Wang |
| 张天阳 | Andrew Zhang | 姚嘉璐 | Jessica Yao |
| 张馨雅 | Xinya Zhang | 杨彬鑫 | Misty Yang |
| 张蕴涵 | Yunhan Zhang | 赵汉黎 | Hailey Zhao |
| 张云想 | Yunxiang Zhang | 祝云姝 | Maggie Zhu |
| 赵君艺 | Victoria Zhao | 石啸天 | Ian Bryant |

100 Years of Chinese Immigration in the United States and Canada

| | | | |
|---|---|---|---|
| 龙可为 | Claire Fillon | 马倩芸 | Annissa Ma |
| 李可欣 | Maggie Li | David田 | David Tian |
| 林昀晖 | Kenny Lin | 吴鸣玥 | Thelia Wu |
| 宋波菲 | Sophia Song | 喻玲珑 | Annie Yu |
| 田芯语 | Melody Tian | 钟琪励 | Qili Zhong |
| 杨咏志 | Robert Yang | 邹安琪 | Angela Zou |
| 殷思齐 | Iris Yin | 程子宁 | Zining Cheng |
| 张薇薇 | Vivian Zhang | 应心玥 | Betty Ying |
| 邓佳怡 | Kelly Deng | 刘阅辰 | Scarlett Liu |
| 邓依然 | Melissa Deng | 叶子思 | Alice Ye |
| 胡锦海 | Elmer Hu | 叶子捷 | Jenny Ye |
| 李炳毅 | Bingyi Li | 茉 莉 | Moli |